Introduction to Python Programming

Maxwell Vector

Contents

3

7

9

Chapter 1

Python Syntax and Execution

Fundamentals of Python Syntax

The syntactic structure of Python is governed by a set of formal rules that are rigorously defined in its underlying grammar. The language's design adheres to a minimalist paradigm wherein a reduced set of syntactic constructs enables concise and precise expression of computational ideas. Lexical tokens such as identifiers, numeric literals (for instance, 42), and string delimiters are recognized by the language's lexical analyzer, which segments the source text into fundamental components. Reserved words play a critical role in establishing the semantic framework of the language, establishing clear distinctions between various classes of operations and control structures. The resulting abstract syntax tree, generated through careful syntactic analysis, provides a structural representation that is essential for subsequent stages of processing and execution.

Spatial Formatting and Block Structures

A distinguishing feature of Python is its reliance on spatial formatting to define code blocks. In lieu of explicit block delimiters such as braces or keywords, Python utilizes indentation as the primary mechanism for indicating nesting and structure. Every compound statement, whether it delineates conditional branches, loops, or function definitions, begins with a header that typically terminates in a colon (:), followed by a series of statements indented to a uniform level. The strict enforcement of consistency in indentation not only enhances readability but also serves as an integral part of the language's syntax, with the parser inferring block boundaries directly from the spatial alignment of text. This design decision underpins a disciplined approach to code organization and enforces a visual and structural clarity that simplifies the cognitive process of parsing program logic.

Python Interpreter Execution Model

The execution of Python source code is characterized by a two-stage process involving an implicit compilation phase followed by interpretation. During the initial phase, the interpreter performs lexical analysis, syntactic parsing, and semantic validation to convert the high-level source code into an intermediate bytecode. This bytecode, which constitutes a lower-level, platform-independent representation of the program, is then executed by the Python Virtual Machine (PVM). The operation of the PVM encompasses dynamic memory management, including techniques such as reference counting and garbage collection, and provides facilities for runtime introspection. The layered nature of execution, from source code to bytecode to virtual machine operations, encapsulates a flexible and dynamic framework that permits the efficient evaluation of constructs and facilitates optimizations that are performed during runtime.

Interactive and Script-Based Command Processing

Python provides a dual modality for command processing that accommodates both interactive and script-based executions. In the interactive mode, the interpreter operates within a read-evaluate-print loop (REPL), whereby expressions are processed in a sequential manner with immediate evaluation feedback. This mode is particularly conducive to exploratory analysis and incremental development, as each command is parsed, evaluated, and the result is immediately presented. Conversely, script-based execution entails the consolidation of source code into a file, which is subsequently read, compiled into bytecode, and executed as a unified unit. The operational characteristics of both modalities are underpinned by the same core execution mechanisms, yet they cater to distinct workflows: one promoting iterative modification and immediate verification, and the other facilitating the execution of comprehensive programs in batch mode.

Python Code Snippet

```python
# A comprehensive demonstration of Python's execution model,
↪  including:
# - Lexical analysis using the tokenize module
# - Parsing source code into an Abstract Syntax Tree (AST) using the
↪  ast module
# - Compiling and executing Python code dynamically
# - A simple Read-Evaluate-Print Loop (REPL) for interactive command
↪  processing

import ast
import tokenize
import io

def print_tokens(source_code):
    """
    Tokenizes the given source code string and prints out its
    ↪  tokens.
    This simulates the initial lexical analysis phase of the Python
    ↪  interpreter.
    """
    print("Tokens from the source code:")
    # Convert the source code string into a bytes stream for
    ↪  tokenize.tokenize
    tokens =
    ↪  tokenize.tokenize(io.BytesIO(source_code.encode('utf-8')).readline)
    for token in tokens:
        # Skip the encoding declaration and end marker for clarity
        if token.type in (tokenize.ENCODING, tokenize.ENDMARKER):
            continue
        token_name = tokenize.tok_name[token.type]
        print(f"Type: {token_name:<12} | Token: {token.string:<15} |
        ↪  Start: {token.start} | End: {token.end}")

def print_ast(source_code):
    """
    Parses the source code into an Abstract Syntax Tree (AST) and
    ↪  prints it.
    This reflects the interpretation and structure analysis
    ↪  performed after lexical processing.
    """
```

```python
    print("\nAbstract Syntax Tree:")
    tree = ast.parse(source_code)
    # Utilize ast.dump with indentation for a readable AST format
    print(ast.dump(tree, indent=4))

def execute_source(source_code):
    """
    Compiles and executes the provided source code.
    This simulates the transition from bytecode generation to
    execution by the Python Virtual Machine (PVM).
    """
    print("\nExecuting the source code:")
    compiled_code = compile(source_code, '<string>', 'exec')
    exec(compiled_code)

def simple_repl():
    """
    Implements a simple Read-Evaluate-Print Loop (REPL) to allow
    interactive command processing. Users can input expressions or
    ↪    statements,
    and the REPL evaluates and prints the results. Type 'exit' to
    ↪    terminate.
    """
    print("\nStarting a simple REPL. Type 'exit' to quit.")
    while True:
        try:
            user_input = input(">>> ")
            if user_input.strip().lower() == 'exit':
                print("Exiting REPL.")
                break
            # Try evaluating as an expression first
            try:
                code = compile(user_input, '<input>', 'eval')
                result = eval(code)
                if result is not None:
                    print(result)
            except SyntaxError:
                # If evaluation fails, compile and execute as a
                ↪    statement
                code = compile(user_input, '<input>', 'exec')
                exec(code)
        except Exception as e:
            print("Error:", e)

# Sample Python code to demonstrate key aspects of Python's syntax
↪    and execution:
# - Function definition with proper indentation (block structure)
# - A recursive algorithm (factorial calculation)
# - Use of numeric literals and printing output
sample_code = '''
def factorial(n):
    """Calculate the factorial of a non-negative integer n
    ↪    recursively."""
```

17

```python
    if n == 0:
        return 1
    else:
        return n * factorial(n - 1)

# Demonstration: Calculate factorial of 5
result = factorial(5)
print("Factorial of 5 is", result)
'''

if __name__ == '__main__':
    print("---- Demonstration of Python Interpreter Mechanics ----")
    # Perform lexical analysis and print tokens
    print_tokens(sample_code)

    # Parse and display the abstract syntax tree (AST)
    print_ast(sample_code)

    # Compile and execute the sample code
    execute_source(sample_code)

    # Uncomment the following line to start the interactive REPL:
    # simple_repl()
```

Chapter 2

Python Keywords and Identifiers

Reserved Keywords

Within the Python programming language, a discrete set of tokens is formally designated as reserved keywords. These tokens are an intrinsic component of the language's grammar and play an indispensable role in demarcating control flow, declaration constructs, and various syntactic operations. The reserved keywords serve as the foundational lexemes that the compiler or interpreter recognizes as having a predefined operational meaning. Their inclusion in the language specification ensures that constructs such as conditional branching, iterative processes, function definitions, and exception handling are implemented in a manner that preserves both semantic clarity and syntactical rigor. As a consequence, the lexical analyzer explicitly prohibits the use of these tokens for any purpose other than their prescribed function, thereby precluding their repurposing as identifiers or variable names.

Identifiers

Identifiers are the symbolic names that delineate entities including variables, functions, classes, and modules within a Python program. Adhering to the formal syntactical rules specified by the language, an identifier must generally commence with an underscore or an alphabetic character, followed by a sequence that may consist of alphanumeric characters and underscores. This implicit regular expression, often represented in abstract notation as $[A - Za - z\_][A - Za - z0 - 9\_]*$, encapsulates the permissible structure of an identifier. Every identifier thus functions as a conduit for referencing an object in memory, allowing the programmer to apply labels to both primitive and composite data structures. The distinction between identifiers and reserved keywords is critical; since the latter are reserved by the system, the lexical rules enforce a strict separation, ensuring that identifiers remain unambiguous and distinct within the syntactic structure of the program.

Naming Conventions

Naming conventions in Python constitute a set of informal guidelines which govern the stylistic choices for forming identifiers. These conventions are aimed at enhancing the readability and maintainability of code by establishing a uniform pattern for the representation of variable names, function names, and class names. The prevalent practice is to utilize lowercase letters and underscores, a style commonly referred to as *snake_case*, for variable and function identifiers. In contrast, class names are typically rendered in *PascalCase* (also known as *CamelCase*), thereby distinguishing them from other entities. The consistent application of these conventions, as documented in widely accepted style guides such as PEP8, supports coherent code development by mitigating potential ambiguities. Furthermore, the deliberate choice of mnemonic identifiers contributes to an expressive code structure that subtly reflects the semantic roles of the entities involved.

Python Code Snippet

```python
import re
import keyword

def is_valid_identifier(identifier):
    """
    Check if a string is a valid Python identifier.

    An identifier must:
      - Begin with a letter (A-Za-z) or underscore (_)
      - Be followed by any combination of letters, digits (0-9), or
    ↪    underscores.
      - Not be a reserved Python keyword.
```

```python
    This regular expression encapsulates the rule:
        ^[A-Za-z_][A-Za-z0-9_]*$
    """
    pattern = r'^[A-Za-z_][A-Za-z0-9_]*$'
    if re.match(pattern, identifier) and not
    ↪   keyword.iskeyword(identifier):
        return True
    return False


def demonstrate_naming_conventions():
    """
    Demonstrates Python naming conventions by defining:
        - A function using snake_case.
        - A class using PascalCase.
        - A special method __init__ that initializes an instance
        ↪   attribute.
    """
    # A function in snake_case used to perform an arithmetic
    ↪   operation
    def calculate_sum(a, b):
        """
        Calculate the sum of two numbers.
        """
        return a + b

    # A class using PascalCase for its name
    class ExampleClass:
        """
        An example class to illustrate naming conventions.
        """
        def __init__(self, value):
            self.value = value  # Instance variable in snake_case

        def display_value(self):
            """
            Display the stored value.
            """
            print(f"Stored Value: {self.value}")

    # Use the function and class
    sum_result = calculate_sum(10, 20)
    print("Sum of 10 and 20 is:", sum_result)

    example_instance = ExampleClass("Hello, Python!")
    example_instance.display_value()


def main():
    # List of sample identifiers to validate
    identifiers = [
        'variable',      # Valid: lowercase, snake_case
        '2ndVariable',   # Invalid: starts with a digit
        '_hidden',       # Valid: starts with an underscore
```

```python
        'class',         # Invalid: reserved keyword in Python
        'CamelCase',     # Valid for a class name (PascalCase)
        'snake_case',    # Valid: common for variables and functions
        'with-dash',     # Invalid: '-' is not allowed
        'var123',        # Valid: contains letters and digits
        '__init__'       # Valid: special method naming convention
    ]

    print("=== Python Identifier Validation ===")
    for ident in identifiers:
        if is_valid_identifier(ident):
            status = "Valid"
        else:
            status = "Invalid"
        print(f"Identifier '{ident}': {status}")

    # List and display reserved keywords from the keyword module
    print("\n=== Python Reserved Keywords ===")
    print(keyword.kwlist)

    # Demonstrate naming conventions through function and class
    ↪ definitions
    print("\n=== Demonstrating Naming Conventions ===")
    demonstrate_naming_conventions()

if __name__ == "__main__":
    main()
```

22

Chapter 3

Variables and Simple Data Types

Variable Binding and Declaration

Variables constitute the fundamental constructs by which symbolic identifiers are bound to values stored in memory. In the programming paradigm under discussion, declaration occurs implicitly through assignment; that is, binding an identifier to a value is accomplished by associating the name with the object at runtime. This dynamic binding obviates the need for explicit type declarations, as the type of each object is determined by its intrinsic properties at the moment of creation. Such a mechanism not only streamlines development but also reinforces the abstract model where a variable functions as a label referencing data, independent of the underlying memory allocation details.

Integers

The integer data type represents elements of the set $\mathbb{Z}$, comprising all whole numbers that do not include any fractional component. Variables that assume integer values adhere to the axioms of discrete arithmetic, wherein operations such as addition, subtraction, multiplication, and integer division maintain the integrity of algebraic properties like associativity and commutativity. The operational semantics of integers ensure that arithmetic manipulations yield results consistent with formal mathematical constructs, thereby providing a robust substrate for computations that demand exactness and discrete granularity.

Floating-Point Numbers

Floating-point numbers offer an approximation to the continuum of real numbers, denoted by $\mathbb{R}$, by representing values in a finite precision format. Their internal architecture is characterized by a sign component, an exponent, and a significand (or mantissa), which together facilitate the expression of a vast range of magnitudes. Nonetheless, the limitations inherent in this finite representation engender rounding errors and precision constraints, which are important considerations in numerical computations. The systematic handling of floating-point arithmetic, guided by established standards, ensures that even these approximations yield reliable and predictable behavior in mathematical operations.

Boolean Values

Boolean values encapsulate the binary logic fundamental to computational reasoning. The data type is confined to two distinct entities, conventionally represented as *True* and *False*, which serve as the cornerstone for controlling conditional expressions and logical flows within a program. The algebraic structure underlying booleans adheres to the principles of boolean algebra, including the laws of identity, complementarity, distributivity, and associativity. This binary framework is integral to the evaluation of conditions and the orchestration of decision-making constructs, ensuring that programmatic logic is both coherent and rigorously defined.

Python Code Snippet

```
# This code snippet demonstrates key concepts covered in the chapter
↪   on Variables and Simple Data Types.
# It covers variable binding (dynamic declaration), integer
↪   arithmetic operations,
# floating-point arithmetic with precision considerations, and
↪   boolean logic.

def variable_binding_demo():
    """
```

```python
    Demonstrates Python's dynamic variable binding.
    Variables are implicitly declared by assignment and can change
    ↪   type throughout execution.
    """
    # Initially bind variable 'x' to an integer.
    x = 10
    print("x as integer:", x)

    # Bind 'x' to a floating-point number.
    x = 3.14159
    print("x as float:", x)

    # Bind 'x' to a boolean.
    x = False
    print("x as boolean:", x)

    # Bind 'x' to a string.
    x = "Dynamic Typing in Python"
    print("x as string:", x)


def integer_arithmetic_demo():
    """
    Demonstrates arithmetic operations on integers.

    Important equations and properties:
        1. Addition: a + b
        2. Subtraction: a - b
        3. Multiplication: a * b
        4. Integer Division: a // b
        5. Modulus: a % b

    Also verifies the associativity of addition:
        (a + b) + c == a + (b + c)
    """
    a = 15
    b = 4
    c = 7

    sum_ab = a + b
    diff_ab = a - b
    prod_ab = a * b
    int_div_ab = a // b
    mod_ab = a % b

    print("Integer Arithmetic:")
    print("Addition: {} + {} = {}".format(a, b, sum_ab))
    print("Subtraction: {} - {} = {}".format(a, b, diff_ab))
    print("Multiplication: {} * {} = {}".format(a, b, prod_ab))
    print("Integer Division: {} // {} = {}".format(a, b,
    ↪   int_div_ab))
    print("Modulus: {} % {} = {}".format(a, b, mod_ab))
```

```python
    # Verify associativity of addition
    left_associative = (a + b) + c
    right_associative = a + (b + c)
    print("Associativity Check: ({} + {}) + {} = {} and {} + ({} +
    ↪   {}) = {}"
        .format(a, b, c, left_associative, a, b, c,
        ↪   right_associative))


def floating_point_demo():
    """
    Demonstrates the behavior of floating-point numbers and
    ↪   highlights precision issues.

    Important points:
        - Floating-point numbers approximate elements of .
        - They are represented by a sign, exponent, and significand
        ↪   which can introduce rounding errors.

    Example:
        0.1 + 0.2 may not exactly equal 0.3.
    """
    x = 0.1
    y = 0.2
    sum_xy = x + y
    print("Floating-Point Arithmetic:")
    print("Sum of {} and {} = {}".format(x, y, sum_xy))

    # Checking equality within a tolerance to account for precision
    ↪   errors.
    if abs(sum_xy - 0.3) < 1e-10:
        print("0.1 + 0.2 is approximately equal to 0.3")
    else:
        print("0.1 + 0.2 is not exactly equal to 0.3 due to
        ↪   floating-point precision issues")


def boolean_logic_demo():
    """
    Demonstrates boolean values and logical operations.

    Boolean Values:
        - True and False represent the two possible states.

    Logical Operators:
        - AND, OR, and NOT.

    The code shows how booleans are used in conditional expressions.
    """
    a = True
    b = False
    print("Boolean Logic Demonstration:")
    print("a =", a, ", b =", b)
```

```python
    print("a and b =", a and b)
    print("a or b =", a or b)
    print("not a =", not a)

    # Using booleans in control flow
    if a and not b:
        print("The expression 'a and not b' is True")
    else:
        print("The expression 'a and not b' is False")


def main():
    """
    Main function to run all demonstration functions.
    """
    print("---- Variable Binding Demo ----")
    variable_binding_demo()

    print("\n---- Integer Arithmetic Demo ----")
    integer_arithmetic_demo()

    print("\n---- Floating-Point Arithmetic Demo ----")
    floating_point_demo()

    print("\n---- Boolean Logic Demo ----")
    boolean_logic_demo()


if __name__ == "__main__":
    main()
```

Chapter 4

Numeric Types and Arithmetic Operations

Overview of Numeric Types in Python

Python implements numeric types that encapsulate both the domain of discrete integers and the continuum represented by real numbers. The integer type, denoted as `int`, is characterized by its support for arbitrary precision, thereby allowing computations that extend beyond fixed-width hardware limitations. Floating-point numbers, represented by the type `float`, are implemented in accordance with the IEEE standard for binary floating-point arithmetic. In addition, Python includes support for complex numbers through the `complex` type, which accommodates numbers of the form $a + bi$, where a and b represent the real and imaginary components, respectively. Each of these types is intrinsically equipped with a suite of arithmetic operators that permit rigorous manipulation of numerical quantities, lending themselves to both theoretical analysis and practical computation.

Fundamental Arithmetic Operators

Arithmetic operators in Python serve as the primary mechanisms for numerical computation, delivering functionality that adheres closely to mathematical operations. The addition operator ($+$) and the subtraction operator ($-$) allow for the combination and separation of numerical values, respectively, while the multiplication operator ($\times$) establishes the product of quantities. Division is expressed through the standard division operator ($/$), which returns a floating-point result even when applied to integer operands. Complementing these operators are the integer division operator ($\lfloor / \rfloor$) and the modulo operator (mod), which provide results conforming to the quotient and remainder from the division algorithm of integers. Furthermore, exponentiation is achieved using the power operator ($**$), encapsulating the action of raising one number to the power of another. The semantics of these operators are interwoven with established algebraic properties such as commutativity, associativity, and distributivity, albeit with necessary caveats in cases where operations on floating-point numbers introduce precision constraints that diverge subtly from the theoretical models.

Arithmetic Expressions and Operational Semantics

Numeric expressions in Python are assembled by combining literals, variables, and arithmetic operators according to a strict hierarchy of precedence and associativity. This precedence model dictates that exponentiation is evaluated prior to multiplication and division, which in turn precede additive operations. Parentheses serve as an overriding structure to enforce specific orders of evaluation, rendering the association explicit even in complex expressions. The intrinsic design of these operators is rooted in the formal calculus of arithmetic, where the integrity of operations on *int* and *float* types is preserved through rules that ensure that the discrete properties of integer arithmetic and the approximation capacity of floating-point arithmetic are both maintained. While the operations on integers maintain an exact correspondence with mathematical definitions due to the nature of arbitrary precision, the operations on floating-point numbers are constrained by finite representation, thereby introducing considerations such as rounding errors and computational inexactness.

Mathematical Consistency and Computational Considerations

The implementation of numeric types and arithmetic operators within Python reflects a confluence of mathematical theory and practical computation. Integer operations conform to the axioms of arithmetic within the set $\mathbb{Z}$, ensuring consistency even when large values transcend traditional hardware limitations through the use of arbitrary precision arithmetic. By contrast, the finite representation inherent in floating-point numbers results in computations that are subject to the limitations imposed by machine precision. These representations employ a sign bit, an exponent field, and a significand, collectively determining the granularity and range of representable values. As a consequence, the application of arithmetic operators to floating-point values demands a rigorous awareness of potential rounding anomalies and the consequent propagation of error in iterative or cumulative computations. The careful orchestration of these numeric operations underpins many facets of scientific computation, numerical analysis, and algorithm development, where both the theoretical and practical aspects of arithmetic are leveraged to yield robust and efficient computational procedures.

Python Code Snippet

```python
# Comprehensive Python code snippet demonstrating Numeric Types and
↪   Arithmetic Operations

# Arbitrary-Precision Integers Demonstration
print("Arbitrary Precision Integer:")
large_int = 2**100  # Python's int type supports arbitrarily large
↪   integers
print("2**100 =", large_int)

# Floating Point Arithmetic and Precision Issues
print("\nFloating Point Arithmetic:")
a = 0.1
b = 0.2
sum_float = a + b
# Note: Due to the limitations of binary floating-point, the result
↪   may not be exactly 0.3.
print("0.1 + 0.2 =", sum_float)  # Expected 0.3, might display
↪   0.30000000000000004

# Using the decimal module for high precision arithmetic to mitigate
↪   rounding issues
from decimal import Decimal, getcontext
getcontext().prec = 28  # Set decimal precision
d1 = Decimal('0.1')
d2 = Decimal('0.2')
decimal_sum = d1 + d2
```

```python
print("Decimal('0.1') + Decimal('0.2') =", decimal_sum)


# Complex Numbers Arithmetic
print("\nComplex Numbers:")
z1 = complex(3, 4)     # Represents 3 + 4i
z2 = complex(1, -2)    # Represents 1 - 2i
print("z1 =", z1)
print("z2 =", z2)
print("z1 + z2 =", z1 + z2)
print("z1 * z2 =", z1 * z2)


# Fundamental Arithmetic Operators Demonstration
print("\nFundamental Arithmetic Operations:")
x = 15
y = 4
print("Addition: 15 + 4 =", x + y)          # Addition
print("Subtraction: 15 - 4 =", x - y)       # Subtraction
print("Multiplication: 15 * 4 =", x * y)    # Multiplication
print("True Division: 15 / 4 =", x / y)     # Division (always
↪    returns a float)
print("Integer Division: 15 // 4 =", x // y) # Integer (floor)
↪    division
print("Modulo: 15 % 4 =", x % y)            # Remainder
print("Exponentiation: 15 ** 4 =", x ** y)  # Power


# Demonstrating Operator Precedence and the Use of Parentheses
print("\nOperator Precedence Examples:")
# Without parentheses: exponentiation is evaluated first, then
↪    multiplication and addition.
result1 = 2 + 3 * 4 ** 2   # Expected: 3 * (4^2) = 3*16 = 48, then
↪    plus 2 gives 50
print("2 + 3 * 4 ** 2 =", result1)

# With parentheses to modify evaluation order:
result2 = (2 + 3) * 4 ** 2   # (2+3)=5, then 5*16=80
print("(2 + 3) * 4 ** 2 =", result2)

# Function to perform a suite of arithmetic operations and return
↪    the results
def arithmetic_operations(a, b):
    """
    Perform basic arithmetic operations on two numbers and return
    ↪    the results.

    Parameters:
        a (int, float): The first operand.
        b (int, float): The second operand.

    Returns:
        dict: A dictionary containing results of addition,
        ↪    subtraction,
            multiplication, true division, integer division,
            ↪    modulo,
```

```python
    and exponentiation.
    """
    if b == 0:
        division = int_division = modulo = None
    else:
        division = a / b
        int_division = a // b
        modulo = a % b

    operations = {
        'addition': a + b,
        'subtraction': a - b,
        'multiplication': a * b,
        'division': division,
        'integer_division': int_division,
        'modulo': modulo,
        'exponentiation': a ** b
    }
    return operations

# Testing the arithmetic_operations function
ops_result = arithmetic_operations(7, 3)
print("\nArithmetic Operations with 7 and 3:")
for op, result in ops_result.items():
    print(f"{op.capitalize()}: {result}")

# Advanced Mathematical Operations Using the math Module
import math
print("\nAdvanced Mathematical Operations:")
angle = math.pi / 4   # 45 degrees in radians
print("Sine of pi/4 =", math.sin(angle))
print("Cosine of pi/4 =", math.cos(angle))
print("Exponential of 3 =", math.exp(3))
print("Natural Logarithm of 10 =", math.log(10))
```

Chapter 5

Boolean Values and Logical Operators

Foundations of Boolean Logic

Boolean logic forms an abstract algebraic structure that under-pins decision-making processes in computational systems and the-oretical computer science. Its origins can be traced to the pio-neering work of George Boole, whose formalism provided a sys-tematic method for representing and manipulating truth values. At its core, Boolean logic is characterized by a binary framework wherein every proposition is assigned one of two possible truth values. This dualistic system elegantly encapsulates notions of af-firmation and negation, which are indispensable in the formation of rigorous conditional expressions. The algebraic properties in-herent to Boolean systems—such as idempotence, absorption, and complementation—are essential facets that afford both clarity and precision when modeling logical relationships and constructing for-mal proofs.

Truth Values in Computational Systems

Within the paradigm of computational logic, truth values are ab-stract entities that represent the outcome of predicate evaluations and binary decisions. The standard truth values, commonly de-noted as *True* and *False*, serve as the sole constituents of the Boolean domain. These values are not merely symbolic; they are endowed with intrinsic algebraic identities that facilitate the definition of logical operations. In computational practice, the correspondence between truth values and binary digits is often employed, with *True* and *False* being associated with 1 and 0, respectively. This representation enables the seamless integration of Boolean logic into digital circuits and algorithmic frameworks. The rigorous treatment of these values is critical in understanding the semantics of conditional expressions, where the evaluation of propositional formulas determines the subsequent flow of execution.

Logical Operators in Conditional Expressions

Logical operators are the fundamental mechanisms by which individual truth values are combined to construct more complex conditional expressions. The primary operators in Boolean logic include logical conjunction, disjunction, and negation, conventionally represented as $\land$, $\lor$, and $\neg$, respectively. The operator $\land$ defines a binary operation that yields a truth value of *True* only when both operands are *True*, while $\lor$ produces *True* if at least one operand is *True*. The negation operator $\neg$ inverts the truth value of its operand. These operators obey strict algebraic laws that govern their interaction and evaluation order, such as commutativity and associativity for both conjunction and disjunction, and the distributive properties that interrelate them. Moreover, these logical constructs provide the foundation for formulating conditionals that are central to both declarative and imperative paradigms in computer science. Their application extends to the evaluation of compound Boolean expressions, where the precedence of $\neg$ over $\land$ and $\lor$ is typically enforced, barring explicit alteration by the use of parentheses. The precise semantics of these operators are critical in ensuring that the logical structure of decision-making constructs is both consistent and unambiguous in the context of formal algorithmic analysis.

Python Code Snippet

```
"""
This script demonstrates key Boolean logic operations and verifies
↪    several
```

34

Boolean algebra identities as discussed in the chapter "Boolean
↪ Values and Logical Operators".

The demonstrated equations and formulas include:

1. Truth Table Calculation for Boolean Operators.
2. Commutative Properties:
*   a and b == b and a,*
*   a or b == b or a.*
3. Associative Properties:
*   a and (b and c) == (a and b) and c,*
*   a or (b or c)   == (a or b) or c.*
4. Idempotence:
*   a and a == a,*
*   a or a == a.*
5. Absorption Laws:
*   a or (a and b) == a,*
*   a and (a or b) == a.*
6. De Morgan's Laws:
*   not(a and b)   == (not a) or (not b),*
*   not(a or b)   == (not a) and (not b).*
7. Operator Precedence:
*   not has higher precedence than and, which in turn is higher*
*   ↪ than or.*

Each function in this script verifies one of these key properties.
"""

```python
def print_truth_table():
    """Prints a truth table of basic Boolean operations."""
    print("Truth Table for Boolean Operators")
    print("-" * 60)
    header = "{:<7} {:<7} {:<12} {:<10} {:<10}".format("a", "b", "a
    ↪  and b", "a or b", "not a")
    print(header)
    print("-" * 60)
    for a in [True, False]:
        for b in [True, False]:
            row = "{:<7} {:<7} {:<12} {:<10} {:<10}".format(str(a),
            ↪  str(b), str(a and b), str(a or b), str(not a))
            print(row)
    print("-" * 60)


def check_commutativity():
    """
    Verifies the commutative properties of 'and' and 'or' operators.
    For all a, b: a and b == b and a, and a or b == b or a.
    """
    for a in [True, False]:
        for b in [True, False]:
            if (a and b) != (b and a):
                raise AssertionError(f"and is not commutative for
                ↪  a={a}, b={b}")
```

```python
        if (a or b) != (b or a):
            raise AssertionError(f"or is not commutative for
            ↪ a={a}, b={b}")
    print("Commutativity verified for 'and' and 'or' operators.")

def check_associativity():
    """
    Verifies the associative properties of 'and' and 'or' operators.
    For all a, b, c: a and (b and c) == (a and b) and c,
                and a or (b or c) == (a or b) or c.
    """
    for a in [True, False]:
        for b in [True, False]:
            for c in [True, False]:
                if (a and (b and c)) != ((a and b) and c):
                    raise AssertionError(f"'and' is not associative
                    ↪ for a={a}, b={b}, c={c}")
                if (a or (b or c)) != ((a or b) or c):
                    raise AssertionError(f"'or' is not associative
                    ↪ for a={a}, b={b}, c={c}")
    print("Associativity verified for 'and' and 'or' operators.")

def check_idempotence():
    """
    Verifies the idempotence of Boolean operations.
    For any Boolean value a: a and a == a, and a or a == a.
    """
    for a in [True, False]:
        if (a and a) != a:
            raise AssertionError(f"Idempotence failed for 'and' with
            ↪ a={a}")
        if (a or a) != a:
            raise AssertionError(f"Idempotence failed for 'or' with
            ↪ a={a}")
    print("Idempotence verified for both 'and' and 'or' operators.")

def check_absorption():
    """
    Verifies the absorption laws:
    For all a, b:
    a or (a and b) == a,
    a and (a or b) == a.
    """
    for a in [True, False]:
        for b in [True, False]:
            if (a or (a and b)) != a:
                raise AssertionError(f"Absorption law 'a or (a and
                ↪ b)' failed for a={a}, b={b}")
            if (a and (a or b)) != a:
                raise AssertionError(f"Absorption law 'a and (a or
                ↪ b)' failed for a={a}, b={b}")
    print("Absorption laws verified.")
```

```python
def check_de_morgan():
    """
    Verifies De Morgan's Laws:
    For all a, b:
        not(a and b) == (not a) or (not b),
        not(a or b)  == (not a) and (not b).
    """
    for a in [True, False]:
        for b in [True, False]:
            if (not (a and b)) != ((not a) or (not b)):
                raise AssertionError(f"De Morgan's law failed for
                ↪ not(a and b) with a={a}, b={b}")
            if (not (a or b)) != ((not a) and (not b)):
                raise AssertionError(f"De Morgan's law failed for
                ↪ not(a or b) with a={a}, b={b}")
    print("De Morgan's Laws verified.")


def precedence_demo():
    """
    Demonstrates operator precedence in Python.
    The expression without parentheses:
        not a and b or c
    is evaluated as:
        ((not a) and b) or c
    which can be verified by explicit calculation.
    """
    a, b, c = True, False, True
    result_without_parentheses = not a and b or c
    result_with_parentheses = ((not a) and b) or c
    print("Precedence Demonstration:")
    print(f"Value of not a and b or c (evaluated as ((not a) and b)
    ↪ or c): {result_without_parentheses}")
    print(f"Value with explicit grouping ((not a) and b) or c :
    ↪ {result_with_parentheses}")
    if result_without_parentheses != result_with_parentheses:
        raise AssertionError("Operator precedence demonstration
        ↪ failed!")
    else:
        print("Operator precedence verified: 'not' > 'and' > 'or'.")


def main():
    print_truth_table()
    print()
    check_commutativity()
    check_associativity()
    check_idempotence()
    check_absorption()
    check_de_morgan()
    print()
    precedence_demo()
    print("\nAll Boolean logic properties have been successfully
    ↪ verified.")
```

```
if __name__ == "__main__":
    main()
```

Chapter 6

String Literals and Basic Operations

Creation of String Literals

A string literal is an ordered sequence of characters defined by delimiters such as quotation marks. In formal terms, a string literal can be represented as a finite sequence

$$s = s_0 s_1 \ldots s_{n-1},$$

where each s_i is a symbol from a predetermined alphabet Σ. The syntactical convention requires that these sequences be enclosed within specific boundary markers, ensuring that the textual data is clearly delimited from surrounding code. The representation of strings often incorporates escape sequences to denote non-printable or special characters. This design choice permits the precise encoding of textual information and ensures that the literal faithfully represents the intended data without ambiguity.

Concatenation of Strings

Concatenation is the binary operation that joins two strings into a single composite string. Formally, given two string literals

$$a, b \in \Sigma^*,$$

their concatenation is defined by the operation

$$a \oplus b,$$

which yields a string c such that

$$c = a_0 a_1 \ldots a_{m-1} b_0 b_1 \ldots b_{n-1},$$

where $a_0 a_1 \ldots a_{m-1}$ represents the sequence of characters in a and $b_0 b_1 \ldots b_{n-1}$ corresponds to the sequence of characters in b. This operation is associative in nature; that is, for any three string literals a, b, and c, the equality

$$a \oplus (b \oplus c) = (a \oplus b) \oplus c$$

holds. Concatenation facilitates the construction of longer, more descriptive strings from shorter substrings and is central to many algorithms that construct dynamic textual outputs from modular components.

Indexing in Strings

Indexing is a fundamental operation that allows access to individual characters within a string literal. Given a string

$$s = s_0 s_1 \ldots s_{n-1},$$

the element at position i, denoted by $s[i]$, is defined for indices satisfying

$$0 \leq i < n.$$

This convention typically follows a zero-based numbering system, wherein the first character of the string is associated with index zero. Indexing operations enable the retrieval and examination of individual symbols, which is crucial in tasks such as pattern matching, character frequency analysis, and error-checking. The underlying structure of indexing adheres to principles from discrete mathematics and sequence theory, affirming the ordered nature of strings as discrete objects.

Slicing of Strings

Slicing is an advanced method for extracting a contiguous subsequence from a string literal. For a given string

$$s = s_0 s_1 \ldots s_{n-1},$$

a slice is denoted by $s[i : j]$ and is defined as the segment

$$s[i : j] = s_i s_{i+1} \ldots s_{j-1},$$

where the indices satisfy

$$0 \leq i \leq j \leq n.$$

This operation is not only instrumental in isolating specific portions of a string but also provides the foundation for transformations whereby substrings are manipulated independently. In many computational systems, the slicing mechanism can be generalized to include stride parameters, thereby allowing the extraction of every k^{th} character from the original sequence. The mathematical rigour inherent in slicing operations assures that the extraction process is well-defined and that the resulting subsequence is a valid string literal complying with the restrictions imposed by the encoding scheme.

Python Code Snippet

```python
def main():
    # =============================================================
    # Creation of String Literals
    # A string literal is formally defined as s = s s ... s,
    # where each s is a character from the alphabet .
    # Strings are enclosed in quotation marks and may include escape
    #   sequences.
    # =============================================================
    s1 = "Hello"
    s2 = "World"
    s3 = "Python is fun!"
    s4 = "Line1\nLine2"   # Using escape sequence for a newline

    print("Created String Literals:")
    print("s1:", s1)
    print("s2:", s2)
    print("s3:", s3)
    print("s4 (with newline):")
    print(s4)


    # =============================================================
    # Concatenation of Strings
    # Given two strings a and b, their concatenation (denoted by )
    #   is:
    # a   b = aa...a bb...b
    # This operation is associative:
```

```python
# a  (b  c) = (a  b)  c
# ================================================================
concat1 = s1 + ", " + s2
print("\nConcatenation:")
print("s1 + ', ' + s2 =", concat1)


# Demonstrate associativity of concatenation
group1 = s1 + ", " + (s2 + " " + s3)
group2 = (s1 + ", " + s2) + " " + s3
print("Group1 (s1 + ', ' + (s2 + ' ' + s3)):", group1)
print("Group2 ((s1 + ', ' + s2) + ' ' + s3):", group2)
print("Associativity holds:", group1 == group2)


# ================================================================
# Indexing in Strings
# For a string s = s s ... s, the element at index i is s[i]
# where 0  i < n, following zero-based indexing.
# ================================================================
print("\nIndexing:")
print("s1:", s1)
try:
    first_char = s1[0]    # First character
    last_char = s1[-1]    # Last character (using negative index)
    print("s1[0] (first character):", first_char)
    print("s1[-1] (last character):", last_char)
except IndexError:
    print("Index out of range!")


# ================================================================
# Slicing of Strings
# Slicing extracts a contiguous subsequence from a string.
# For s = s s ... s, the slice s[i:j] yields:
# s[i:j] = s s ... s, where 0  i  j  n.
# A stride can be added to select every kth element.
# ================================================================
print("\nSlicing:")
# Extract 'Python' from s3 ("Python is fun!")
slice_python = s3[0:6]    # Characters at indices 0 to 5
# Extract 'is' from s3
slice_is = s3[7:9]        # Characters at indices 7 to 8
# Extract 'fun' from s3, ignoring the exclamation mark
slice_fun = s3[10:-1]     # From index 10 to the second last
↪    character
print("s3:", s3)
print("s3[0:6] =", slice_python)
print("s3[7:9] =", slice_is)
print("s3[10:-1] =", slice_fun)


# Slicing with a step: extract every 2nd character from s3
slice_step = s3[::2]
print("s3[::2] (every second character) =", slice_step)


# ================================================================
```

```python
# Utility Functions Demonstrating String Operations
# ================================================================
def concatenate(a, b):
    """
    Concatenate two string literals a and b.
    This mimics the operation: a  b = a + b.
    """
    return a + b


def slice_string(s, start, end, step=1):
    """
    Return a slice of string s from index 'start' to 'end'-1
    ↪  with a given 'step'.
    Corresponds to: s[start:end:step] = s s ... sd.
    """
    return s[start:end:step]


# Testing the utility functions
a = "Data"
b = "Science"
concatenated = concatenate(a, b)
sliced_segment = slice_string(s3, 7, 9)

print("\nFunction Tests:")
print("concatenate('Data', 'Science') =", concatenated)
print("slice_string(s3, 7, 9) =", sliced_segment)

if __name__ == "__main__":
    main()
```

Chapter 7

String Methods and Formatting

Overview of Built-In String Methods

The collection of built-in string methods constitutes a comprehensive toolkit for the systematic transformation and analysis of character sequences. These methods operate on immutable string objects and, by design, yield new string instances that embody the desired modifications. The operations provided encompass a broad spectrum of functionalities, ranging from elementary case transformations to more intricate search-and-replace procedures. In mathematical terms, a string can be represented as an element of

$Sigma^n$, where

$Sigma$ denotes the alphabet and n the number of characters. The methods discussed here serve as mappings of the form

$$f : Sigma^n rightarrow Sigma^n,$$

ensuring that the integrity of the original string is maintained through the creation of a new, modified sequence.

Case Transformation and Whitespace Manipulation

Transformations pertaining to character case and the handling of whitespace are fundamental operations that facilitate subsequent text processing tasks. The conversion of a string to either uppercase or lowercase is formally viewed as an application of a bijective function

$$g : Sigma^n rightarrow Sigma^n,$$

where each character in the domain is systematically mapped to its corresponding case-transformed counterpart. Additionally, methods for managing extraneous whitespace—including the elimination of leading and trailing spaces, as well as the consolidation of interstitial whitespace—play a critical role in preparing strings for lexical analysis and formatted output. These operations, instituted through well-defined functions, promote data uniformity and mitigate ambiguities in subsequent processing stages.

Search, Replace, and Subsequence Extraction

The ability to locate and modify specific subsequences within a string is central to advanced text manipulation. Search-and-replace operations are designed to identify occurrences of a designated substring and substitute them with an alternative sequence. This process may be rigorously defined by a transformation function

$$R : Sigma^n times Sigma^{n'} times Sigma^{n''} rightarrow Sigma^m,$$

where
$Sigma^{n'}$ represents the target substring and
$Sigma^{n''}$ the replacement sequence, with m signifying the length of the resultant string. Equally important are methods for extracting specific segments from the overall string by leveraging index-based slicing. Such techniques embrace the ordered nature of the sequence and allow for the retrieval of substrings through operations that conform to rules of the form

$$s[i : j] = s_i s_{i+1} ldots s_{j-1},$$

with indices satisfying 0
leqi

leqj
leqn.

Structured String Formatting

Structured formatting techniques provide a mechanism for embedding dynamic values within a predetermined textual template. The process is underpinned by the concept of placeholders, which serve as markers for variable substitution during the assembly of the final output. Mathematically, this operation can be modeled as a function

$$F : Sigma^n times V rightarrow Sigma^m,$$

where
$Sigma^n$ is the original format string, V denotes the set of substitution variables, and
$Sigma^m$ represents the fully formatted output. The formatting functions enable the specification of alignment, field width, numerical precision, and padding, thereby ensuring that the output adheres to a systematic and aesthetically consistent structure. The inherent precision of these formatting constructs is particularly vital in contexts where data presentation must conform to rigorous standards.

Advanced Applications of Formatting Functions

Beyond the elementary formatting capabilities, advanced constructs enable precise control over the layout and presentation of complex textual data. Such constructs support the specification of field dimensions, alignment directionality, and intricate precision settings, facilitating the generation of output that is both semantically robust and visually coherent. The interplay between string substitution, alignment directives, and numerical formatting is governed by a series of well-articulated rules that integrate combinatorial principles with stream processing theories. This confluence of theoretical foundations and practical applications epitomizes the efficacy of built-in formatting functions in producing clear, structured output without recourse to external formatting utilities.

Python Code Snippet

```python
# Comprehensive Python Code Demonstrating Important String
↪   Operations
#
# This code illustrates the concepts and functions described in the
↪   chapter:
# 1. transform_string(s): Represents the mapping f: ^n → ^n by
↪   applying a series of built-in string methods.
# 2. convert_case(s): Demonstrates the bijective mapping g: ^n → ^n
↪   by transforming the string to uppercase.
# 3. remove_whitespace(s): Removes leading, trailing, and excessive
↪   interstitial whitespace.
# 4. search_replace(s, target, replacement): Implements the
↪   transformation R: ^n × ^(n') × ^(n'') → ^m by replacing
↪   substrings.
# 5. extract_subsequence(s, i, j): Retrieves a substring s[i:j] as
↪   defined by the slice notation.
# 6. format_string(template, **kwargs): Represents F: ^n × V → ^m by
↪   performing structured string formatting.
#
# The demo() function exercises these functions on a sample string
↪   to reflect the theories
# and equations presented in the chapter.

import re

def transform_string(s: str) -> str:
    """
    Represents the mapping f: ^n → ^n.
    Applies multiple transformations on the string and returns a new
    ↪   string.
    """
    # Remove extraneous whitespace and capitalize the first
    ↪   character.
    result = s.strip()
    result = result.capitalize()
    return result

def convert_case(s: str) -> str:
    """
    Represents the bijective mapping g: ^n → ^n.
    Converts every character in the string to its uppercase
    ↪   equivalent.
    """
    return s.upper()

def remove_whitespace(s: str) -> str:
    """
    Removes leading and trailing whitespace, and collapses multiple
    interstitial spaces into a single space.
    """
```

47

```python
    s = s.strip()
    s = re.sub(r'\s+', ' ', s)
    return s

def search_replace(s: str, target: str, replacement: str) -> str:
    """
    Implements the function R: ^n × ^(n') × ^(n'') → ^m.
    Replaces all occurrences of 'target' with 'replacement' in the
    ↪ string.
    """
    return s.replace(target, replacement)

def extract_subsequence(s: str, i: int, j: int) -> str:
    """
    Returns the subsequence s[i:j] = s_i s_(i+1) ... s_(j-1),
    where 0   i   j   len(s).
    """
    return s[i:j]

def format_string(template: str, **kwargs) -> str:
    """
    Represents a structured formatting function F: ^n × V → ^m.
    Formats the string using a template with placeholders and
    ↪ substitution variables.
    """
    return template.format(**kwargs)

def demo():
    # Sample string with extra spaces and mixed cases.
    original = "   Python is a powerful, expressive, and versatile
    ↪  programming language.   "
    print("Original String:")
    print(repr(original))

    # Demonstrate transformation f: ^n → ^n.
    transformed = transform_string(original)
    print("\nTransformed String (f: ^n → ^n):")
    print(transformed)

    # Demonstrate case conversion g: ^n → ^n.
    upper_str = convert_case(original)
    print("\nUpper Case Conversion (g: ^n → ^n):")
    print(upper_str)

    # Demonstrate removal of extraneous whitespace.
    cleaned = remove_whitespace(original)
    print("\nWhitespace Removed:")
    print(cleaned)

    # Demonstrate search and replace: R: ^n × ^(n') × ^(n'') → ^m.
    replaced = search_replace(cleaned, "powerful", "robust")
    print("\nAfter Search and Replace (R: ^n × ^(n') × ^(n'') →
    ↪  ^m):")
```

```python
    print(replaced)

    # Demonstrate subsequence extraction using slice notation.
    # Locate the starting index of the word "expressive" and extract
    ↪ it.
    start = replaced.find("expressive")
    end = start + len("expressive")
    subsequence = extract_subsequence(replaced, start, end)
    print("\nExtracted Subsequence (s[i:j]):")
    print(subsequence)

    # Demonstrate structured string formatting: F: ⌒n × V → ⌒m.
    template = "Language: {lang}, Quality: {quality}"
    formatted_output = format_string(template, lang="Python",
    ↪ quality="highly readable")
    print("\nFormatted String:")
    print(formatted_output)

    # Combined example consolidating multiple operations:
    combined = format_string(
        "Processed Output: {text}",
        text = search_replace(remove_whitespace(original),
        ↪ "programming", "coding")
    )
    print("\nCombined Transformation:")
    print(combined)

if __name__ == "__main__":
    demo()
```

Chapter 8

Lists: Basics and Indexing

Definition and Construction of List Data Structures

A list is an ordered collection of elements that can be formally represented as an ordered tuple

$$L = (a_0, a_1, \ldots, a_{n-1}),$$

where each element a_i is drawn from an underlying set Σ and the index i satisfies $0 \leq i < n$. The construction of lists is typically achieved through the explicit specification of elements, where the literal representation employs enclosing square brackets, as in

$$[a_0, a_1, \ldots, a_{n-1}].$$

In mathematical terms, this representation embodies a finite sequence, clearly delineating the order inherent to the structure. The mutability of lists permits successive modifications after their initial creation, thereby distinguishing them from immutable sequence types.

Indexing as a Fundamental Operation

The process of indexing is critical to the manipulation and utilization of lists. Given a list L of length n, the operation of indexing is defined as a mapping

$$I : \{0, 1, \ldots, n - 1\} \to \Sigma,$$

such that for each index i, the relation

$$I(i) = a_i$$

holds. This mapping guarantees the ordered retrieval of elements, ensuring that the position of each element within the sequence is unambiguously determined by its corresponding index. In systems that permit negative indexing, an index of -1 is interpreted as corresponding to the final element of the list, thereby extending the conventional indexing scheme through the relation

$$I(-1) = a_{n-1}.$$

This flexible indexing mechanism reinforces the list's utility in accessing elements randomly, while also maintaining the sequential integrity of the stored data.

Accessing Elements and Extraction of Subsequences

Element access within a list extends beyond the retrieval of individual items to encompass the extraction of contiguous segments from the sequence. For indices i and j satisfying

$$0 \leq i \leq j \leq n,$$

the operation

$$L[i : j]$$

defines the subsequence

$$(a_i, a_{i+1}, \ldots, a_{j-1}).$$

This slicing mechanism functions as a mapping from pairs of indices to a new sequence—effectively a sublist—that preserves the ordered nature of the original list. Such operations are essential in numerous computational contexts, allowing for the partitioning, analysis, and transformation of data embedded within the list structure. The formalism of list indexing and slicing underscores the mathematical precision with which these data structures are manipulated in both theoretical and applied settings.

51

Python Code Snippet

```
# Python Code to Demonstrate List Construction, Indexing, and
↪  Slicing

# The list L is conceptually defined as:
#     L = [a0, a1, ..., a_{n-1}]
# where each a_i is an element of an underlying set and n is the
↪  length of the list.
L = [10, 20, 30, 40, 50, 60]
print("Original List L:", L)


# ------------------------------------------------------------
# Indexing as a Fundamental Operation
# ------------------------------------------------------------
# Access individual elements using positive indexing:
# For 0 <= i < n, the element at position i is accessed as L[i]
print("Element at index 0 (a0):", L[0])
print("Element at index 2 (a2):", L[2])
print("Element at index 4 (a4):", L[4])

# Negative indexing offers an alternative:
# In systems supporting negative indexing, L[-1] returns the last
↪  element a_{n-1}
print("Element at index -1 (last element, a_{n-1}):", L[-1])
print("Element at index -3:", L[-3])

# ------------------------------------------------------------
# Accessing Elements and Extraction of Subsequences
# ------------------------------------------------------------
# Slicing operation: For indices i and j satisfying 0 <= i <= j <=
↪  n,
# the slice L[i:j] returns the subsequence (a_i, a_{i+1}, ...,
↪  a_{j-1}).

# Example: Extracting a sublist from index 1 to 3 (i.e., a1, a2, a3)
sublist_1_4 = L[1:4]
print("Sublist L[1:4] (elements a1 to a3):", sublist_1_4)

# Slicing with omitted start or end index:
# L[:3] returns the first three elements (a0, a1, a2)
print("Sublist L[:3] (first three elements):", L[:3])
# L[3:] returns all elements from index 3 to the end (a3, ...,
↪  a_{n-1})
print("Sublist L[3:] (elements from index 3 to end):", L[3:])

# Demonstrate that lists are mutable:
# Modify the element at index 2 (initially 30) to 35
L[2] = 35
print("Modified List L after setting L[2] = 35:", L)

# Iterate through the list using indexing:
```

```
print("Iterating over list using indices:")
for i in range(len(L)):
    print("Index", i, "has element:", L[i])

# Creating a shallow copy of the list using slicing:
L_copy = L[:]
print("A shallow copy of List L:", L_copy)

# Full slice returns the entire list:
print("Full slice L[:] returns:", L[:])
```

Chapter 9

List Manipulation and Methods

Appending Elements to a List

The append operation is defined as an augmentation of a list represented as a finite sequence

$$L = (a_0, a_1, \ldots, a_{n-1}),$$

by introducing an additional element x at the terminal position. This operation transforms the original sequence into

$$L' = (a_0, a_1, \ldots, a_{n-1}, x).$$

The operation is executed without the need to specify a position explicitly, thereby guaranteeing that the appended element occupies the end of the list. The underlying dynamic adjustment of the list's storage, typically managed via reallocation strategies, contributes to an amortized time complexity of $O(1)$. An analytical perspective on this process considers both the memory management implications and the preservation of the sequential order inherent to the list structure.

Inserting Elements at Arbitrary Positions

Insertion within a list is formalized by the introduction of an element x at an arbitrary index i, where $0 \leq i \leq n$. Consider a list

$$L = (a_0, a_1, \ldots, a_{n-1});$$

the insertion of x at position i yields a new sequence

$$L' = (a_0, a_1, \ldots, a_{i-1}, x, a_i, \ldots, a_{n-1}).$$

This operation requires a positional shift of the elements originally at indices $i, i+1, \ldots, n-1$ to accommodate the new element, a process that enforces the maintenance of the list's order. The computational cost of this element-shifting mechanism is characterized by a worst-case time complexity of $O(n)$. The method of insertion is instrumental in preserving the structure while providing a flexible mechanism to modify the sequence in situ.

Removing Elements from a List

The removal operation is concerned with the elimination of an element from the list, which may be specified either by its positional index or by its value. For an element located at index j, the removal leads to the reconfiguration of the list

$$L = (a_0, a_1, \ldots, a_{j-1}, a_j, a_{j+1}, \ldots, a_{n-1})$$

into a contracted form

$$L' = (a_0, a_1, \ldots, a_{j-1}, a_{j+1}, \ldots, a_{n-1}).$$

This operation necessitates that all successive elements a_{j+1} through a_{n-1} be shifted one position to the left in order to close the gap created by the removed element. Similar to insertion, the worst-case time complexity for removal is proportional to $O(n)$ due to the required element shifting. When the removal is based on a matching criterion, the first occurrence of the specified value is identified, excised, and the integrity of the list's ordering is preserved by the subsequent re-indexing of the remaining elements.

Iterating over List Items

Iteration is a fundamental operation that involves the sequential traversal of the elements within the list. Given a list L of length

n, the iteration process can be mathematically formulated as the application of the mapping

$$I : \{0, 1, \ldots, n-1\} \to \Sigma,$$

where each index i is associated with the corresponding element $a_i = I(i)$. This ordered traversal allows for the systematic examination and potential transformation of each element within the collection. The operation of iteration, though conceptually simple, is optimized in practical implementations to maximize memory locality and processor cache efficiency. These optimizations are particularly significant in the context of large-scale data processing, where the cost of sequential access and iteration may have a pronounced impact on overall system performance.

Python Code Snippet

```
#!/usr/bin/env python3
"""
This script demonstrates fundamental list manipulation operations
↪   inspired by the chapter.
Operations include:
  - Appending an element to a list.
  - Inserting an element at an arbitrary position.
  - Removing an element (by index and by value) from a list.
  - Iterating over list items.

The operations follow these mathematical formulations:

1. Append Operation:
   Given a list L = (a_0, a_1, ..., a_{n-1}),
   appending an element x produces L' = (a_0, a_1, ..., a_{n-1}, x).
   (Amortized time complexity: O(1))

2. Insertion Operation:
   Inserting an element x at index i (0  i  n) transforms
   L = (a_0, a_1, ..., a_{n-1}) into L' = (a_0, a_1, ..., a_{i-1},
   ↪   x, a_i, ..., a_{n-1}).
   (Worst-case time complexity: O(n) due to shifting)

3. Removal Operation:
   Removing the element at index j from
   L = (a_0, a_1, ..., a_{j-1}, a_j, a_{j+1}, ..., a_{n-1})
   results in L' = (a_0, a_1, ..., a_{j-1}, a_{j+1}, ..., a_{n-1}).
   (Worst-case time complexity: O(n))
"""

def append_element(lst, x):
```

```python
    """
    Append element x to the end of list lst.
    This operation leverages Python's built-in append method which
    ↪  has an amortized O(1) cost.
    """
    lst.append(x)
    return lst

def insert_element(lst, index, x):
    """
    Insert element x at the specified index in list lst.
    This operation shifts elements starting at 'index' to the right,
    ↪  with O(n) worst-case complexity.
    """
    lst.insert(index, x)
    return lst

def remove_element_by_index(lst, index):
    """
    Remove and return the element at the specified index in list
    ↪  lst.
    This uses the pop() function, shifting subsequent elements to
    ↪  occupy the emptied position.
    """
    removed = lst.pop(index)
    return removed, lst

def remove_element_by_value(lst, value):
    """
    Remove the first occurrence of 'value' in list lst.
    This operation searches for 'value' and removes it; worst-case
    ↪  time complexity is O(n).
    """
    lst.remove(value)
    return lst

def iterate_list_items(lst):
    """
    Iterate over lst and print index-value pairs.
    This demonstrates sequential access over the list.
    """
    for index, element in enumerate(lst):
        print(f"Index {index}: Value {element}")

def main():
    # Define an initial sample list representing L = (a_0, a_1, ...,
    ↪  a_{n-1})
    sample_list = [10, 20, 30, 40, 50]
    print("Original list:", sample_list)

    # Demonstrate the append operation:
    # Resulting list should be: [10, 20, 30, 40, 50, 60]
    appended_list = append_element(sample_list.copy(), 60)
```

```python
    print("After appending 60:", appended_list)

    # Demonstrate the insertion operation:
    # Insert 99 at index 2: [10, 20, 99, 30, 40, 50]
    inserted_list = insert_element(sample_list.copy(), 2, 99)
    print("After inserting 99 at index 2:", inserted_list)

    # Demonstrate the removal operation by index:
    # Remove element at index 3 (element 40): [10, 20, 30, 50]
    removed_value, list_after_index_removal =
    ↪   remove_element_by_index(sample_list.copy(), 3)
    print(f"Removed element at index 3 (value: {removed_value}):",
    ↪   list_after_index_removal)

    # Demonstrate the removal operation by value:
    # Remove the first occurrence of 30: [10, 20, 40, 50]
    list_after_value_removal =
    ↪   remove_element_by_value(sample_list.copy(), 30)
    print("After removing the first occurrence of 30:",
    ↪   list_after_value_removal)

    # Demonstrate iteration over list items:
    print("Iterating over list items:")
    iterate_list_items(sample_list)

if __name__ == "__main__":
    main()
```

Chapter 10

Tuples: Immutable Sequences

Definition and Fundamental Properties

A tuple is defined as a finite, ordered collection of elements that, once constructed, cannot be altered. This inherent immutability implies that for any tuple

$$T = (a_0, a_1, \ldots, a_{n-1}),$$

the sequence of elements along with its cardinality remains invariant throughout its existence. The unchangeable nature of tuples guarantees that the ordering and the identity of the elements are preserved, thereby providing a stable structure that supports rigorous reasoning about data integrity and consistency in computational processes.

Mathematical Underpinnings of Immutable Sequences

The theoretical framework of tuples can be grounded in the concept of ordered n-tuples, where each element a_i is associated with a unique position in a sequence. Formally, the construction of a tuple may be viewed as a mapping

$$T : \{0, 1, \ldots, n-1\} \to \Sigma,$$

with Σ representing the universe of admissible elements. In this formulation, immutability manifests as the nonexistence of any operation capable of altering the mapping after T has been defined. This static mapping underpins the reliability of tuples in contexts where a constant data representation is mandatory, as it precludes inadvertent or unauthorized modifications that could compromise the system's state.

Comparative Analysis with Mutable Structures

In contrast to mutable sequence types, such as lists, tuples offer a set of characteristics that are particularly advantageous in specific computational paradigms. The fixed nature of tuples facilitates their use as keys in associative data structures that require objects with stable hash values. Additionally, the assurance that a tuple's elements will remain unmodified eliminates a class of side effects commonly encountered in mutable structures, thereby simplifying reasoning about program correctness and behavior. This delineation underscores the importance of discerning between mutable and immutable constructs when designing algorithms that rely on fixed structural invariants.

Semantic Applications and Use Cases

The employment of tuples is especially appropriate in scenarios where the encapsulation of heterogeneous yet constant data elements is required. When multiple values are produced as a coherent unit—such as the output from a deterministic function—the tuple serves as an ideal container that preserves the operational semantics of the data. The use of tuples is further justified in cases where the integrity of the constituent elements is vital to the subsequent execution of a system, ensuring that the data remains in a trusted state across various stages of processing. In these applications, the immutability of tuples provides not only a guarantee of order but also an intrinsic protection against unintended modifications, thereby reinforcing the robustness of the computational model.

Python Code Snippet

```python
# This Python code snippet demonstrates key concepts from the
↪    chapter on tuples.
# It provides a comprehensive example covering:
# 1. Creation of tuples, representing the immutable sequence T =
↪    (a_0, a_1, ..., a_{n-1})
# 2. A mapping from indices to tuple elements (analogous to T:
↪    {0,1,...,n-1} -> )
# 3. Verification of tuple immutability
# 4. Usage of tuples as keys in dictionaries for stable hash values
# 5. A sample algorithm (Fibonacci sequence) that returns a tuple,
↪    emphasizing immutability.

def create_tuple(*args):
    """
    Create a tuple from provided arguments.
    Represents the mathematical concept T = (a_0, a_1, ...,
    ↪    a_{n-1}).
    """
    return tuple(args)

def display_mapping(t):
    """
    Build a dictionary mapping each index to its corresponding tuple
    ↪    element.
    This simulates the mapping:
        T : {0, 1, ..., n-1} -> ,
    where   is the set of admissible elements.
    """
    mapping = {i: t[i] for i in range(len(t))}
    return mapping

def is_immutable(t):
    """
    Verify that the tuple is immutable.
    Attempting to modify any element of a tuple should raise a
    ↪    TypeError.
    """
    try:
        t[0] = 'modified'
    except TypeError:
        return True
    return False

def demo_dictionary_with_tuple_keys():
    """
    Demonstrate the use of tuples as keys in a dictionary.
    Due to their immutability, tuples can serve as keys (unlike
    ↪    lists).
    """
    dict_with_tuple_keys = {}
```

```python
    t1 = (1, 2, 3)
    t2 = (4, 5, 6)
    dict_with_tuple_keys[t1] = "First Tuple"
    dict_with_tuple_keys[t2] = "Second Tuple"
    return dict_with_tuple_keys

def algorithm_returning_tuple(n):
    """
    Sample algorithm: Compute the first n Fibonacci numbers and
    ↪   return them as an immutable tuple.
    The Fibonacci tuple maintains the data integrity of the
    ↪   sequence.
    """
    if n <= 0:
        return tuple()
    if n == 1:
        return (0,)

    fib = [0, 1]
    for i in range(2, n):
        fib.append(fib[i - 1] + fib[i - 2])
    # Convert the mutable list to an immutable tuple before
    ↪   returning.
    return tuple(fib)

if __name__ == "__main__":
    # Creating a tuple T using create_tuple:
    print("Creating tuple T:")
    T = create_tuple(10, 20, 30, 40, 50)
    print("T =", T)

    # Display the mapping from indices to tuple elements:
    print("\nMapping of indices to elements:")
    mapping = display_mapping(T)
    for index, value in mapping.items():
        print(f"Index {index}: {value}")

    # Check the immutability of T using is_immutable:
    print("\nIs T immutable?")
    print(is_immutable(T))

    # Using tuples as keys in a dictionary:
    print("\nDictionary with tuples as keys:")
    dict_keys = demo_dictionary_with_tuple_keys()
    for key, description in dict_keys.items():
        print(f"Key {key}: {description}")

    # Demonstrate a computational algorithm that returns a tuple
    ↪   (Fibonacci sequence):
    print("\nFibonacci sequence as an immutable tuple:")
    fib_tuple = algorithm_returning_tuple(10)
    print("Fibonacci tuple:", fib_tuple)
```

Chapter 11

Sets: Basics of Unordered Collections

Definition and Fundamental Concepts

In mathematical and computational contexts, a set is defined as a collection of distinct objects, commonly referred to as elements, in which the order of appearance holds no intrinsic significance. Formally, a set S is denoted by

$$S = \{a_0, a_1, \ldots, a_{n-1}\},$$

where each a_i is an element and the condition $a_i \neq a_j$ is maintained for every pair of indices with $i \neq j$. The absence of any prescribed order differentiates sets from ordered collections, emphasizing that the identity of a set is entirely determined by its constituent elements rather than by any sequential arrangement. This conceptualization has its roots in classical set theory, where sets serve as the fundamental constructs upon which much of modern mathematics is built.

Unordered Nature and Abstract Properties

The defining characteristic of sets is their unordered nature, which signifies that the internal representation of a set does not encode any positional or sequential information about its elements. This invariance under permutation means that two sets containing the same elements are considered equal, irrespective of the order in which the elements are presented. Such an equivalence is formalized by the axiom of extensionality, which states that for any two sets A and B, the relation $A = B$ holds if and only if every element of A is also an element of B, and every element of B is likewise contained in A.

The abstract properties derived from this unordered structure include the ability to perform operations such as union, intersection, and set difference. These operations adhere to well-defined algebraic identities that are critical in both theoretical analysis and practical computation. Furthermore, the absence of order simplifies the conceptual framework for membership testing, as the verification of whether an object belongs to a set is based solely on the identity of the elements without the need to consider their arrangement.

Storage of Unique Elements and Its Implications in Computation

A salient feature of sets is their inherent guarantee of element uniqueness. By definition, sets do not permit duplicate entries; when an element is inserted into a set, any subsequent attempt to insert an equivalent element is effectively disregarded. Mathematically, this is encapsulated in the principle that each element $a \in S$ is unique, thus reinforcing the condition that for any set S, if an element appears once, it cannot manifest further within the same set.

This property of maintaining unique elements has significant implications in computational contexts. The enforcement of uniqueness facilitates the elimination of redundancy and ensures the integrity of data within collections. In algorithms that process large volumes of data, the capability to swiftly confirm membership and to preserve only non-duplicative elements often results in enhanced performance and efficiency. The theoretical underpinnings of these operations frequently involve mechanisms designed to optimize membership testing, such as the use of hash functions or balanced search structures, thereby reducing the computational complexity involved in managing collections of distinct items.

The combination of unordered structure and assured uniqueness forms the foundational basis for the utilization of sets in a variety

64

of applications, ranging from data deduplication and indexing to the implementation of algorithmic strategies that demand rapid and reliable membership evaluation.

Python Code Snippet

```python
# Comprehensive Python Code Demonstrating Set Concepts

def check_extensionality(setA, setB):
    """
    Check if two sets are equal based on the axiom of
    ↪ extensionality.
    Two sets A and B are considered equal if every element in A is
    ↪ also in B
    and every element in B is in A.
    """
    # First, if the sizes differ, the sets cannot be equal.
    if len(setA) != len(setB):
        return False
    # Check that every element in setA exists in setB.
    for element in setA:
        if element not in setB:
            return False
    return True


def manual_union(setA, setB):
    """
    Manually compute the union of two sets.
    The union includes all unique elements from both setA and setB.
    """
    result = set()
    for elem in setA:
        result.add(elem)
    for elem in setB:
        result.add(elem)
    return result


def manual_intersection(setA, setB):
    """
    Manually compute the intersection of two sets.
    The intersection includes only those elements found in both setA
    ↪ and setB.
    """
    result = set()
    for elem in setA:
        if elem in setB:
            result.add(elem)
    return result


def manual_difference(setA, setB):
```

```python
    """
    Manually compute the difference of two sets (setA - setB).
    The result contains elements that are in setA but not in setB.
    """
    result = set()
    for elem in setA:
        if elem not in setB:
            result.add(elem)
    return result

def demonstrate_set_operations():
    # Demonstrate the uniqueness property of sets.
    # Duplicate elements in the literal are automatically removed.
    set1 = {1, 2, 3, 4, 5, 5, 3}
    set2 = {4, 5, 6, 7, 8}

    print("Set 1:", set1)
    print("Set 2:", set2)

    # Membership testing: the unordered property of sets allows for
    ↪  efficient lookup.
    test_value = 3
    if test_value in set1:
        print(f"{test_value} is a member of Set 1")
    else:
        print(f"{test_value} is not a member of Set 1")

    # Perform set operations using built-in methods.
    union_builtin = set1.union(set2)
    intersection_builtin = set1.intersection(set2)
    difference_builtin = set1.difference(set2)

    print("Union using built-in method:", union_builtin)
    print("Intersection using built-in method:",
    ↪  intersection_builtin)
    print("Difference (Set1 - Set2) using built-in method:",
    ↪  difference_builtin)

    # Use manual implementations of set operations.
    union_manual = manual_union(set1, set2)
    intersection_manual = manual_intersection(set1, set2)
    difference_manual = manual_difference(set1, set2)

    print("Union using manual implementation:", union_manual)
    print("Intersection using manual implementation:",
    ↪  intersection_manual)
    print("Difference (Set1 - Set2) using manual implementation:",
    ↪  difference_manual)

    # Demonstrate the axiom of extensionality.
    # Even if the order is different, two sets with the same
    ↪  elements are equal.
    set3 = {5, 4, 3, 2, 1}
```

66

```
    print("Set 1 equals Set 3 (using built-in equality):", set1 ==
    ↪  set3)
    print("Set 1 equals Set 3 (using manual extensionality check):",
    ↪  check_extensionality(set1, set3))

if __name__ == "__main__":
    demonstrate_set_operations()
```

Chapter 12

Set Operations and Methods

Union Operation

The union operation is defined as the combination of two sets by aggregating all distinct elements found in either of the operands. Denoted mathematically as $A \cup B$, this operation yields a set composed of every element x for which the membership condition $x \in A$ or $x \in B$ holds true. The formal definition is given by

$$A \cup B = \{x \mid x \in A \text{ or } x \in B\}.$$

This operation exhibits several algebraic properties that underscore its theoretical and practical importance. In particular, the union is commutative, meaning that $A \cup B = B \cup A$, and associative, as indicated by $(A \cup B) \cup C = A \cup (B \cup C)$. Furthermore, the idempotence property, expressed as $A \cup A = A$, reinforces the principle that the representation of a set is entirely determined by the uniqueness of its elements, independent of duplication. The union operation gracefully encapsulates the conceptual unification of disparate collections into a comprehensive aggregate, and its theoretical formulation finds extensive applications in both abstract set theory and algorithmic implementations.

Intersection Operation

The intersection operation extracts the commonality between two sets, yielding a new set that contains precisely those elements shared by both operands. Represented by $A \cap B$, the operation is formally described by

$$A \cap B = \{x \mid x \in A \text{ and } x \in B\}.$$

Intrinsic to this operation are its fundamental algebraic properties. The symmetric nature of intersection is evident through its commutativity, as any permutation of the sets leaves the result invariant, i.e., $A \cap B = B \cap A$. In addition, the associative property, expressed by $(A \cap B) \cap C = A \cap (B \cap C)$, permits the extension of this operation to more than two sets without ambiguity. The properties of idempotence and absorption further delineate the behavior of intersection in relation to union and other set operations. In theoretical and applied contexts, the intersection operation serves as a mechanism for isolating the mutual elements inherent within multiple collections, and its rigorously defined behavior supports advanced analyses in combinatorial optimization and relational algebra.

Difference Operation

The set difference operation, which is often denoted by $A \setminus B$, isolates the elements that belong exclusively to one set in the context of a pairwise comparison. Formally defined as

$$A \setminus B = \{x \mid x \in A \text{ and } x \notin B\},$$

this operation is inherently asymmetric, as the expression $A \setminus B$ is generally not equivalent to $B \setminus A$. The distinction underlines the operation's sensitivity to the order of operands, thus facilitating the subtraction of one collection from another. The theoretical framework governing set difference is deeply rooted in the principles of extensionality and the axioms of set theory, ensuring that every element is considered solely once in the outcome. In analytical contexts, the set difference is instrumental in delineating exclusive classifications and in the formulation of difference-based algorithms that rely on the removal of redundant or overlapping data.

Built-in Set Methods

In practice, many computational environments provide intrinsic methods to perform set operations, thereby streamlining the implementation of union, intersection, and difference without necessitating manual iteration or conditional comparisons. These built-in methods not only encapsulate the mathematical definitions but also implement optimization strategies that leverage efficient data representations, such as hash-based structures or balanced trees, to facilitate rapid membership testing and aggregation of elements. Emphasis is placed on preserving the fundamental properties of sets, including uniqueness and the inherent lack of order among elements, while ensuring that the operations conform to the rigor of classical set theory. The built-in functions abstract complexities and offer standardized interfaces that reduce the liability of human error, thereby enabling high-performance execution of set operations in both theoretical investigations and practical applications.

Python Code Snippet

```python
def demonstrate_set_operations():
    # Define example sets representing different collections
    A = {1, 2, 3, 4, 5}
    B = {4, 5, 6, 7, 8}
    C = {5, 6, 9}

    # Display the defined sets
    print("Set A:", A)
    print("Set B:", B)
    print("Set C:", C)

    # Union Operation: Combine all unique elements from A and B
    # Mathematical representation: A   B = { x | x in A or x in B }
    union_operator = A | B
    union_method = A.union(B)
    print("\nUnion of A and B:")
    print("Using | operator:", union_operator)
    print("Using union() method:", union_method)

    # Intersection Operation: Extract common elements between A and
    ↪ B
    # Mathematical representation: A   B = { x | x in A and x in B }
    intersection_operator = A & B
    intersection_method = A.intersection(B)
    print("\nIntersection of A and B:")
    print("Using & operator:", intersection_operator)
```

```python
    print("Using intersection() method:", intersection_method)

    # Difference Operation: Elements in A that are not in B and vice
    ↪ versa
    # Mathematical representation: A \ B = { x | x in A and x not in
    ↪ B }
    difference_A_B_operator = A - B
    difference_A_B_method = A.difference(B)
    difference_B_A_operator = B - A
    difference_B_A_method = B.difference(A)
    print("\nDifference of A and B (A \\ B):")
    print("Using - operator:", difference_A_B_operator)
    print("Using difference() method:", difference_A_B_method)
    print("\nDifference of B and A (B \\ A):")
    print("Using - operator:", difference_B_A_operator)
    print("Using difference() method:", difference_B_A_method)

    # Demonstrating algebraic properties
    # 1. Idempotence: A  A == A and A  A == A
    print("\nIdempotence Property:")
    print("A  A:", A | A)
    print("A  A:", A & A)

    # 2. Commutativity: A  B == B  A and A  B == B  A
    print("\nCommutative Property:")
    print("A  B == B  A:", (A | B) == (B | A))
    print("A  B == B  A:", (A & B) == (B & A))

    # 3. Associativity: (A  B)  C == A  (B  C) and (A  B)  C == A
    ↪ (B  C)
    print("\nAssociative Property (Union):")
    print("(A  B)  C:", (A | B) | C)
    print("A  (B  C):", A | (B | C))

    print("\nAssociative Property (Intersection):")
    print("(A  B)  C:", (A & B) & C)
    print("A  (B  C):", A & (B & C))

if __name__ == "__main__":
    demonstrate_set_operations()
```

71

Chapter 13

Dictionaries: Key-Value Mapping

Formal Definition and Abstract Model

A dictionary is rigorously defined as an abstract data type that embodies a collection of ordered pairs (k, v), where k denotes a key and v denotes its corresponding value. More formally, let $\mathcal{K}$ represent the set of all admissible keys and $\mathcal{V}$ represent the set of available values. The dictionary D is then characterized as a finite subset of the Cartesian product $\mathcal{K} \times \mathcal{V}$ subject to the constraint that for each key $k \in \mathcal{K}$ there exists at most one value $v \in \mathcal{V}$ such that $(k, v) \in D$. In this formulation, the mapping inherent in the dictionary is expressed as a function

$$\phi \colon \mathcal{K} \to \mathcal{V},$$

satisfying the condition that $\phi(k) = v$ if and only if (k, v) is an element of D. This formalism underlines the property of uniqueness for keys, which is central to the integrity of the mapping structure.

Structural Characteristics of Dictionaries

The internal structure of a dictionary is defined by its organization as a collection that maintains unique associations between keys and values. The keys, serving as unique identifiers, are required to be of types that possess an invariant notion of identity, often realized through immutability and hashability. Specifically, the property of hashability implies the existence of a hash function

$$h \colon \mathcal{K} \to \mathbb{Z},$$

which deterministically maps each key to an integer in a manner that preserves the uniqueness of distinct keys under standard conditions. By virtue of the uniqueness condition, duplicate keys are precluded, thereby ensuring that the dictionary represents a well-defined, finite partial function from $\mathcal{K}$ to $\mathcal{V}$. Moreover, the inherent lack of ordering among the constituent key-value pairs distinguishes the dictionary from linear data structures, thereby emphasizing its paradigm as an associative rather than sequential data repository.

Mapping Mechanisms and Operational Semantics

The operational semantics of a dictionary are intrinsically linked to its role as a mapping mechanism. The assignment of values to keys is performed through well-defined operations that encapsulate insertion, deletion, and lookup procedures. The retrieval of a value associated with a given key is governed by the function ϕ, which yields the associated value when the key exists within the dictionary; otherwise, the function remains undefined for that key. This behavior confirms that the dictionary is effectively a finite partial function. From an algorithmic perspective, carefully designed implementations based on hash tables are capable of approximating constant-time performance, denoted as $O(1)$, for the majority of dictionary operations under average-case conditions. Such performance characteristics are a direct consequence of the probabilistic distribution of hash values and the efficient resolution of collisions in practical computational environments.

Theoretical Considerations in Key-Value Associations

The theoretical foundation of dictionaries is predicated on the principles of functional mappings and the axioms of set theory. Under this lens, a dictionary is viewed as an isomorphic representation of a finite function, with the uniqueness constraint on keys ensuring that the function is well-defined. This abstraction provides a

73

robust framework for the analysis and design of algorithms that leverage key-value associations. In addition, the algebraic properties of dictionaries facilitate operations analogous to those in relational algebra, such as the union and intersection of mappings, when combined with appropriate disambiguation strategies. Although such operations extend beyond the basic definition, their study contributes to a deeper understanding of the complexities inherent in data association tasks. The concept of a dictionary thus not only encapsulates a practical tool for efficient data storage and retrieval but also serves as a subject of theoretical inquiry within the broader context of computer science and discrete mathematics.

Python Code Snippet

```python
class CustomDict:
    def __init__(self, capacity=10):
        """
        Initialize the custom dictionary with a fixed capacity.
        The buckets list holds sub-lists for chaining in case of
        ↪ collisions.
        """
        self.capacity = capacity
        self.buckets = [[] for _ in range(capacity)]

    def _hash(self, key):
        """
        Compute the hash index of a key.
        This method uses Python's built-in hash function and maps
        ↪ the result
        to an index within the range of available buckets.

        The mapping mimics the mathematical function:
            h: →
        where   is the set of admissible keys.
        """
        return hash(key) % self.capacity

    def insert(self, key, value):
        """
        Insert a key-value pair into the dictionary.
        If the key already exists, its value is updated.

        This operation is analogous to defining the finite partial
        ↪ function:
            : →
        such that (key) = value, ensuring uniqueness of keys.
        """
        index = self._hash(key)
```

```python
        # Check if key exists. If so, update its value.
        for i, (k, _) in enumerate(self.buckets[index]):
            if k == key:
                self.buckets[index][i] = (key, value)
                return
        # If key does not exist, append the new key-value pair.
        self.buckets[index].append((key, value))

    def lookup(self, key):
        """
        Retrieve the value associated with the given key.
        This function represents the mapping  in the dictionary: if
        ↪  key exists,
        it returns the corresponding value; otherwise, it raises a
        ↪  KeyError.
        """
        index = self._hash(key)
        for k, v in self.buckets[index]:
            if k == key:
                return v
        raise KeyError(f"Key {key} not found.")

    def delete(self, key):
        """
        Delete the key-value pair associated with the key.
        Traverses the appropriate bucket to remove the pair if it
        ↪  exists.
        """
        index = self._hash(key)
        for i, (k, _) in enumerate(self.buckets[index]):
            if k == key:
                del self.buckets[index][i]
                return
        raise KeyError(f"Key {key} not found.")

    def items(self):
        """
        Generator to yield all key-value pairs stored in the
        ↪  dictionary.
        This is useful for iterating over the finite partial
        ↪  function .
        """
        for bucket in self.buckets:
            for key, value in bucket:
                yield (key, value)

    def __str__(self):
        """
        Create a readable string representation of the dictionary.
        """
        items_list = []
        for bucket in self.buckets:
            items_list.extend([f"{k}: {v}" for k, v in bucket])
```

```python
        return "{" + ", ".join(items_list) + "}"


def union(dict1, dict2):
    """
    Compute the union of two CustomDict instances.

    The union operation is analogous to the set-theoretic union of
    ↪    the
    key-value mappings. In the case of duplicate keys, the value
    ↪    from dict2
    will overwrite the value from dict1.
    """
    # Use the maximum capacity for the result to reduce re-hashing.
    result = CustomDict(capacity=max(dict1.capacity,
    ↪    dict2.capacity))
    for key, value in dict1.items():
        result.insert(key, value)
    for key, value in dict2.items():
        result.insert(key, value)
    return result


def intersection(dict1, dict2):
    """
    Compute the intersection of two CustomDict instances.

    The intersection contains only the keys that are present in both
    ↪    dictionaries.
    The associated value is taken from dict1. This mimics a
    ↪    relational algebra
    like operation on the key-value pairs.
    """
    # Use the minimum capacity of the two for the result.
    result = CustomDict(capacity=min(dict1.capacity,
    ↪    dict2.capacity))
    for key, value in dict1.items():
        try:
            # If the key also exists in dict2, include it in the
            ↪    intersection.
            _ = dict2.lookup(key)
            result.insert(key, value)
        except KeyError:
            continue
    return result


def main():
    # Create two custom dictionaries with a smaller capacity for
    ↪    demonstration.
    dict_a = CustomDict(capacity=5)
    dict_b = CustomDict(capacity=5)
```

76

```python
    # Insert elements into dict_a representing the mapping :  ↵ .
    dict_a.insert("apple", 1)
    dict_a.insert("banana", 2)
    dict_a.insert("cherry", 3)

    # Insert elements into dict_b.
    dict_b.insert("banana", 20)
    dict_b.insert("date", 4)
    dict_b.insert("elderberry", 5)

    print("Dictionary A:", dict_a)
    print("Dictionary B:", dict_b)

    # Demonstrate the lookup operation (retrieving value via ).
    try:
        key_to_lookup = "banana"
        value = dict_a.lookup(key_to_lookup)
        print(f"Lookup in Dictionary A: {key_to_lookup} -> {value}")
    except KeyError as error:
        print(error)

    # Demonstrate deletion operation.
    dict_a.delete("apple")
    print("Dictionary A after deleting 'apple':", dict_a)

    # Demonstrate union: merging the two dictionaries.
    union_dict = union(dict_a, dict_b)
    print("Union of Dictionary A and B:", union_dict)

    # Demonstrate intersection: common key-value pairs between the
    ↵  dictionaries.
    intersection_dict = intersection(dict_a, dict_b)
    print("Intersection of Dictionary A and B:", intersection_dict)

if __name__ == "__main__":
    main()
```

Chapter 14

Dictionary Methods and Iteration

Analytical Framework of Dictionary Operations

The dictionary, as an abstract data type, is characterized by its representation of a finite partial function $\phi\colon \mathcal{K} \to \mathcal{V}$, where $\mathcal{K}$ denotes the set of admissible keys and $\mathcal{V}$ represents the corresponding set of values. This formalism provides a rigorous foundation upon which the primary methods of dictionary manipulation are constructed. Each operation, whether it involves the insertion of a new key-value pair, the deletion of an existing association, or the retrieval of a value given a key, is defined in terms of its effect on the underlying mapping ϕ. The operations maintain the property that for any key $k \in \mathcal{K}$, there exists at most one value $v \in \mathcal{V}$ satisfying $\phi(k) = v$. The mathematical underpinning is critical when analyzing both the correctness and the efficiency of these methods.

Dictionary methods are designed to manipulate the finite partial function while preserving the invariant properties of the data structure. For example, operations that update a dictionary are constrained by the uniqueness of keys, thus ensuring that any modification results in a well-defined mapping. The semantics of these operations are described by preconditions and postconditions that typically involve the preservation of function properties and the maintenance of finite cardinality. In doing so, the structural integrity of the dictionary is upheld, which is essential for subsequent iterative processes that traverse its key-value pairs.

Techniques for Iterative Traversal of Key-Value Pairs

Iteration over a dictionary is accomplished through methods that provide systematic access to its constituent elements. These iterative techniques are employed to traverse the set of keys, the collection of values, or the assemblage of key-value pairs. The concept of an iterator in this context is a structural mechanism that encapsulates the state of the traversal, thereby allowing successive yields of elements without exposing the underlying representation.

Mathematically, the iteration process can be viewed as the generation of a sequence $\langle (k_1, v_1), (k_2, v_2), \ldots, (k_n, v_n) \rangle$, where each ordered pair belongs to the dictionary and n is the number of elements in the mapping. This sequence need not adhere to any predefined order, reflecting the inherent non-sequential nature of the dictionary. Nonetheless, in certain implementations the preservation of insertion order may be observed, which introduces additional structural constraints and can affect the performance of iterative algorithms.

The iterative methods are typically implemented as lazy evaluators, producing elements on-demand rather than materializing the complete sequence in memory. This design choice is particularly pertinent when dealing with large mappings, as the memory overhead is minimized and the iterative process can be integrated seamlessly with functional constructs and stream processing techniques. The abstraction provided by the iterator encapsulates both the control flow and the current state of traversal, thus facilitating termination analysis and ensuring termination conditions are well-defined.

Performance Considerations and Structural Implications

The performance of both dictionary methods and iteration techniques is intimately connected to the underlying data structures, such as hash tables or balanced trees, that implement the abstract mapping $\phi \colon \mathcal{K} \to \mathcal{V}$. In hash-based implementations, the average time complexity of basic dictionary operations, including the retrieval of key-value pairs, is typically constrained to $O(1)$ under the assumption of a uniform hash distribution and effective collision resolution. However, the iteration over every element in a dictionary incurs a linear time complexity of $O(n)$, where n denotes the number of key-value pairs stored in the structure.

The structural design of the dictionary directly influences the efficiency of its methods and the characteristics of its iterators. For instance, in implementations that leverage chaining techniques for collision resolution, the internal representation consists of an array of buckets, with each bucket containing a secondary structure such as a linked list. The design decisions revolving around bucket capacity, load factors, and resizing policies have a direct impact on the performance bottlenecks encountered during both single-element operations and full dictionary traversal. An in-depth algorithmic analysis often reveals trade-offs between execution time, memory consumption, and the overhead caused by iterator state management.

Iterative methods may also be combined with other higher-order operations, such as filtering and mapping, to yield composite behaviors within the framework of functional programming paradigms. The theoretical treatment of these composite operations requires a careful balance between the abstract mathematical model and the practical considerations of algorithm design. In such cases, a rigorous analysis of time and space complexities further serves to elucidate the implications of various design choices, reinforcing the broader understanding of dictionary methods as both a theoretical model and a practical tool in the realm of computer science.

Python Code Snippet

```
"""
This Python script demonstrates the theoretical framework of
↪   dictionary operations as discussed in the chapter.
The dictionary is considered as a finite partial function : K → V,
↪   where each key in K maps to
a unique value in V. This example includes operations such as
↪   insertion, deletion, update, lazy iteration,
and filtering using list comprehensions.

Key concepts illustrated:
- Insertion and update: Ensuring that each key remains unique,
↪   reflecting the property of a mathematical function.
```

- *Deletion: Removing a key-value pair from the mapping.*
- *Iteration: Both eager (using a custom iterator method) and lazy*
  ↪ *(using a generator function) evaluation.*
- *Invariant validation: Confirming that the mapping maintains the*
  ↪ *uniqueness of keys.*

```python
class DictMapping:
    """
    A class that encapsulates a dictionary to simulate the
    ↪  mathematical mapping : K → V.
    Each key corresponds to a unique value and the operations
    ↪  maintain the mapping invariant.
    """
    def __init__(self, initial_data=None):
        # Initialize the internal mapping as an empty dictionary or
        ↪  from provided initial data.
        if initial_data is None:
            self.mapping = {}
        else:
            # Convert initial_data to a dict ensuring the uniqueness
            ↪  of keys.
            self.mapping = dict(initial_data)

    def insert(self, key, value):
        """
        Insert a key-value pair into the mapping.
        If the key already exists, the value is updated, maintaining
        ↪  the invariant that each key maps to a single value.
        """
        if key in self.mapping:
            print(f"Key '{key}' exists. Updating its value to
            ↪  {value}.")
        else:
            print(f"Inserting key '{key}' with value {value}.")
        self.mapping[key] = value

    def delete(self, key):
        """
        Delete a key from the mapping if it exists.
        """
        if key in self.mapping:
            del self.mapping[key]
            print(f"Deleted key '{key}' from the mapping.")
        else:
            print(f"Key '{key}' not found. No deletion performed.")

    def update(self, key, value):
        """
        Update the value associated with an existing key.
        If the key does not exist, it inserts the key-value pair.
        """
        if key in self.mapping:
```

```python
            print(f"Updating key '{key}' to new value {value}.")
            self.mapping[key] = value
        else:
            print(f"Key '{key}' not found. Inserting new key with
            ↪    value {value}.")
            self.mapping[key] = value

    def get(self, key, default=None):
        """
        Retrieve the value associated with a key with an optional
        ↪    default.
        """
        return self.mapping.get(key, default)

    def iterate(self):
        """
        Return an iterator over the key-value pairs.
        The iterator yields tuples (key, value) corresponding to the
        ↪    mapping .
        """
        for key, value in self.mapping.items():
            yield key, value

def validate_invariant(mapping):
    """
    Validate that the mapping adheres to the function invariant:
    For each key in the mapping there is a unique corresponding
    ↪    value.
    In a proper Python dictionary, this invariant is inherently
    ↪    satisfied.
    """
    keys = list(mapping.keys())
    assert len(keys) == len(set(keys)), "Invariant violated:
    ↪    Duplicate keys found!"
    print("Invariant check passed: All keys are unique.")

def lazy_iterator(dictionary):
    """
    A generator function that lazily yields key-value pairs from the
    ↪    given dictionary.
    This function demonstrates lazy evaluation where elements are
    ↪    produced on-demand.
    """
    for key, value in dictionary.items():
        yield key, value

def main():
    # Representing the abstract mapping : K → V with initial
    ↪    key-value pairs.
    initial_data = {'a': 1, 'b': 2, 'c': 3}
    dict_map = DictMapping(initial_data)

    print("Initial mapping:")
```

82

```python
    for k, v in dict_map.iterate():
        print(f"{k} → {v}")

    # Insertion of a new key-value pair.
    dict_map.insert('d', 4)

    # Update of an existing key ('b').
    dict_map.update('b', 20)

    # Deletion of key 'a'.
    dict_map.delete('a')

    print("\nMapping after insertion, update, and deletion:")
    for k, v in dict_map.iterate():
        print(f"{k} → {v}")

    # Validate that the dictionary maintains the function invariant.
    validate_invariant(dict_map.mapping)

    # Demonstrate lazy iteration over the dictionary using a
    ↪   generator.
    print("\nLazy iteration over the mapping:")
    for k, v in lazy_iterator(dict_map.mapping):
        print(f"{k} → {v}")

    # Using a dictionary comprehension to filter entries with even
    ↪   values.
    even_entries = {k: v for k, v in dict_map.mapping.items() if v %
    ↪   2 == 0}
    print("\nFiltered mapping (even values only):")
    for k, v in even_entries.items():
        print(f"{k} → {v}")

if __name__ == '__main__':
    main()
```

Chapter 15

Conditional Statements

Foundational Concepts in Conditional Evaluation

1 Boolean Expressions in Decision Processes

In formal programming semantics, a boolean expression is an evaluative construct that yields one of two logical outcomes, *True* or *False*, upon computation. Such expressions are grounded in the principles of Boolean algebra, which utilizes logical operators such as conjunction ($\land$), disjunction ($\lor$), and negation ($\neg$). The binary nature of these evaluations establishes a rigorous framework for decision-making in programming, where each conditional test produces a definitive logical value that governs subsequent execution flow.

2 Decision Structures as Mappings

The construct of a conditional statement may be understood as a mapping from a set of logical predicates to discrete blocks of execution. Given a condition C, the mapping associates the evaluation outcome *True* with a specific block of statements; conversely, if C evaluates to *False*, control is transferred to an alternative branch. When the structure is extended to incorporate additional conditions through *elif* clauses and a fallback alternative via an *else* clause, the overall decision mechanism is modeled as a sequential cascade of mutually exclusive mappings. Each mapping guarantees that only a single branch is activated, ensuring that the functional invariant of unique execution paths is maintained.

Syntactic and Semantic Analysis of if, elif, and else Constructs

1 Syntactic Structure of Conditional Constructs

The syntactic formulation of conditional statements is characterized by a hierarchical arrangement wherein the primary clause is introduced with the keyword if. This clause is directly followed by a boolean expression and a corresponding block of instructions, encapsulated in a structured and indented format. The structure is further refined by the incorporation of one or more $elif$ clauses, each introducing a supplemental condition and its associated block. The final structural element, the $else$ clause, does not comprise a condition but instead serves as a default branch. This layered syntax enforces a clear separation between alternative execution paths and preserves the deterministic nature of the conditional construct.

2 Semantics of Conditional Evaluation

The semantics underlying conditional statements dictate that the associated boolean expressions are evaluated in a deterministic sequence. Initially, the expression following the if keyword is computed; should it evaluate to $True$, the corresponding block of instructions is executed, and any subsequent conditions are bypassed. In the absence of a positive evaluation, the interpreter proceeds to sequentially evaluate each $elif$ condition. The inherent design of this construct adheres to a short-circuit evaluation strategy, whereby only the minimal necessary set of conditions is investigated until a valid branch is identified. In scenarios where all preceding conditions evaluate to $False$, the $else$ clause—if present—provides a guaranteed pathway, thereby solidifying the semantic model of a complete and exhaustive decision-making construct.

Execution Dynamics and Control Flow Mechanisms

1 Operational Semantics and Branching Strategy

The operational dynamics of conditional statements are encapsulated in an ordered evaluation process which systematically traverses the sequence of conditions. Each condition serves as a decision node within an abstract decision tree, where the evaluation result directs the flow of control along one of several discrete branches. The execution of this construct is governed by well-defined operational semantics which ensure that the transition from one state to another is both deterministic and reproducible. Within this framework, the guarantee that only one branch is executed in any given evaluation cycle is of paramount importance, as it sustains the invariant of mutually exclusive execution paths.

2 Implications for Complexity and Efficiency

The implementation of conditional statements carries significant ramifications for both algorithmic complexity and overall computational efficiency. As conditions are processed in sequential order, the worst-case scenario involves a linear series of evaluations, yielding a time complexity of $O(n)$ for n conditions. However, the short-circuit nature of conditional evaluation often mitigates this linear performance constraint by terminating the evaluation process upon the first occurrence of a $True$ condition. This operational characteristic not only optimizes runtime performance but also reinforces the strategic importance of condition ordering in scenarios where computational efficiency is critical. The rigorous analysis of these constructs, from both a theoretical and a practical standpoint, underscores their central role in the controlled management of execution flow.

Python Code Snippet

```
#!/usr/bin/env python3
"""
This script demonstrates the key concepts of conditional statements,
```

```
boolean expressions, and decision mappings as discussed in the
↪   chapter.

Key concepts illustrated:
    1. Boolean Expressions and Operators:
        - Conjunction: (a > 0) and (b > 0)   # Represents: (a > 0)
        ↪   (b > 0)
        - Disjunction: (a < 0) or (b < 0)       # Represents: (a < 0)
        ↪   (b < 0)
        - Negation: not (a == b)                 # Represents: ¬(a ==
        ↪   b)

    2. Decision Mapping using if, elif, and else constructs:
        - Mapping numeric values to descriptive categories.

    3. Short-circuit Evaluation:
        - Processing a list of condition-action pairs and stopping at
        ↪   the first True condition.
"""


def evaluate_boolean_expressions(a, b):
    """
    Evaluate boolean expressions using conjunction, disjunction, and
    ↪   negation.

    Equations:
        Conjunction: (a > 0) and (b > 0)
        Disjunction: (a < 0) or (b < 0)
        Negation: not (a == b)

    Parameters:
        a (int or float): First input number.
        b (int or float): Second input number.

    Returns:
        dict: Dictionary with the result of each boolean expression.
    """
    conjunction = (a > 0) and (b > 0)    # Represents: (a > 0)  (b >
    ↪   0)
    disjunction = (a < 0) or (b < 0)        # Represents: (a < 0)  (b
    ↪   < 0)
    negation = not (a == b)                   # Represents: ¬(a == b)
    return {
        "conjunction": conjunction,
        "disjunction": disjunction,
        "negation": negation
    }


def decision_mapping(value):
    """
    Map a numeric value to its descriptive category using
    ↪   conditional statements.
```

```
Decision structure:
    if value < 0:
        "Negative"
    elif value == 0:
        "Zero"
    elif 0 < value < 10:
        "Single Digit Positive"
    else:
        "Large Number"

Parameters:
    value (int or float): The numeric value to categorize.

Returns:
    str: Description of the value's category.
"""
if value < 0:
    return "Negative"
elif value == 0:
    return "Zero"
elif 0 < value < 10:
    return "Single Digit Positive"
else:
    return "Large Number"

def process_conditions(conditions):
    """
    Process a list of condition-action pairs to demonstrate
    ↪   short-circuit evaluation.

    The function iterates over a list of tuples. Each tuple
    ↪   contains:
    (lambda function for condition, lambda function for
    ↪   associated action)

    The first condition that evaluates to True triggers its
    ↪   corresponding action,
    and no further conditions are checked.

    Parameters:
        conditions (list): List of tuples with (condition, action).

    Returns:
        The result from the action corresponding to the first True
        ↪   condition,
        or a default message if none of the conditions are met.
    """
    for condition, action in conditions:
        if condition():
            return action()
    return "No conditions met"

def main():
```

```python
# Example 1: Evaluate Boolean Expressions
a, b = 5, -3
print("Evaluating Boolean Expressions for a = {} and b =
↪  {}:".format(a, b))
results = evaluate_boolean_expressions(a, b)
for expr, result in results.items():
    print("  {}: {}".format(expr, result))


print("\n" + "-" * 50 + "\n")

# Example 2: Decision Mapping
test_values = [-10, 0, 7, 15]
print("Decision Mapping Results:")
for val in test_values:
    category = decision_mapping(val)
    print("  Value {}: {}".format(val, category))


print("\n" + "-" * 50 + "\n")

# Example 3: Demonstrate Short-circuit Evaluation in Conditional
↪  Processing
print("Processing Conditions with Short-circuit Evaluation:")
conditions = [
    (lambda: False, lambda: "Condition 1 met (This will not be
    ↪  executed)"),
    (lambda: 2 + 2 == 5, lambda: "Condition 2 met (This will not
    ↪  be executed)"),
    (lambda: 3 * 3 == 9, lambda: "Condition 3 met (First True
    ↪  condition)"),
    (lambda: True, lambda: "Condition 4 met (This will not be
    ↪  reached)")
]
result = process_conditions(conditions)
print("Result from process_conditions: {}".format(result))

if __name__ == "__main__":
    main()
```

89

Chapter 16

While Loops

Syntactic Structure of While Loops

The syntactic formulation of while loops is characterized by a clearly defined structure that integrates a looping keyword, a conditional predicate, and an encapsulated block of statements. The construct is initiated by the keyword *while*, immediately followed by a boolean expression C that functions as the loop guard. This predicate, which is evaluated to yield either $True$ or $False$, determines whether the statements within the loop body, denoted by S, are permitted to execute. The grammatical representation may be abstractly expressed as

$$\texttt{while } C \ \{S\},$$

where the braces delimit the compound statement that constitutes the loop body. Under this syntactic paradigm, the evaluation of C is conducted prior to each execution of S, thereby enforcing a disciplined approach to iterative execution.

Operational Semantics and Iterative Dynamics

The operational semantics of while loops are defined by the mechanism of condition-controlled iteration. Prior to every potential execution of the loop body, the condition C is evaluated; if the evaluation yields $True$, the state transformation prescribed by S

is applied, and control is subsequently returned to a re-evaluation of C. This iterative process is succinctly captured by the following semantic equivalence:

while C do S $\equiv$ if C then $(S;$ while C do $S)$ else skip.

This equivalence establishes a recursive definition wherein the execution cycle repeats as long as C remains satisfied, thus creating a self-referential loop construct. The iterative dynamics, when analyzed in terms of state transitions, reveal that each execution of S may be interpreted as a deterministic function mapping an initial state s to a subsequent state s'. Consequently, the iterative process can be regarded as the sequential application of a state transformer until the condition C is invalidated.

Loop Invariants and Termination Conditions

Central to the formal analysis of while loops is the concept of a loop invariant, commonly denoted by I. A loop invariant is a property of the system state that is preserved before and after each execution of the loop body S. The establishment of such an invariant is essential for the rigorous verification of the correctness of iterative constructs. Concurrently, the termination of a while loop depends on the progressive evolution of the state such that the condition C is eventually rendered *False*. The design of a termination argument typically involves demonstrating a monotonic progression or identifying a well-founded ordering within the state space that precludes infinite descent. When combined, the mechanism of loop invariants and the proof of termination conditions provide a robust framework for analyzing the correctness and behavior of while loops within the broader context of program semantics.

Python Code Snippet

```
# This code snippet demonstrates key concepts from the While Loops
↪   chapter:
# 1. The syntactic structure and operational semantics of while
↪   loops.
# 2. The use of loop invariants and termination conditions.
# 3. The equivalence of a while loop to a recursive conditional
↪   construct.
```

```
#
# The following function uses a while loop to compute the sum of
↪   consecutive
# natural numbers until adding the next number would exceed a given
↪   limit.
def compute_sum_until(limit):
    """
    Compute the sum of natural numbers while ensuring the sum
    ↪   remains below 'limit'.

    Loop Invariant:
        At the beginning of each iteration, current_sum < limit.

    Termination Condition:
        When adding the next natural number would cause current_sum
        ↪   to exceed limit.

    Parameters:
        limit (int): The upper bound for the sum.

    Returns:
        int: The final sum which is the accumulation of natural
        ↪   numbers.
    """
    current_sum = 0       # Initial state for the accumulated sum.
    current_number = 1    # Starting from the first natural number.

    # Execute the loop as long as the loop invariant holds.
    while current_sum < limit:
        # Display current status and invariant information.
        print(f"Before Adding: current_sum = {current_sum}, next
        ↪   number = {current_number}")

        # Check termination: adding the next number exceeds the
        ↪   limit.
        if current_sum + current_number > limit:
            print("Termination condition met: Next addition would
            ↪   exceed the limit.")
            break  # Exit the loop if the invariant would be
            ↪   violated.

        # Update the state: add the current number to the sum.
        current_sum += current_number
        print(f"After Adding: current_sum = {current_sum}")

        # Ensure monotonic progress by incrementing the number.
        current_number += 1

    return current_sum

# The following function models a while loop recursively,
↪   demonstrating the equivalence:
#    while C do S      if C then (S; while C do S) else skip
```

```python
# In this case, C is "n > 0" and S is to print the current value and
# ↪ decrement n.
def while_loop_recursion(n):
    """
    Recursively simulate the execution of a while loop.

    Operational Semantics:
        If n > 0, then execute the body (print n and call
        ↪ recursively with n - 1);
        otherwise, do nothing (skip).

    Parameters:
        n (int): The current state used for the condition check.

    Returns:
        None
    """
    if n > 0:
        print(f"Recursive call with n = {n}")
        # Simulate S and the recursive call of the while loop.
        while_loop_recursion(n - 1)
    else:
        # 'skip' equivalent: base case, do nothing.
        return

# Main block to execute and test the above functions.
if __name__ == "__main__":
    print("Demonstration of compute_sum_until:")
    final_sum = compute_sum_until(20)
    print(f"Final computed sum: {final_sum}\n")

    print("Demonstration of while_loop_recursion:")
    while_loop_recursion(5)
```

Chapter 17

For Loops

Syntactic and Structural Properties

The for loop construct represents a fundamental iterative control structure, distinguished by its declarative syntax and its ability to traverse collections and sequences with succinct precision. In its canonical form, the construct encapsulates an iterator mechanism that extracts each element from a given collection S and binds it to a loop variable for the duration of one iteration. This high-level abstraction obviates the necessity for explicit index arithmetic, thereby reducing potential sources of error and enhancing both code readability and maintainability. The intrinsic design of the for loop guarantees that each element, whether drawn from an ordered sequence or an unordered collection, is processed in a consistent manner, while the underlying iterator protocol manages state and progression through S.

Operational Semantics and the Iterative Process

The operational semantics of the for loop can be formally understood through a reduction semantics framework. Consider a collection represented as an ordered tuple $S = \langle e_0, e_1, \ldots, e_{n-1} \rangle$. The for loop systematically decomposes S by binding each element e_i successively to the loop variable and invoking the associated loop body

$B(e_i)$. This process is succinctly modeled as a state transition:

$$\langle s, \texttt{for } e \in S \ \{B(e)\}\rangle \to \langle s', \texttt{skip}\rangle,$$

where s denotes the initial program state, $B(e)$ represents the loop body parameterized by the current element e, and s' is the resultant state after the complete iteration over S. Within each iteration, the deterministic application of $B(e)$ ensures that state modifications occur in an orderly and isolated fashion, thereby validating the correctness of the iterative process through consistent state transformation.

Iteration over Sequences and Collections

Within the realm of data structures, the for loop exhibits a pronounced versatility by adapting its iteration scheme to both sequences and collections. When the target data structure is an ordered sequence, the for loop adheres strictly to the inherent order of elements, ensuring that each successive element e_i is processed in the same order as defined by the sequence. In the case of unordered collections, such as sets, the iteration order is determined by the internal management of the collection; however, the semantic intent remains unchanged. The abstraction afforded by the for loop permits an uninterrupted delineation of the iteration process, effectively decoupling the mechanics of element retrieval from the operational logic contained within $B(e)$.

Efficiency and Computational Considerations

The efficiency inherent in the for loop construct derives from its reliance on an optimized iterator protocol that minimizes overhead by abstracting the process of element retrieval. In typical implementations, the cost associated with advancing to the next element in a collection is constant, thereby yielding an overall time complexity of $O(n)$ for a collection of n elements. This property, combined with the elimination of explicit index management, contributes to both the clarity and the computational efficiency of the for loop construct. Compiler optimizations further enhance performance by exploiting memory locality and reducing per-iteration overhead, thereby attesting to the performance benefits of this iterative paradigm in the systematic processing of sequences and collections.

Python Code Snippet

```
# This code snippet demonstrates the fundamental operational
↪    semantics of the for loop.
# It simulates the reduction semantics of a for loop over a
↪    collection S with an
# initial state s, following the transition:
#    ( s, for e in S {B(e)} ) -> ( s', skip )
# where each element e in the collection S is processed by a loop
↪    body B(e) that modifies
# the state s in a deterministic manner.

def loop_body(e, state):
    """
    Simulate the loop body B(e) which processes element e and
    ↪    updates the state.
    In this example, we add the element's value to a running sum and
    ↪    record the element.
    """
    # Before processing, state is printed in the calling function.
    state["sum"] += e            # update the running sum
    state["elements"].append(e)  # record the processed element
    print(f"Processing element {e}: updated state sum =
    ↪    {state['sum']}")
    return state

def for_loop_simulation(S, initial_state):
    """
    Simulate the reduction semantics of the for loop over an ordered
    ↪    collection S.
    The state transition:
        ( s, for e in S {B(e)} ) -> ( s', skip )
    is performed by iterating over each element e in S and updating
    ↪    the state.
    """
    state = initial_state
    for e in S:
        print(f"Before iteration with e = {e}, state = {state}")
        state = loop_body(e, state)
        print(f"After iteration with e = {e}, state = {state}\n")
    return state

def for_loop_simulation_set(S, initial_state):
    """
    Simulate a similar iterative process for an unordered collection
    ↪    (set).
```

96

```python
    Here, we demonstrate a different loop body that computes the
    ↪   product of the elements.
    The order of iteration is determined by the set's internal
    ↪   management.
    """
    state = initial_state

    def loop_body_product(e, state):
        """
        Loop body for processing elements in a set: update the
        ↪   product and record the element.
        """
        state["product"] *= e         # update the running product
        state["elements"].append(e)   # record the processed element
        print(f"Processing element {e}: updated state product =
        ↪   {state['product']}")
        return state

    for e in S:
        print(f"Before iteration with e = {e}, state = {state}")
        state = loop_body_product(e, state)
        print(f"After iteration with e = {e}, state = {state}\n")
    return state

def main():
    # Example 1: Iteration over an ordered sequence (list)
    ordered_sequence = [1, 2, 3, 4, 5]
    initial_state_ordered = {"sum": 0, "elements": []}
    print("Simulating for loop over ordered sequence:")
    final_state_ordered = for_loop_simulation(ordered_sequence,
    ↪   initial_state_ordered)
    print("Final state for ordered sequence:", final_state_ordered)
    print("\n" + "="*60 + "\n")

    # Example 2: Iteration over an unordered collection (set)
    unordered_set = {10, 20, 30, 40, 50}
    initial_state_unordered = {"product": 1, "elements": []}
    print("Simulating for loop over unordered set:")
    final_state_unordered = for_loop_simulation_set(unordered_set,
    ↪   initial_state_unordered)
    print("Final state for unordered set:", final_state_unordered)

if __name__ == "__main__":
    main()
```

Chapter 18

Loop Control Statements

Break Statement

The break statement constitutes an imperative mechanism for terminating an ongoing loop before the exhaustion of its natural iterations. In formal operational semantics, when a break instruction is encountered within a loop body, the current execution state, denoted by s, is instantaneously redirected to a state s' that lies immediately beyond the loop construct. This abrupt interruption of iteration is facilitated without the execution of the residual statements in the current iteration, thereby effectuating a non-local transfer of control. In nested loop scenarios, the execution of a break statement is confined to the innermost loop, unless explicit measures are undertaken to propagate the control transfer to an outer loop level. The insertion of a break statement alters the conventional linear progression of loop execution, contributing an additional control flow edge in the underlying control flow graph. Consequently, the break statement serves as a potent tool for the implementation of conditional loop termination in contexts where a predetermined condition invalidates the need to perform further iterations.

Continue Statement

The continue statement operates as a selective bypass mechanism within loop constructs. Upon its execution, the current iteration is immediately abandoned, and control is transferred directly to the loop's iterative mechanism, thereby reinitiating the verification of the loop's continuation condition. Mathematically, if the loop is represented by an iterative process over a sequence of states, then executing continue in a state s results in a transition that effectively skips the remaining statements in the current iteration while preserving the invariant state conditions required for initiating the subsequent iteration. The continue statement does not terminate the loop, but rather preserves the loop's overall structural integrity by ensuring that the iterative process resumes in a deterministic manner. Its utilization is particularly advantageous in scenarios where certain conditions necessitate the omission of the residual processing associated with the current cycle, without compromising the overarching semantic guarantees provided by the iterative construct.

Pass Statement

In contrast to the break and continue statements, the pass statement is employed as a syntactically obligatory placeholder in constructs that mandate a statement without imposing any operational effect. Its execution is semantically characterized as a no-operation, with the state transition formally represented as $s \rightarrow s$, wherein the program state remains invariant. The pass statement fulfills a critical role in satisfying the syntactic requirements of the language, particularly in the context of empty loop bodies or conditional branches where an operative statement is syntactically demanded but functionally unnecessary. By not altering the control flow or the state of the execution environment, the pass statement contributes to code clarity and uniformity, upholding the invariant properties of the loop construct while enforcing structural consistency according to grammatical constraints.

Python Code Snippet

```python
# This script demonstrates the use of loop control statements:
↪   break, continue, and pass.
# It also simulates state transitions representing the formal
↪   semantics discussed in the chapter.
# In our simulation, we consider each loop iteration as a state "s"
↪   and show how "break" can
# transition to a new state "s'" immediately, while "continue" skips
↪   to the next iteration,
# and "pass" maintains the state (s → s).

def find_first_even(numbers):
    """
    Searches for the first even number in the list.
    When an even number is found, the break statement causes an
    ↪   immediate transition
    from the current state s to a new state s' (i.e., exit of the
    ↪   loop).
    """
    for num in numbers:
        if num % 2 == 0:
            print(f"First even number found: {num}")
            # Break out of the loop, representing the state
            ↪   transition: s -> s'
            break
    else:
        # This block executes only if the loop completes without
        ↪   encountering a break.
        print("No even number found.")

def process_numbers(numbers):
    """
    Processes a list of numbers by summing even, non-negative
    ↪   numbers.
    - Uses 'continue' to skip negative numbers, thus preserving
    ↪   state conditions for the next iteration.
    - Demonstrates the 'pass' statement as a placeholder for odd
    ↪   numbers where no action is taken.
    """
    total = 0
    for num in numbers:
        if num < 0:
            # Continue: Skip processing for negative numbers and
            ↪   move to the next state.
            continue

        # If the number is odd, we use pass as a placeholder.
        if num % 2 != 0:
            # The pass statement here does not change the state: s
            ↪   -> s
            pass
```

100

```python
        else:
            total += num
            print(f"Adding {num}, total so far: {total}")
    return total

def nested_loop_example(matrix):
    """
    Demonstrates the use of break in nested loops.
    Searches for a target value within a 2D matrix. When the target
    ↪   is found, the inner loop
    is broken (transition from state s to s' within the inner
    ↪   context), and then the outer loop is also terminated.
    """
    target = 42
    found = False
    for i, row in enumerate(matrix):
        for j, value in enumerate(row):
            if value == target:
                print(f"Target {target} found at position ({i},
                ↪   {j}).")
                found = True
                # Break out of the inner loop
                break
        if found:
            # Break out of the outer loop as well, representing
            ↪   nested state transitions
            break
    if not found:
        print(f"Target {target} not found in the matrix.")

def simulate_state_transitions():
    """
    Simulates state transitions within a loop.
    Each iteration of the loop represents a state 's'. The following
    ↪   control statements affect
    the state transition:
    - 'break' causes an abrupt jump from the current state s to a
    ↪   final state s' (exiting the loop).
    - 'continue' skips the remaining processing in the current
    ↪   state, moving directly to the next state.
    - 'pass' acts as a no-operation, keeping the state unchanged (s
    ↪   -> s).
    """
    state = 0  # Initial state s.
    while state < 10:
        print(f"Current state: {state}")

        if state == 5:
            print("Condition met at state 5, transitioning out of
            ↪   loop (s -> s').")
            # Immediate state transition out of the loop using
            ↪   break.
            break
```

```python
        elif state % 2 == 0:
            print("Even state encountered, skipping processing for
            ↪  this iteration using continue.")
            state += 1
            # The continue statement moves to the next iteration
            ↪  without further modifications.
            continue
        else:
            print("Processing state normally.")

            # The pass statement here is a placeholder and does not
            ↪  affect the state.
            pass

        state += 1

if __name__ == "__main__":
    # Demonstration of break: finding the first even number.
    numbers_list = [1, 3, 5, 7, 8, 9, 10]
    find_first_even(numbers_list)

    print("\nProcessing a mixed list of numbers with loop control:")
    mixed_numbers = [4, -3, 7, -1, 2, 9, 0]
    total_sum = process_numbers(mixed_numbers)
    print(f"Total sum of even, non-negative numbers: {total_sum}")

    print("\nNested loop search in a matrix:")
    matrix = [
        [10, 20, 30],
        [40, 42, 50],
        [60, 70, 80]
    ]
    nested_loop_example(matrix)

    print("\nSimulating state transitions using loop control
    ↪  statements:")
    simulate_state_transitions()

# End of demonstration code.
```

Chapter 19

List Comprehensions

Conceptual Foundations

A list comprehension constitutes a syntactic form that encapsulates the dual notions of element generation and conditional filtering within a single, compact expression. In formal terms, the mechanism may be viewed as a transformation function applied to each element in an iterable structure. This transformation is succinctly captured by an expression analogous to

$$L = \{f(x) \mid x \in S \text{ and } P(x)\},$$

where S represents the domain of iteration, $f(x)$ is the transformation applied to each element, and $P(x)$ is a predicate that governs the inclusion of elements in the resulting list. The notation emphasizes the integration of mapping and filtering operations into a singular construct that yields an ordered collection.

Formal Syntax and Operational Semantics

The formal grammar of a list comprehension is characterized by its intrinsic components: an output expression, an iteration variable, a source iterable, and an optional conditional clause. The canonical form is represented as

$$[e \text{ for } x \text{ in } S \text{ if } C(x)],$$

where e denotes the expression subject to evaluation, x is the bound variable that spans the iterable set S, and $C(x)$ serves as a condition restricting the domain. In the operational semantics of the construct, the evaluation proceeds by iterating over each element $x \in S$, evaluating the condition $C(x)$, and, contingent upon its truth value, computing e. The computed value is then appended to the resulting list. This mechanism embodies the fundamental principles of functional abstraction and encapsulates the effect of both the mapping of a function and the filtration of elements in a single syntactic entity.

Transformative Capabilities

The transformative essence of list comprehensions lies in their ability to perform complex manipulations on sequential data with a minimalistic notation. The expression within the comprehension defines a transformation logic that is applied uniformly across all elements satisfying the conditional predicate. This uniformity ensures that the operational semantics preserve immutability during the iterative process, as each element is processed in isolation before being aggregated. The construct offers the possibility of nesting multiple iterative clauses, which, in a formal sense, corresponds to the composition of multiple mappings and filters. Such nested configurations underscore the expressive power of the comprehension, allowing for the compact representation of multivariate transformations that might otherwise require verbose iterative constructs in conventional loop paradigms.

Computational Efficiency and Expressiveness

From a computational perspective, list comprehensions are lauded for their conciseness and the clarity they afford in representing data transformations. The inherent structural optimization reduces the syntactic overhead associated with explicit looping constructs, thereby facilitating improved readability and maintainability. Internally, the evaluation model of a list comprehension leverages optimizations that minimize temporary storage and duplicate traversals. Such efficiencies can be formally related to the reduction of control flow complexity, as the collection of resultant values is achieved through an implicit, yet rigorously defined, accumulation process. Consequently, list comprehensions exemplify an intersection of theoretical elegance and practical performance, embodying a design that is both mathematically rigorous and operationally efficient.

Python Code Snippet

```python
# This Python code demonstrates several key concepts from the
↪    chapter on List Comprehensions.
# The mathematical notation L = { f(x) | x in S and P(x) } is
↪    implemented here by defining
# a transformation function f(x) and a predicate P(x).

# Define a transformation function: f(x) = x**2 (squaring the input)
def transformation(x):
    return x ** 2

# Define a predicate function: P(x) checks if x is even
def predicate(x):
    return x % 2 == 0

# Create a source list S with numbers from 1 to 20
S = list(range(1, 21))

# Use list comprehension to generate L by applying transformation on
↪    x if predicate(x) is True
L = [transformation(x) for x in S if predicate(x)]
print("Transformed list (squares of even numbers):", L)
# This list comprehension directly implements the formula:
# L = { f(x) | x in S and P(x) }

# Nested list comprehensions: Generate all distinct pairs (x, y)
↪    where x < y from S
pairs = [(x, y) for x in S for y in S if x < y]
print("\nAll distinct pairs (x, y) with x < y:")
print(pairs)

# Multiplication Table using nested list comprehensions:
# Create a 10x10 multiplication table where each cell is the product
↪    of its row and column numbers.
multiplication_table = [[x * y for y in range(1, 11)] for x in
↪    range(1, 11)]
print("\nMultiplication Table (10x10):")
for row in multiplication_table:
    print(row)

# Advanced Example: Compute factors for a given number using list
↪    comprehension.
```

```python
def compute_factors(n):
    # Generate a list of factors for the number n.
    return [i for i in range(1, n + 1) if n % i == 0]

# List of numbers for which to compute factors.
numbers = [10, 15, 21, 28]
# Use dictionary comprehension to map each number to its list of
#   factors.
factors_dict = {n: compute_factors(n) for n in numbers}
print("\nFactors of given numbers:")
for n, factors in factors_dict.items():
    print(f"{n}: {factors}")

# Additional nested comprehension: Flatten a 2D matrix into a 1D
#   list.
matrix = [
    [1, 2, 3],
    [4, 5, 6],
    [7, 8, 9]
]
flattened = [element for row in matrix for element in row]
print("\nFlattened matrix:")
print(flattened)
```

Chapter 20

Functions: Definition and Calling

Theoretical Foundations of Function Definition

Within computational theory, a function is understood as an abstract mapping that associates elements from one set to those of another. Formally, a function may be denoted by the expression $f : D \to C$, where D represents the domain of inputs and C the codomain of outputs. This abstraction is further refined in programming language semantics to encapsulate both computational behavior and scope. In this context, a function is not merely a static relation but an operational entity that, when invoked, performs a predetermined sequence of actions to compute a result. The definition of a function thus forms both a conceptual and syntactic cornerstone, providing the mechanism by which reusable computational procedures are established.

Structural Aspects of Function Declaration

The declaration of a function is characterized by its clear partitioning into a header and a body. The header defines the function's signature, which comprises an identifier and a list of formal parameters. Symbolically, the signature may be represented as

$$N(P_1, P_2, \ldots, P_n) \rightarrow R,$$

where N is the function name, P_i are symbols corresponding to input parameters, and R denotes the type or nature of the returned result, if applicable. The body of the function is an ordered collection of statements that implement the desired sequence of operations. The delineation between the header and the body establishes a clear interface for function invocation and assures that the inner workings of the function remain encapsulated, thus promoting a modular design philosophy.

Mechanisms of Function Invocation

Function invocation, or calling, is the process by which control is transferred from a calling context to the encapsulated function. Upon invocation, an activation record is typically established by the underlying runtime environment. This record allocates space for local parameters, temporary variables, and maintains a reference to the return address. In formal terms, the invocation sets in motion the evaluation of the expression $f(x)$, wherein the argument x is substituted into the function's computational expression. The mechanism of parameter passing—whether by value or by reference—determines the mode by which the input is transmitted to the function's local context. Subsequently, the function's body is executed in isolation, offering a deterministic transformation of the provided input that culminates in an output being returned to the calling environment. This systematic procedure ensures that the abstraction of the function is preserved across multiple invocations, thereby reinforcing the principles of encapsulation and controlled state transition.

Reusability Through Modular Function Abstraction

The capacity to define functions as discrete, reusable modules forms a fundamental aspect of modern software engineering. The abstraction provided by functions allows computational procedures to be decomposed into coherent, self-contained units that can be invoked numerous times with varying inputs. Such modularity not only minimizes redundancy but also enhances the clarity and maintainability of complex systems. In mathematical abstraction, a function may be represented as a tuple (N, P, B), where N is the unique identifier, P represents the ordered collection of parameters, and B encapsulates the block of operations detailing the transformation. This formalism underpins the reusability of function definitions, as the invariant nature of the signature boundary between the interface and its implementation precludes unintended interference. The repeated and consistent application of these modules across diverse contexts is central to achieving scalability and rigorous program correctness within computational systems.

Python Code Snippet

```
"""
This script demonstrates the theoretical foundations, structural
↪   aspects, and
mechanisms of function definition and invocation as discussed in the
↪   chapter
"Functions: Definition and Calling". It illustrates:

1. Function declaration with a clear header and a detailed
↪   docstring.
2. Simulation of an activation record by printing parameter values.
3. Modular design of functions to promote reusability.
4. Invocation mechanics through iterative calls.
5. Use of lambda (anonymous) functions for inline operations.
6. Representation of a function signature as a tuple for
↪   abstraction.
"""

def compute_quadratic(a, b, c, x):
    """
    Computes the quadratic function f(x) = a * x^2 + b * x + c.

    Parameters:
        a (float): Coefficient for the x^2 term.
        b (float): Coefficient for the x term.
        c (float): Constant term.
        x (float): Input value from the domain D.

    Returns:
        float: The computed result representing an element from the
        ↪   codomain C.
    """
    # Simulate the creation of an activation record
    print("Activation Record: a = {}, b = {}, c = {}, x = {}"
        .format(a, b, c, x))
```

```python
    result = a * x**2 + b * x + c
    return result

def demonstrate_function_invocation():
    """
    Demonstrates the process of function invocation and modular
    ↪  function abstraction.

    It shows:
      - The usage of a defined function (compute_quadratic) with
      ↪  constant coefficients.
      - Iterative invocation over a set of input values.
      - The formulation of a simple lambda function for a linear
      ↪  transformation.
      - Representation of the function signature as a tuple (N, P,
      ↪  B), where:
            N = Name of function
            P = Tuple of parameter names
            B = The function body (reference to compute_quadratic)
    """
    # Define coefficients for the quadratic equation f(x) = a*x^2 +
    ↪  b*x + c
    a, b, c = 1.0, -2.0, 1.0  # Example coefficients
    x_values = [0, 1, 2, 3, 4]  # Sample values for x in the domain
    ↪  D

    print("Function Signature: compute_quadratic(a, b, c, x) -> R")
    print("Demonstrating multiple invocations of
    ↪  compute_quadratic:")

    # Iterate over sample x values to simulate function calls
    for x in x_values:
        print("\nInvoking compute_quadratic for x =", x)
        result = compute_quadratic(a, b, c, x)
        print("Result: f({}) = {}".format(x, result))

    # Demonstrate a lambda function (anonymous function) for a
    ↪  simple linear mapping
    linear_transform = lambda m, x: m * x + 10  # Symbolically: f(x)
    ↪  = m*x + 10
    print("\nLambda Function Demonstration: linear_transform(m, x) =
    ↪  m*x + 10")
    m = 3
    x_example = 5
    print("linear_transform({}, {}) = {}"
          .format(m, x_example, linear_transform(m, x_example)))

    # Represent the function signature as a tuple (N, P, B)
    func_signature = ("compute_quadratic", ("a", "b", "c", "x"),
    ↪  compute_quadratic)
    print("\nModular Function Signature Representation:")
    print("Function Name: {}".format(func_signature[0]))
    print("Parameters: {}".format(", ".join(func_signature[1])))
```

```python
def main():
    """
    Main function to execute the demonstration.

    It coordinates the invocation of example functions and simulates
    activation record creation along with modular function
    ↪ abstractions.
    """
    print("----- Function Demonstration Start -----")
    demonstrate_function_invocation()
    print("----- Function Demonstration End -----")

if __name__ == "__main__":
    main()

# End of Python Code Demonstration
```

Chapter 21

Function Parameters and Return Values

Formal Definitions and Semantic Considerations

Within the realm of abstract computation, a function is conceptualized as a mapping from an input space to an output space. The ordered collection of formal parameters, denoted as $(p_1, p_2, \ldots, p_n)$, constitutes the interface through which a function receives its inputs. This interface defines a contract that specifies the nature and form of the data required for its execution. The process of parameter binding—where actual arguments are associated with these formal parameters—is governed by the evaluation strategy of the underlying computational model. Such a mechanism ensures that values supplied upon invocation are integrated into the function's local environment, thereby isolating the internal computational process from external influences. The abstraction provided by this binding process is central to achieving modular design, as it delineates the boundaries between the function's internal logic and its external usage context.

The semantics of parameter passing are critical to maintaining consistency and predictability in function behavior. In formal terms, the substitution of actual arguments in place of formal parameters mirrors the mathematical operation of function application, where a function f applied to a set of arguments is expressed as $f(p_1, p_2, \ldots, p_n)$. This substitution not only facilitates the encapsulation of computational details but also allows for the adoption of various parameter passing paradigms—such as call-by-value or call-by-reference—that further influence the modularity of the system. The precise definition of these parameters transcends simple syntactical placeholders; they form the structural foundation for self-contained operational units within complex computational architectures.

Semantic Frameworks for Return Values

Return values are the mechanism by which functions communicate the outcomes of their computations to the external environment. Formally, a function defined by the mapping $f : D \to C$ associates elements from the domain D with elements in the codomain C, and the returned value represents the element in C corresponding to the given inputs. The act of returning a value demarcates the conclusion of the function's execution, providing a discrete and encapsulated result that can be seamlessly integrated into broader computational workflows. This process is intrinsic to the function's operational semantics, establishing the function as a self-contained unit with a well-defined output.

The mechanism for returning values involves the creation of an output that encapsulates the result of the function's computational logic. This output is typically stored in a designated memory space or represented symbolically, underscoring the distinction between the internal state of the function and the externally observable outcome. The explicit representation of return values as part of the function's interface enhances type safety and facilitates the composition of functions in a systematic manner. By strictly delineating the domain of inputs and the corresponding outputs, the process of returning values supports the development of reliable and maintainable systems, where the behavior of individual functions remains predictable and invariant under reorganization or refactoring.

Integration of Parameters and Return Values in Modular Design

The interplay between parameter acceptance and value return forms an essential framework for modular design in computational systems. The specification of a function's parameters and its corresponding return value creates a contract that governs the interaction between discrete functional units. This contract, characterized by a clearly defined input-output relationship, enables functions to be composed in a manner that minimizes unintended dependencies and promotes reusability. By treating functions as black-box entities—with well-articulated interfaces that include both the parameter list and the return value—one can ensure that the internal mechanisms remain concealed, thereby allowing independent evolution of components without compromising overall system integrity.

In a modular context, the segregation of a function's interface from its internal implementation fosters an environment in which individual functions can be interconnected to yield complex computational behavior. The explicit separation between the data injected through parameters and the outcomes delivered via return values contributes to a robust architecture, wherein each function operates as an autonomous, self-contained module. This architectural paradigm not only simplifies reasoning about program behavior but also enhances the maintainability of the system by permitting modifications within a function's internal logic without affecting its externally defined interface. The rigorous formalism underlying parameter binding and value return is thus instrumental in advancing the goals of modularity and reusability in sophisticated software engineering endeavors.

Python Code Snippet

```
# -*- coding: utf-8 -*-
"""
This module illustrates the core concepts discussed in the chapter:
    - Function parameters as a formal interface (f: D -> C)
    - Parameter binding: substituting actual arguments for formal
    ↪   parameters
    - Encapsulation of computational logic through return values
    - Modular design using clear input-output contracts

Each function below is annotated with its mathematical abstraction.
"""

def function_mapping(f, domain):
    """
    Apply a function f to each element of a given domain.

    Mathematically:
        Let f : D -> C and x  D,
        then f(x)  C.
```

114

    """

```python
mapping = {}
for x in domain:
    mapping[x] = f(x)   # Actual parameter 'x' is bound to the
    ↪  formal parameter of f.
return mapping
```

```python
def square(x):
```
    """
    """
```python
return x * x
```

```python
# Using a lambda function to define the cube operation inline.
# Mathematical representation: f(x) = x^3
cube = lambda x: x ** 3
```

```python
def advanced_function(a, b, operation, verbose=False):
```
    """

```python
        Given f is applied as f(a, b), actual arguments a and b
        ↪  replace the formal parameters.
    """
    if verbose:
        print(f"Executing operation with parameters: a = {a}, b =
        ↪  {b}")
    result = operation(a, b)
    if verbose:
        print(f"Operation result: {result}")
    return result

def add(x, y):
    """
    Perform addition on two numbers.

    Mathematical formulation:
        f(x, y) = x + y

    Parameters:
        x (int or float): First number.
        y (int or float): Second number.

    Returns:
        int or float: The sum of x and y.
    """
    return x + y

def multiply(x, y):
    """
    Perform multiplication on two numbers.

    Mathematical formulation:
        f(x, y) = x * y

    Parameters:
        x (int or float): First number.
        y (int or float): Second number.

    Returns:
        int or float: The product of x and y.
    """
    return x * y

def inner_outer_example(x):
    """
    Demonstrates the isolation of variable scope in nested
    ↪  functions.

    The outer function accepts a parameter x, which is then used by
    ↪  an inner function.
    This encapsulation simulates the modular design where the
    ↪  internal logic is hidden.
```

```python
    Specifically:
        Define inner_function(y) such that:
            inner_function(y) = x + y
        Then outer_function(x) returns inner_function(10).

    Parameters:
        x (int or float): An input value.

    Returns:
        int or float: The result of x + 10.
    """
    def inner_function(y):
        # 'x' is bound from the outer scope.
        return x + y
    return inner_function(10)


def main():
    # Define a domain for mapping functions.
    domain = [1, 2, 3, 4, 5]

    # Demonstrate mapping using the square function: f(x) = x^2.
    squares = function_mapping(square, domain)
    print("Mapping using square (f(x) = x^2):", squares)

    # Demonstrate mapping using the cube lambda function: f(x) =
    ↪   x^3.
    cubes = function_mapping(cube, domain)
    print("Mapping using cube (f(x) = x^3):", cubes)

    # Use advanced_function to perform addition and multiplication.
    sum_result = advanced_function(10, 5, add, verbose=True)
    product_result = advanced_function(10, 5, multiply,
    ↪   verbose=True)

    # Using a dispatch dictionary to select the operation based on a
    ↪   key.
    operations = {
        "add": add,
        "multiply": multiply
    }
    selected_op = "add"
    if selected_op in operations:
        result = advanced_function(20, 30, operations[selected_op],
        ↪   verbose=True)
        print(f"Result using operation '{selected_op}' on (20,
        ↪   30):", result)

    # Demonstrate inner function scope isolation.
    scope_result = inner_outer_example(15)  # Expected to compute 15
    ↪   + 10.
    print("Result from inner_outer_example (should be 25):",
    ↪   scope_result)
```

```
if __name__ == "__main__":
    main()
```

Chapter 22

Variable Scope

Local Variables and Their Lifetimes

The delineation of local variables is fundamental in the architecture of formal computational models. Variables declared within a confined syntactical block, function, or subroutine are intrinsically associated with a restricted scope. Let L denote the set of variables introduced in a particular lexical block B, and consider that each $l \in L$ is accessible solely within B and its nested sub-blocks. The lifetime of any variable in L is strictly limited to the dynamic activation period of its defining block. This temporally bounded existence alleviates the potential for inadvertent side-effects and promotes tighter control over memory allocation and reclamation. The binding of local variables occurs at the entry of their block scope, with an adherence to static lexical scoping rules, ensuring that the substitution of identifiers with their associated values remains unequivocal and context-sensitive.

Global Variables and Their Lifetimes

In contrast, global variables are declared in the outermost module or program-level context, thereby assuming a ubiquitous scope across the entirety of the codebase. Denote by G the set of global variables defined in the global namespace; each $g \in G$ remains accessible from any subsequent portion of the program subsequent to its declaration. The lifetime of a global variable extends over the entire duration of the program's execution or until an explicit

119

re-assignment or disposal is enacted. This persistent visibility provides a mechanism for maintaining state or shared information across diverse components. However, the extended lifetime and unconfined accessibility necessitate stringent measures to avert unintended interferences between independent computational modules, as the potential for namespace pollution and inadvertent shadowing increases.

Scope Resolution and Binding Mechanisms

The systematic resolution of identifiers and the subsequent binding of variables constitute the foundation upon which variable scope is managed. Under static scoping conventions, the resolution process examines the program's lexical structure to locate the most immediate declaration corresponding to a given identifier. Formally, if an identifier x is referenced within a nested block, the search criterion is to traverse the hierarchical chain of lexical contexts until a binding for x is encountered. In the absence of a local declaration, the resolution process defaults to the global namespace represented by G. This hierarchical binding mechanism not only enforces modularity by isolating local computational environments but also engenders the phenomenon of shadowing. When a local declaration of an identifier x coexists with a global counterpart sharing the same name, the local binding takes precedence within its scope, thereby concealing the global identifier and preserving the integrity of localized computations.

Interaction Between Local and Global Environments

The interplay between local and global environments is governed by a well-defined hierarchical structure that delineates the accessibility and temporal persistence of variables. Consider the scenario wherein a local variable x_{local} exists within a block while an identically named global variable x_{global} is accessible throughout the program. Under an unambiguous resolution protocol, any reference to x within the local context is unequivocally bound to x_{local}, irrespective of the existence of x_{global}. This stratification ensures that local computations are insulated from external modifications, while global variables serve as shared resources across disparate scopes. The contrast in lifetimes—local variables being ephemeral and closely tied to dynamic activation records, and global variables persisting over the full execution timeline—illustrates the inherent trade-offs in design, balancing modularity against the convenience of omnipresent state accessibility.

Python Code Snippet

```python
# Global variable declaration (G)
x_global = 100  # This variable belongs to the global namespace (G)

def demonstrate_local_scope():
    # Local variable declarations (L)
    x = 10  # Local variable; accessible only within
    ↪   demonstrate_local_scope()
    y = 20  # Another local variable
    print("Inside demonstrate_local_scope:")
    print("Local x:", x)
    print("Local y:", y)

    # Nested function to further illustrate local scope and lifetime
    def nested_function():
        # 'z' is local to nested_function; it captures the value of
        ↪   'x' from the enclosing scope
        z = x * 2
        print("Inside nested_function:")
        print("Nested local variable z (computed as 2 * x):", z)

    nested_function()

def demonstrate_scope_binding():
    # Demonstrates scope resolution and shadowing of global
    ↪   variables.
    x = 5  # This local 'x' shadows any global 'x' (if existed)
    ↪   within this function's scope
    print("\nInside demonstrate_scope_binding:")
    print("Local x (before inner modification):", x)

    def inner():
        # Initially, inner() accesses the 'x' from the enclosing
        ↪   scope due to static (lexical) scoping.
        print("In inner (accessing parent's x):", x)
        # To modify 'x' from the enclosing scope, we use the
        ↪   nonlocal keyword.
        nonlocal x
        x = 15
        print("In inner after modifying parent's x:", x)

    inner()
```

```python
    print("After inner, modified local x:", x)

def demonstrate_global_access():
    # Illustrates accessing and modifying a global variable.
    global x_global
    print("\nInside demonstrate_global_access:")
    print("Global x_global (before modification):", x_global)
    # Modify the global variable
    x_global = x_global + 50
    print("Global x_global (after modification):", x_global)

def closure_example():
    # Demonstrates the closure property where a nested function
    ↪   captures and retains
    # the local variable 'a' even after the outer function execution
    ↪   completes.
    a = 25  # Local variable in closure_example
    print("\nInside closure_example, local variable a:", a)

    def inner_closure():
        # Captures 'a' from the enclosing scope
        print("In inner_closure, captured variable a from closure:",
        ↪   a)
    return inner_closure

def main():
    print("Demonstrating Variable Scope, Lifetime, and Binding in
    ↪   Python\n")
    print("Initial global x_global:", x_global)

    # Demonstrate local variable scope and lifetime through a simple
    ↪   function call
    demonstrate_local_scope()

    # Demonstrate scope resolution, shadowing, and the nonlocal
    ↪   mechanism
    demonstrate_scope_binding()

    # Demonstrate access and modification of a global variable
    demonstrate_global_access()
    print("Final global x_global:", x_global)

    # Demonstrate that closures capture local variables from their
    ↪   defining context
    closure_func = closure_example()
    # Even though closure_example() has ended, inner_closure still
    ↪   has access to 'a'
    closure_func()

if __name__ == "__main__":
    main()
```

122

Chapter 23

Lambda Functions and Anonymous Functions

Abstract Foundations of Lambda Expressions

Lambda expressions are conceptualized as function objects that are defined without a formal identifier, thus operating as anonymous functions within a program's structure. In formal notation, an expression of the form $\lambda x.E$ denotes an abstraction that accepts a parameter x and returns an expression E. This abstract formulation draws its origins from lambda calculus, a mathematical system that underpins many functional programming paradigms. The absence of an explicit name in such constructions is indicative of their design purpose: to serve as transient, inline function objects that are instantiated, utilized, and discarded without cluttering the global namespace with superfluous identifiers.

Syntax and Structural Representations

A precise examination of lambda expressions reveals a highly compact syntactical framework. Generally, a lambda expression is represented as

$$\lambda x_1, x_2, \ldots, x_n.E,$$

where $x_1, x_2, \ldots, x_n$ are formal parameters and E constitutes the resultant expression upon the function's application. This notation

encapsulates both parameter contraction and the intended computation within a single, succinct form. The dot notation serves as a
syntactical delimiter, distinguishing the list of parameters from the
expression that constitutes the function's body. This structure not
only simplifies the formulation of functions that perform narrowly
defined tasks but also accentuates the role of these constructs as
first-class citizens that seamlessly integrate within larger functional
chains.

Binding Mechanisms and Closure Forma-
tion

The operational semantics of lambda expressions are intrinsically
tied to the principles of binding and lexical scoping. Upon invocation, the lambda abstraction engages in a binding process where
formal parameters are correspondingly matched to actual arguments, a procedure that aligns with the substitution model prevalent in formal semantics. In this process, the parameters within
the lambda abstraction are locally bound to the argument expressions, ensuring that variable references within the body E are resolved according to the immediate lexical environment. Furthermore, lambda functions inherently support closure formation; that
is, they capture and retain access to non-local variables from the
encompassing scope in which they were defined. This characteristic
enables lambda expressions to persist with contextual knowledge,
thereby facilitating the construction of higher-order functions and
contributing to the modular decomposition of intricate computational processes.

In-line Function Object Construction in
Functional Paradigms

The utility of lambda functions is most pronounced when they are
employed as in-line function objects that are crafted without the
overhead associated with traditional function declarations. Such
constructions are particularly advantageous in contexts where brief,
one-off computations are required as components of larger functional compositions. The ability to define these compact function
objects directly at the point of use leads to a more expressive and

streamlined codebase, where the intent of the computation is immediately apparent. The mathematical underpinnings drawn from the principles of lambda calculus enable these constructs to be rigorously analyzed in terms of fixed-point combinators and recursive patterns, thereby ensuring that their behavior is both predictable and amenable to formal reasoning. In effect, lambda functions serve as the prototypical embodiment of in-line abstraction, reinforcing the paradigms of modularity and conciseness that are central to advanced computational theory.

Python Code Snippet

```python
# 1. Single-Argument Lambda Function: compute the square of a
↪   number.
square = lambda x: x ** 2
print("Square of 5:", square(5))

# 2. Multi-Argument Lambda Functions: calculate the sum and product
↪   of two numbers.
add = lambda x, y: x + y
prod = lambda x, y: x * y
print("Sum of 3 and 4:", add(3, 4))
print("Product of 3 and 4:", prod(3, 4))

# 3. Using lambda with higher-order functions: map and filter.
numbers = list(range(1, 11))
squares = list(map(lambda x: x ** 2, numbers))
evens = list(filter(lambda x: x % 2 == 0, numbers))
print("Numbers:", numbers)
print("Squares:", squares)
print("Even Numbers:", evens)

# 4. Sorting with lambda as the key function.
students = [
    {"name": "Alice", "score": 88},
    {"name": "Bob", "score": 95},
    {"name": "Charlie", "score": 70}
]
# Sort students by score in descending order.
sorted_students = sorted(students, key=lambda student:
↪   student["score"], reverse=True)
print("Students sorted by score (desc):", sorted_students)

# 5. Demonstration of Closure: lambda functions capturing variables
↪   from their lexical scope.
def make_multiplier(n):
    """
    Returns a lambda function that multiplies its input by a
    ↪   captured factor n.
```

```
    This demonstrates closure formation where the lambda retains
    ↪  access to n.
    """
    return lambda x: n * x

double = make_multiplier(2)
triple = make_multiplier(3)
print("Double of 4:", double(4))
print("Triple of 4:", triple(4))

# 6. Y Combinator for Recursive Lambda (Fixed-Point Combinator
↪  Example)
def Y(f):
    """
    Implements the Y combinator in Python to enable recursion with
    ↪  lambda functions.
    f: A function that takes a recursive function as an argument and
    ↪  returns another function.
    """
    return (lambda x: f(lambda *args: x(x)(*args)))(lambda x:
    ↪  f(lambda *args: x(x)(*args)))

# Define a factorial function using the Y combinator.
factorial = Y(lambda f: lambda n: 1 if n == 0 else n * f(n - 1))
print("Factorial of 5:", factorial(5))

# End of comprehensive lambda examples.
```

Chapter 24

Built-in Functions Overview

Conceptual Foundations and Theoretical Underpinnings

Python's built-in functions epitomize a design philosophy that integrates theoretical principles of computation with pragmatic programming methodologies. These functions are conceived as intrinsic operations that are interwoven into the language's runtime, thereby providing an optimized mechanism for executing frequently encountered tasks. Their design is informed by abstract models of computation, such as the λ calculus, and by formal semantic frameworks that emphasize minimalism and orthogonality. In this context, built-in functions act as both fundamental primitives and as high-level abstractions, encapsulating operations that would otherwise necessitate extensive bespoke implementations. Their existence within the language core reflects a synthesis of mathematical rigor and empirical efficiency, offering a standardized means to perform operations that range from elementary arithmetic and type conversion to advanced introspection and sequence manipulation.

Taxonomical Classification and Structural Organization

The assortment of built-in functions in Python is systematically categorized to address a broad spectrum of computational tasks. This taxonomical structure is indicative of a deliberate division into function classes that correspond to specific semantic roles. One prominent category encompasses functions that facilitate numerical computations and perform elementary arithmetic operations. Another distinct category is devoted to type conversion and object construction, wherein functions provide deterministic pathways for transforming inputs into canonical forms. Additional classifications cover operations related to collections and sequences, such as iteration, aggregation, and sorting routines, as well as functions that enable reflective operations on objects and support metaprogramming paradigms. Such a structured organization not only simplifies the theoretical analysis of their properties but also enhances their practical utility by providing a clear, predictable interface for routine tasks. The resulting architectural clarity contributes to the overall expressiveness of the language, promoting both consistency and reliability in program design.

Operational Mechanisms and Efficiency Considerations

A defining characteristic of Python's built-in functions is their integration into the interpreter's core, which affords them a performance profile that is often superior to that of functions implemented entirely in Python. This efficiency is achieved via implementations in lower-level languages such as C, which enable direct access to system-level routines and memory management strategies. The operational semantics of these functions are founded on a precise protocol that governs parameter binding, argument evaluation, and return value computation. In many cases, theoretical guarantees are provided in terms of computational complexity, as evidenced by time complexity bounds expressed in asymptotic notation such as $O(1)$ or $O(n)$, where applicable. The interpreter employs a series of optimizations, including caching and short-circuit evaluations, to ensure that built-in functions execute with minimal overhead. This internal orchestration of performance and reliability highlights the dual commitment to theoretical robustness and practical expediency, rendering these functions indispensable in the construction of efficient and maintainable programs.

Interoperability within the Pythonic Ecosystem

Within the dynamic environment of Python, built-in functions serve as the connective tissue that unifies disparate aspects of the programming model. Their design facilitates seamless interoperability with both user-defined functions and the broader infrastructure of Python's data types and object models. Conformance to a uniform calling convention and consistent error handling protocols ensures that built-in functions integrate effortlessly with constructs such as higher-order functions, iterators, and generators. This uniformity not only reinforces the syntactic and semantic cohesion of the language, but also embeds resilience within program execution by guaranteeing predictable responses to both valid and aberrant input conditions. The inherent flexibility of these functions enables them to participate in complex functional compositions without sacrificing clarity or performance. As such, they substantively contribute to the expressiveness and robustness of Python's computational framework by providing a reliable, high-performance substrate upon which more elaborate algorithms and abstractions can be constructed.

Python Code Snippet

```
# Comprehensive Python Code Snippet Demonstrating Built-in Functions
↪    and Operational Mechanisms

import functools
import math

def arithmetic_mean(data):
    """
    Compute the arithmetic mean using built-in functions sum() and
    ↪    len().
    Time Complexity: O(n)
    """
    if len(data) == 0:
        return None  # Avoid division by zero
    return sum(data) / len(data)
```

```python
def sort_by_second_element(data):
    """
    Sort a list of tuples based on the second element using sorted()
    ↪    and a lambda function.
    Time Complexity: O(n log n)
    """
    return sorted(data, key=lambda x: x[1])


@functools.lru_cache(maxsize=None)
def fibonacci(n):
    """
    Compute the nth Fibonacci number using recursion with caching.
    Without caching, the recursive approach is exponential; with
    ↪    lru_cache, it achieves O(n) time.
    """
    if n < 2:
        return n
    return fibonacci(n-1) + fibonacci(n-2)


def functional_transformations(data):
    """
    Demonstrate functional programming by transforming a sequence.
    This function squares even numbers using map() and filter()
    ↪    combined with lambda functions.
    Time Complexity: O(n)
    """
    squared_evens = list(map(lambda x: x ** 2, filter(lambda x: x %
    ↪    2 == 0, data)))
    return squared_evens


def demonstrate_zip_enumerate():
    """
    Illustrate the use of zip() and enumerate() to combine
    ↪    collections and iterate with indices.
    Time Complexity: O(n)
    """
    letters = ["A", "B", "C"]
    numbers = [1, 2, 3]
    combined = list(zip(letters, numbers))
    print("Zipped List:", combined)
    for idx, (letter, number) in enumerate(combined):
        print(f"Index {idx}: {letter} -> {number}")


def demonstrate_introspection():
    """
    Showcase introspection using built-in functions such as id(),
    ↪    type(), and len().
    """
    sample_list = [10, 20, 30]
    print("ID of sample_list:", id(sample_list))
    print("Type of sample_list:", type(sample_list))
    print("Length of sample_list:", len(sample_list))
```

```python
    # Uncomment the following line to see interactive help on the
    ↪  built-in function 'len'
    # help(len)

def main():
    print("----- Python Code Snippet Demonstration -----")

    # 1. Arithmetic Mean Calculation (O(n))
    data = [15, 25, 35, 45, 55]
    mean_value = arithmetic_mean(data)
    print("Arithmetic Mean:", mean_value)

    # 2. Sorting Tuples by Second Element (O(n log n))
    items = [("orange", 2), ("apple", 5), ("banana", 3)]
    sorted_items = sort_by_second_element(items)
    print("Sorted Items:", sorted_items)

    # 3. Fibonacci Sequence Generation using recursion with caching
    ↪  (O(n))
    n = 10
    fib_sequence = [fibonacci(i) for i in range(n)]
    print("Fibonacci Sequence (first", n, "terms):", fib_sequence)

    # 4. Functional Transformation: Square Even Numbers (O(n))
    numbers = list(range(1, 11))
    squared_evens = functional_transformations(numbers)
    print("Squared Even Numbers:", squared_evens)

    # 5. Using zip() and enumerate() for Collection Manipulation
    ↪  (O(n))
    demonstrate_zip_enumerate()

    # 6. Introspection of Built-in Functions
    demonstrate_introspection()

if __name__ == "__main__":
    main()
```

Chapter 25

The Math Module

Historical Context and Design Objectives

The math module emerges from a tradition of integrating rigorous mathematical theory with computational efficiency. Its design reflects a synthesis of classical numerical analysis and modern software engineering principles. Functions and constants within the module are implemented in lower-level languages, thereby providing a level of performance and precision that is critical for advanced arithmetic operations. The module embodies an intrinsic commitment to the formal semantics of numerical computation, where every function is purposefully aligned with theoretical models such as the
lambda calculus and the IEEE 754 standard for floating-point arithmetic.

Numerical Constants and Their Computational Properties

A core aspect of the math module is its provision of immutable numerical constants. Among these, the constant
pi is defined as the mathematical ratio of a circle's circumference to its diameter, while *e* represents the base of the natural logarithm. Additional constants, such as
tau (which equals 2
pi) and other values representing positive infinity (
infty) and not-a-number (

$mboxNaN$), are provided to facilitate a wide range of computations. These values are stored in double-precision format and serve as fundamental benchmarks for the evaluation of trigonometric, logarithmic, and exponential functions. Their inclusion within the module ensures consistency in numerical precision across diverse computational tasks.

Elementary Arithmetic Functions and Their Operational Characteristics

The module encompasses a broad array of functions that perform elementary arithmetic operations. Functionality such as the computation of square roots, absolute values, and factorials is rendered through dedicated routines like
$sqrtcdot$,
$fabs($
$cdot$), and
$factorial($
$cdot$), respectively. Trigonometric functions—including
$sin($
$cdot$),
$cos($
$cdot$), and
$tan($
$cdot$)—are implemented to deliver rapid evaluations of angle-based calculations. The establishment of these functions adheres to well-defined mathematical principles, ensuring that the operations support a precise mapping between theoretical arithmetic formulations and their practical computational realization.

Advanced Functions in Trigonometry and Logarithmic Computations

Beyond elementary operations, the math module provides a suite of advanced functions that extend the boundaries of traditional arithmetic computation. Functions such as
$atan2(y, x)$ allow for the determination of an angle in a two-dimensional plane by considering the signs of both inputs, thus addressing quadrant-specific behaviors. The module's logarithmic functions, including

log(
cdot) and
*log*10(
cdot), are designed to accommodate various bases and scaling properties, while the inclusion of functions like
*expm*1(
cdot) and
*log*1*p*(
cdot) ensures numerical stability in cases where the magnitude of the operand is very small. Such careful implementations highlight the dual emphasis on mathematical accuracy and computational efficiency.

Mathematical Precision and Numerical Stability Considerations

Each function within the math module is rigorously engineered to preserve numerical precision and stability across a spectrum of computational scenarios. Intrinsic domain restrictions are enforced, whereby operations that are mathematically undefined—for example, the computation of
sqrt−1 in the realm of real numbers—result in the generation of corresponding exceptions. The implementation of these functions in a compiled language affords a level of computational efficiency that minimizes error propagation and rounding discrepancies. Moreover, the module's reliance on fixed-precision arithmetic necessitates a careful treatment of issues related to overflow, underflow, and rounding errors, thereby ensuring that each operation maintains a verifiable balance between speed and accuracy.

Integration within the Computational Ecosystem

The math module functions as an integral component of the programming language's standard library, interfacing seamlessly with other facets of the computational ecosystem. Its functions are designed to operate under a unified calling convention, thereby harmonizing with user-defined routines and other system components. The module's design is a testament to the meticulous calibration of mathematical theory and practical implementation, providing advanced arithmetic operations that are both robust and performant. By encapsulating sophisticated mathematical routines within a standardized interface, the module establishes a foundation for complex numerical computation that is both theoretically sound and practically efficient.

Python Code Snippet

```python
import math

def demonstrate_constants():
    # Displaying immutable numerical constants provided by the math
    ↪ module.
    print("Math Constants:")
    print("pi =", math.pi)              # Ratio of a circle's
    ↪ circumference to its diameter
    print("e =", math.e)                # Base of the natural logarithm
    print("tau =", math.tau)            # tau, which equals 2*pi
    print("inf =", math.inf)            # Representation of positive
    ↪ infinity
    print("nan =", math.nan)            # Not-a-Number (NaN)

def demonstrate_arithmetic():
    # Demonstrating elementary arithmetic functions.
    num = 16
    print("\nElementary Arithmetic:")
    print("Square root of", num, "=", math.sqrt(num))
    print("Absolute value of -10 =", math.fabs(-10))
    print("Factorial of 5 =", math.factorial(5))

def demonstrate_trigonometry():
    # Showcasing trigonometric functions and two-argument arctan.
    angle_degrees = 45
    angle_radians = math.radians(angle_degrees)   # Converting
    ↪ degrees to radians
    print("\nTrigonometric Functions:")
    print("sin({}°) =".format(angle_degrees),
    ↪ math.sin(angle_radians))
    print("cos({}°) =".format(angle_degrees),
    ↪ math.cos(angle_radians))
    print("tan({}°) =".format(angle_degrees),
    ↪ math.tan(angle_radians))
    # atan2 accounts for the quadrant by considering the sign of
    ↪ both inputs.
    print("atan2(1, 1) =", math.atan2(1, 1))

def demonstrate_logarithmic():
    # Demonstrating logarithmic computations including advanced
    ↪ functions for numerical stability.
```

```
    num = 10
    print("\nLogarithmic Functions:")
    print("Natural log of", num, "=", math.log(num))
    print("Log base 10 of", num, "=", math.log10(num))

    # For small numbers, expm1 and log1p help maintain numerical
    ↪  precision.
    small_number = 1e-10
    print("expm1({}) =".format(small_number),
    ↪  math.expm1(small_number))
    print("log1p({}) =".format(small_number),
    ↪  math.log1p(small_number))

def demonstrate_error_handling():
    # Illustrating how math module enforces domain restrictions and
    ↪  provides error feedback.
    try:
        # Attempting to compute the square root of a negative number
        ↪  in real numbers.
        result = math.sqrt(-1)
    except ValueError as e:
        print("\nError Handling:")
        print("Error computing sqrt(-1):", e)

def main():
    print("Demonstration of the math Module Functionalities:\n")
    demonstrate_constants()
    demonstrate_arithmetic()
    demonstrate_trigonometry()
    demonstrate_logarithmic()
    demonstrate_error_handling()

if __name__ == "__main__":
    main()
```

136

Chapter 26

Exception Handling

Motivation for Exception Handling

Unforeseen conditions during program execution, whether arising from invalid data, unexpected system states, or violations of logical constraints, pose significant challenges to maintaining algorithmic continuity. Exception handling mechanisms were developed to address this discontinuity by providing a structured framework that isolates error-prone operations from the principal logic. In modern computational systems, disruptions caused by anomalous events necessitate a systematic approach wherein irregular conditions are not treated as terminal failures but as events that can be intercepted and remedied within a controlled execution scope.

Mechanics of the Try and Except Constructs

Encapsulating a sequence of operations within a try block constitutes a formal declaration that these operations are susceptible to exceptional conditions. During the execution of such a block, each operation is monitored for deviations from normative behavior. Upon detection of an anomaly, the standard control flow is preemptively interrupted, transferring execution to a corresponding except block. This subsequent block is tasked with evaluating the nature of the raised exception and executing tailored recovery procedures. The process involves a dynamic matching of the raised exception against a hierarchy of potential handlers, thereby ensuring that only the most contextually appropriate remediation strategy is invoked. The design of try and except constructs is fundamentally influenced by principles of modularity and separation of concerns, thereby promoting error management as an intrinsic component of program robustness.

Role and Semantics of the Finally Block

The articulation of a finally block within this structured exception handling paradigm introduces an invariant mechanism dedicated to the execution of cleanup operations. Independent of whether an exception is detected or an explicit recovery path is invoked, the finally block is guaranteed to execute once the try block terminates. This unconditional execution is particularly critical for the management of resources such as file descriptors, network sockets, or allocated memory, ensuring that resource deallocation and state restoration occur reliably. The semantic role of the finally block, therefore, is to enforce the maintenance of system invariants and to prevent the propagation of resource inconsistencies or memory leaks within the computational environment.

Propagation of Exceptions and Execution Semantics

When a raised exception is not immediately intercepted by an associated except block, the exception is propagated upward through the hierarchy of active execution contexts. This propagation continues until a matching handler is encountered or the runtime environment terminates the program. The propagation mechanism embodies a disciplined approach to error resolution, permitting localized exception management while simultaneously enabling the centralization of error reporting and logging in higher-level constructs. This hierarchical search and resolution scheme is integral to maintaining a balance between precise control flow and comprehensive error diagnosis, thereby ensuring that the system remains resilient in the face of unpredictable operational conditions.

Python Code Snippet

```python
#!/usr/bin/env python3

# Define a custom exception class for demonstration
class CustomError(Exception):
    """
    Custom exception to be raised when specific error conditions are
    ↪  met.
    """
    def __init__(self, message="A custom error occurred during
    ↪  operation"):
        super().__init__(message)

def divide_numbers(a, b):
    """
    Performs division of two numbers with comprehensive exception
    ↪  handling.

    Parameters:
        a (int or float): The numerator.
        b (int or float): The denominator.

    Returns:
        float: The result of the division if successful.

    Raises:
        ZeroDivisionError: If b is zero.
        TypeError: If either a or b is not a number.
        CustomError: Wrapping ZeroDivisionError to provide a custom
        ↪  message.
    """
    try:
        # Check if the arguments are numbers; raise TypeError if
        ↪  not.
        if not (isinstance(a, (int, float)) and isinstance(b, (int,
        ↪  float))):
            raise TypeError("Both operands must be numeric.")

        # Perform the division which may raise ZeroDivisionError
        result = a / b

    except ZeroDivisionError as e:
        print("Error: Attempted division by zero encountered.")
        # Raise a custom exception, chaining from the original
        ↪  error.
        raise CustomError("Division by zero is not allowed.") from e

    except TypeError as e:
        # Handle cases where non-numeric types are provided.
        print("Type error:", e)
        # Propagate the exception after logging.
```

```python
        raise

    else:
        # This block executes if no exception was raised in the try
        ↪  block.
        print("Division successful. The result is:", result)
        return result

    finally:
        # This block executes no matter what, useful for cleanup or
        ↪  logging.
        print("Exiting the divide_numbers function.")

def complex_calculation(numbers):
    """
    Iterates over a list of numbers, performing a division operation
    ↪  on each element.
    Uses exception handling to manage failures and always executes
    ↪  cleanup in the loop.

    Parameters:
        numbers (list): A list containing elements to use as
        ↪  divisors for 100.

    Returns:
        list: List of results. If an error occurs for an element,
        ↪  None is stored.
    """
    results = []
    for i, num in enumerate(numbers):
        try:
            print(f"\nProcessing element at index {i}: {num}")
            # Divide 100 by the current number
            res = divide_numbers(100, num)
        except Exception as e:
            # Log the error specific to the current computation.
            print(f"Calculation failed for element at index {i}:
            ↪  {e}")
            results.append(None)
        else:
            # Store the successful result.
            results.append(res)
        finally:
            # Always indicate completion of processing for the
            ↪  current element.
            print(f"Finished processing element at index {i}.")
    return results

def main():
    """
    Main function to execute the complex_calculation.
    Demonstrates exception propagation, handling, and cleanup using
    ↪  finally blocks.
```

140

```python
    """
    # A list of test values including valid numbers, a zero (to
    ↪   trigger ZeroDivisionError),
    # and a non-numeric value (to trigger TypeError).
    test_values = [50, 0, "a", 25]
    print("Starting complex calculations...")

    # Execute the calculation and capture the results.
    final_results = complex_calculation(test_values)

    print("\nFinal Calculation Results:", final_results)

if __name__ == '__main__':
    main()
```

Chapter 27

Custom Exception Classes

Conceptual Foundations of User-Defined Exception Classes

User-defined exception classes constitute an integral component within the error-handling architecture of robust software systems. These classes are expressly designed to encapsulate error conditions that extend beyond the scope of standard, built-in exceptions. In this paradigm, an exception is regarded as a first-class object that embodies detailed diagnostic information and semantic context. The creation of such classes empowers a system to delineate nuanced failure modes and to maintain invariant conditions across complex computational workflows. Concretely, a custom exception class formalizes the notion of an error by associating it with specialized metadata, thereby facilitating precise differentiation among multiple error states.

Design Principles and Structural Considerations

The architectural formulation of custom exception classes is firmly rooted in fundamental object-oriented design principles, most notably inheritance. By deriving a bespoke exception from a canonical base exception, the resulting class integrates seamlessly into an existing error-handling framework. This hierarchical approach assures that the custom exception inherits essential properties while concurrently enabling augmentation with additional attributes and behaviors specific to the operational domain. The deliberate structuring of these classes involves a careful design of constructors to accept parameters—such as descriptive text, error codes, or contextual state identifiers—that provide a rich representation of the failure condition. As a consequence, custom exception classes support not only the centralized capturing of errors but also the systematic categorization essential for complex exception propagation schemes.

Error Taxonomy and Domain-Specific Integration

The utilization of custom exception classes is intimately related to the formulation of a comprehensive error taxonomy, particularly in the context of specialized applications. By defining exception classes tailored to represent domain-specific error states, the error-handling mechanism becomes capable of conveying precise semantic information. Each custom exception class occupies a distinct position within the error taxonomy, enabling explicit differentiation among classes of errors such as validation failures, resource constraints, or state inconsistencies. This integration of domain knowledge into the exception model guarantees that exceptional conditions are communicated with exactitude. Moreover, the structured taxonomy permits the implementation of finely grained catch mechanisms that are aligned to the particularities of each error condition, thereby enhancing both the diagnostic resolution and the subsequent remedial strategies.

Methodological Considerations in Implementation

The process of implementing custom exception classes necessitates a rigorous methodological approach, balancing minimal redundancy with comprehensive descriptive capability. The design involves a systematic determination of the attributes required to fully characterize the error state, along with the precise specification of the inheritance chain to ensure congruence with the overarching exception hierarchy. Special attention is given to the encapsulation of contextual data and the potential need for error chaining, whereby an instance of a custom exception retains a reference to an original underlying error. This strategy not only enhances clarity in error propagation but also facilitates later stages of error analysis and logging. Through such methodological rigor, custom exception classes are positioned as an essential facility within high-assurance software systems, ensuring that the propagation and handling of domain-specific errors align with stringent standards of reliability and maintainability.

Python Code Snippet

```python
# Custom Exception Hierarchy demonstrating user-defined exceptions
↪   with detailed context,
# error codes, and error chaining for enhanced diagnostics.

class CustomError(Exception):
    """
    Base class for custom errors in the system.

    Attributes:
        message (str): A human-readable explanation of the error.
        error_code (int, optional): A numeric code identifying the
        ↪   error type.
        context (dict, optional): Additional contextual information
        ↪   about the error.
    """
    def __init__(self, message, error_code=None, context=None):
        super().__init__(message)
        self.error_code = error_code
        self.context = context or {}

    def __str__(self):
        base_message = super().__str__()
        if self.error_code is not None:
            base_message += f" (Error Code: {self.error_code})"
        if self.context:
            base_message += f" | Context: {self.context}"
        return base_message


class ValidationError(CustomError):
    """
    Exception raised for errors in the input validation process.
    """
    def __init__(self, field, value, message="Validation error"):
```

```python
        context = {"field": field, "value": value}
        error_code = 1001
        full_message = f"{message}: Invalid value '{value}' for
        ↪    field '{field}'"
        super().__init__(full_message, error_code, context)


class ResourceError(CustomError):
    """
    Exception raised when there is an issue with resource allocation
    ↪    or availability.
    """
    def __init__(self, resource, message="Resource constraint
    ↪    error"):
        context = {"resource": resource}
        error_code = 2001
        full_message = f"{message}: Problem with resource
        ↪    '{resource}'"
        super().__init__(full_message, error_code, context)


class StateError(CustomError):
    """
    Exception raised for inconsistencies or mismatches in system
    ↪    state.
    """
    def __init__(self, state, message="State inconsistency
    ↪    detected"):
        context = {"state": state}
        error_code = 3001
        full_message = f"{message}: Encountered unexpected state
        ↪    '{state}'"
        super().__init__(full_message, error_code, context)


# Example functions that use the custom exceptions to perform
↪    validations and error handling.

def calculate_inverse(value):
    """
    Calculate the multiplicative inverse of a number.

    Raises:
        ValidationError: If the value is not numeric or is zero
        ↪    (division by zero).
    """
    if not isinstance(value, (int, float)):
        raise ValidationError("value", value, message="Input type
        ↪    error")
    if value == 0:
        raise ValidationError("value", value, message="Division by
        ↪    zero error")
    return 1 / value
```

```python
def process_resource(resource):
    """
    Simulate resource allocation, raising an exception if the
    ↪ resource is unavailable.

    Raises:
        ResourceError: If the specified resource is not in the list
        ↪ of available resources.
    """
    available_resources = ["cpu", "memory", "disk"]
    if resource not in available_resources:
        raise ResourceError(resource, message="Requested resource is
        ↪ unavailable")
    return f"{resource} is allocated."


def verify_state(state):
    """
    Verify that the provided state matches the expected state.

    Raises:
        StateError: If the state does not match the expected state
        ↪ 'active'.
    """
    expected_state = "active"
    if state != expected_state:
        raise StateError(state, message="State mismatch error")
    return "State verified successfully."


def complex_operation(value, resource, state):
    """
    Perform a complex operation that involves multiple steps.
    Demonstrates error chaining to capture and provide context for
    ↪ failures in sub-operations.

    Parameters:
        value: Input for which the inverse is calculated.
        resource: Resource to be allocated.
        state: System state verification parameter.

    Returns:
        dict: A summary of the successful results from each
        ↪ operation.

    Raises:
        CustomError: Wrapped exceptions from individual operations
        ↪ with enhanced context.
    """
    try:
        inverse_result = calculate_inverse(value)
```

146

```
        except CustomError as ce:
            raise CustomError("Failed in calculate_inverse",
                            context={"value": value}) from ce

    try:
        resource_result = process_resource(resource)
    except CustomError as ce:
        raise CustomError("Failed in process_resource",
                        context={"resource": resource}) from ce

    try:
        state_result = verify_state(state)
    except CustomError as ce:
        raise CustomError("Failed in verify_state",
                        context={"state": state}) from ce

    return {
        "inverse": inverse_result,
        "resource_status": resource_result,
        "state_verification": state_result
    }


# Main execution block to test the custom exceptions and error
↪   chaining mechanism.
if __name__ == "__main__":
    test_cases = [
        {"value": 0, "resource": "gpu", "state": "inactive"},  #
        ↪ Expected to trigger validation and resource errors.
        {"value": "a", "resource": "disk", "state": "active"},   #
        ↪ Expected to trigger type error.
        {"value": 5, "resource": "memory", "state": "active"},   #
        ↪ Expected to succeed.
    ]

    for idx, case in enumerate(test_cases, start=1):
        print(f"Test Case {idx}: {case}")
        try:
            result = complex_operation(case["value"],
                ↪ case["resource"], case["state"])
            print("Operation Result:", result)
        except CustomError as e:
            print("Caught Exception:", e)
        print("-" * 60)
```

Chapter 28

Modules and Importing

Conceptual Foundations of Modular Programming

Modular programming is predicated upon the principle of decomposing a software system into discrete, encapsulated units that each embody a coherent subset of the system's functionality. This paradigm is not merely a matter of code organization; it constitutes a rigorous commitment to the separation of concerns, where each module represents an independent abstraction endowed with a well-defined interface. Such a design philosophy facilitates improved maintainability, parallel development, and an enhanced capacity for formal reasoning regarding program behavior. Indeed, the formal abstraction associated with a module is characterized by a unique namespace and the encapsulation of implementation details, thereby ensuring that interactions with the module occur exclusively through carefully controlled, public interfaces.

Architectural Considerations in Module Design

The architectural strategy for module design emphasizes the establishment of clear boundaries between functional components. In the process of structuring code into modules, intrinsic properties such as high cohesion and loose coupling are targeted; these principles serve as cornerstones in the development of scalable, robust

148

systems. Each module is envisioned as a self-contained package, wherein related data structures, functions, and object definitions are consolidated to support domain-specific tasks. The deliberate isolation of functionalities minimizes inter-module dependencies and enables independent testing and evolution of system components. Furthermore, the explicit declaration of a module's public interface—separating externally exposed elements from internal implementation details—embodies the object-oriented ideals of encapsulation and information hiding, which are critical in preventing inadvertent interference across disparate segments of the system.

Mechanics and Semantics of the Import Process

The process of importing modules represents a fundamental mechanism by which software systems assemble independent components into a cohesive whole. This mechanism involves the resolution of module identifiers against a structured search path, followed by the execution of module-level initialization routines, and culminates in the integration of the module's namespace with the importing context. The semantic process underlying module importation is characterized by a sequence of operations that guarantee both the isolation and the controlled sharing of code. Upon invocation of the import directive, the system locates the corresponding module file, compiles it if necessary, and executes its top-level definitions in a dedicated namespace. This ensures that the module's internal state and symbols are managed independently, thereby precluding namespace collisions when multiple modules are aggregated within the same project. The syntactic and semantic structure of the import operation, hence, serves as the bridge that allows independently developed modules to interact in a predictable and formally justifiable manner.

Python Code Snippet

```
# File: mymodules/__init__.py
"""
The mymodules package provides modular functionalities for
↪    mathematical and utility operations.
This package is structured to demonstrate high cohesion and loose
↪    coupling, in line with the
```

architectural principles of modular programming.
"""

```
# File: mymodules/module_math.py
"""
module_math.py: Provides mathematical functions including the
↪    computation of quadratic roots
and the generation of Fibonacci numbers via an iterative algorithm.
"""
import math

def quadratic_roots(a, b, c):
    """
    Compute the real roots of a quadratic equation: ax^2 + bx + c =
    ↪    0.

    Parameters:
        a (float): Coefficient of x^2.
        b (float): Coefficient of x.
        c (float): Constant term.

    Returns:
        tuple: A tuple containing the two real roots if the
        ↪    discriminant is non-negative.
              Returns None if there are no real roots.
    """
    discriminant = b ** 2 - 4 * a * c
    if discriminant < 0:
        return None
    sqrt_disc = math.sqrt(discriminant)
    root1 = (-b + sqrt_disc) / (2 * a)
    root2 = (-b - sqrt_disc) / (2 * a)
    return (root1, root2)

def compute_fibonacci(n):
    """
    Generate the Fibonacci sequence up to n elements using an
    ↪    iterative algorithm.

    Parameters:
        n (int): Number of Fibonacci elements to generate.

    Returns:
        list: A list containing the Fibonacci sequence.
    """
    fib_sequence = []
    a, b = 0, 1
    for _ in range(n):
        fib_sequence.append(a)
        a, b = b, a + b
    return fib_sequence

if __name__ == "__main__":
```

```python
    # When executed directly, run simple test cases to verify
    ↪ functionality.
    print("Testing module_math functions:")
    print("Quadratic roots for 2x^2 - 4x - 6 = 0:",
    ↪ quadratic_roots(2, -4, -6))
    print("First 10 Fibonacci numbers:", compute_fibonacci(10))
```

```python
# File: mymodules/module_utils.py
"""
module_utils.py: Provides utility functions such as the recursive
↪ computation of factorial.
"""
def factorial(n):
    """
    Compute the factorial of a non-negative integer n recursively.

    Parameters:
        n (int): A non-negative integer.

    Returns:
        int: The factorial of n.

    Raises:
        ValueError: If n is a negative number.
    """
    if n < 0:
        raise ValueError("Factorial is not defined for negative
        ↪ numbers")
    if n == 0:
        return 1
    return n * factorial(n - 1)

if __name__ == "__main__":
    # Test the factorial function when module is run directly.
    print("Testing module_utils function:")
    print("Factorial of 5:", factorial(5))
```

```python
# File: main.py
"""
main.py: Demonstrates modular programming by importing modules from
↪ the 'mymodules' package
and integrating their functionalities through clear, maintained
↪ boundaries.
"""
from mymodules import module_math, module_utils

def main():
    print("=== Modular Programming Demonstration ===")

    # Demonstrate the use of the quadratic_roots function from
    ↪ module_math:
    # Solve the quadratic equation 2x^2 - 4x - 6 = 0.
    a, b, c = 2, -4, -6
```

```python
    roots = module_math.quadratic_roots(a, b, c)
    if roots is not None:
        print(f"Quadratic roots of equation {a}x^2 + ({b})x + {c} =
        ↪    0: {roots}")
    else:
        print("The equation has no real roots.")

    # Generate and display the first 10 Fibonacci numbers.
    n = 10
    fib_numbers = module_math.compute_fibonacci(n)
    print(f"First {n} Fibonacci numbers: {fib_numbers}")

    # Demonstrate the use of the factorial function from
    ↪    module_utils.
    number = 5
    fact_result = module_utils.factorial(number)
    print(f"Factorial of {number}: {fact_result}")

if __name__ == "__main__":
    main()
```

Chapter 29

Package Structuring

Theoretical Foundations of Package Structuring

The modern paradigm of software organization recognizes that a robust project structure is predicated upon the deliberate aggregation of related modules into well-defined packages. In formal terms, a package is understood as a directory that encapsulates a set of modules along with the necessary initialization markers, thereby creating a distinct namespace. This systematic grouping is not merely a matter of physical arrangement; it embodies the principles of high cohesion and low coupling, which are central to contemporary theories in software architecture. The notion that each package should serve as a self-contained unit of logical functionality is analogous to the concept of a mathematical set, where every element shares an intrinsic relationship to the defining property of the set itself. The establishment of these discrete organizational boundaries aids in preventing namespace collisions and ensures that the internal mechanics of one package remain abstracted from others, in line with the principle of information hiding.

Organizational Strategies and Modularity Techniques

The process of aggregating modules into a cohesive package requires a rigorous design approach that begins with the identifica-

153

tion of coherent functional domains. Each package is fashioned as a composite of modules that interact through well-specified interfaces, rendering the overall structure amenable to formal analysis. The directory layout of a scalable project is typically arranged such that packages are nested in a hierarchy that reflects the logical stratification of system functionalities. This may be formalized by considering a package P as a tuple (M, I), where M represents the collection of modules and I denotes the explicit public interface that governs inter-package interactions. Strategic deployment of naming conventions and the disciplined use of initialization files (__init__.py) serve as mechanisms to instantiate these theoretical constructs in a tangible project structure. Such structuring fosters an environment wherein the inherent complexities of module interdependencies are mitigated by a clear delineation of responsibilities, allowing for both localized reasoning and scalable evolution of the system.

Implications for Scalability and Project Maintainability

The adoption of a structured package architecture exerts a profound influence on the scalability and maintainability of extensive software systems. When modules are organized into packages that reflect specific conceptual domains, the resultant system exhibits improved modularity, which in turn permits the incremental evolution of each independent component. In larger projects, this architectural decomposition translates into a form of formal separation that not only simplifies debugging and testing but also enhances the intellectual tractability of the codebase. The compartmentalization inherent in package structuring underpins numerous best practices in source code management, including version control, dependency resolution, and automated integration testing. Moreover, the segregation of modules into coherent packages creates an environment conducive to parallel development, as independent research and development efforts can be pursued concurrently without incurring significant interface conflicts. The resultant project structure, therefore, constitutes a scalable framework that is both robust in its present form and flexible enough to accommodate future enhancements through disciplined adherence to modular design methodologies.

Python Code Snippet

```python
# This code demonstrates the principles of package structuring
↪   discussed in the chapter.
# We formalize a package P as a tuple (M, I) where:
#    M: A dictionary of modules (each providing related
↪   functionality)
#    I: A dictionary representing the public interface exposed by the
↪   package


# Module representing mathematical operations.
class ModuleMath:
    """Module for mathematical computations."""
    def add(self, a, b):
        """Return the sum of a and b."""
        return a + b

    def subtract(self, a, b):
        """Return the difference between a and b."""
        return a - b

    def multiply(self, a, b):
        """Return the product of a and b."""
        return a * b

    def divide(self, a, b):
        """Return the division of a by b. Raise an error if b is
↪   zero."""
        if b == 0:
            raise ValueError("Cannot divide by zero")
        return a / b

# Module representing string operations.
class ModuleString:
    """Module for string manipulations."""
    def to_upper(self, s):
        """Convert the string s to uppercase."""
        return s.upper()

    def to_lower(self, s):
        """Convert the string s to lowercase."""
        return s.lower()

    def capitalize(self, s):
        """Capitalize the first letter of string s."""
        return s.capitalize()

# The Package class encapsulates the modules and their public
↪   interface.
class Package:
    def __init__(self):
        """
```

```python
        Initialize package P as (M, I) where:
          M: a dictionary of module instances (cohesive grouping)
          I: a public interface exposing specific functions from the
          ↪ modules
        """
        # Collection of modules
        self.modules = {
            'math': ModuleMath(),
            'string': ModuleString()
        }
        # Public interface: mapping descriptive names to module
        ↪ functions.
        self.interface = {
            'add': self.modules['math'].add,
            'subtract': self.modules['math'].subtract,
            'multiply': self.modules['math'].multiply,
            'divide': self.modules['math'].divide,
            'to_upper': self.modules['string'].to_upper,
            'to_lower': self.modules['string'].to_lower,
            'capitalize': self.modules['string'].capitalize
        }

    def get_interface(self):
        """Return the public interface of the package."""
        return self.interface

    def list_modules(self):
        """List the keys (names) of all modules in the package."""
        return list(self.modules.keys())

    def execute(self, func_name, *args, **kwargs):
        """
        Execute a function from the public interface.
        Raises an AttributeError if the function is not found.
        """
        if func_name not in self.interface:
            raise AttributeError(f"Function '{func_name}' not
            ↪ provided in the package interface")
        return self.interface[func_name](*args, **kwargs)

# Main algorithm demonstrating the usage of the Package.
def main():
    # Instantiate the package, formally representing P = (M, I)
    pkg = Package()

    # Display the available modules (reflecting high cohesion)
    print("Modules in the package:", pkg.list_modules())

    # Retrieve the public interface and perform operations.
    interface = pkg.get_interface()

    # Math operations demonstration
    print("Addition (10 + 5):", pkg.execute('add', 10, 5))
```

156

```python
print("Subtraction (10 - 5):", pkg.execute('subtract', 10, 5))
print("Multiplication (10 * 5):", pkg.execute('multiply', 10,
↪  5))
print("Division (10 / 5):", pkg.execute('divide', 10, 5))

# String operations demonstration
sample_string = "hello world"
print("To Upper:", pkg.execute('to_upper', sample_string))
print("To Lower:", pkg.execute('to_lower', sample_string))
print("Capitalize:", pkg.execute('capitalize', sample_string))

# Exception handling demonstration: Division by zero.
try:
    print("Division (10 / 0):", pkg.execute('divide', 10, 0))
except ValueError as e:
    print("Caught an error during division:", e)

# If this script is executed directly, run the main demonstration.
if __name__ == "__main__":
    main()
```

Chapter 30

File I/O: Reading Files

Fundamental Concepts in File Input Handling

File input operations in Python are underpinned by a well-defined abstraction that decouples the high-level programming interface from the underlying operating system mechanisms. In its essence, a file represents a contiguous sequence of data stored in secondary memory, and the corresponding file object in Python encapsulates this sequence along with a cursor that tracks the current read position. The act of opening a file invokes operating system calls that establish a communication channel through which data is streamed into the runtime environment. This structural separation is manifested in the various modes of operation, whereby textual and binary forms of file representations are clearly delineated via specific mode indicators. The implementation in Python is further enhanced by buffering strategies that optimize the number of system calls; these buffers temporarily store blocks of data read from the file, thereby reducing the overhead associated with continuous I/O requests. Such a design conforms to the principles of modularity and abstraction, ensuring that file handling complexities remain internally managed while exposing a consistent and intuitive interface to the programmer.

Techniques for Sequential Reading and Buffer Management

The sequential access of file data is achieved through systematic methods that enable the progressive consumption of information from the file stream. Among these techniques, methods that read a predefined number of bytes or a complete line epitomize the granularity of access required in diverse application contexts. Internally, these methods interact with the file buffer—a memory-resident store that holds a fragment of the file's content. The buffer is populated by the underlying system based on a predetermined block size, often denoted by a parameter b, which can be tuned according to the size of the file and the performance requirements of the application. When a read operation is invoked, the file pointer is advanced by the number of bytes that have been successfully transferred from the buffer to the program's memory. This mechanism not only confers predictability to the file reading process but also enables a controlled environment for handling files too voluminous to be loaded entirely into memory. The underlying algorithmic design strikes a balance between minimizing latency in data retrieval and optimizing the utilization of system resources.

Data Interpretation, Encoding Considerations, and Error Management

The accurate interpretation of the data read from a file is contingent upon a rigorous handling of character encoding and a robust strategy for error detection. In textual files, the translation from byte sequences to human-readable characters is governed by specific encodings such as UTF-8 or ASCII. The file object in Python, when opened in text mode, automatically decodes the byte stream into a string representation; this process requires that the encoding parameter be correctly specified to prevent misinterpretation of the data. The mathematical mapping of byte sequences to characters may be conceptualized as a function $f : B \to C$, where B represents the set of possible byte sequences and C the set of characters in the target encoding. Error management in file reading is equally critical; it encompasses the detection of interrupt-driven anomalies—ranging from end-of-file conditions to permissions-related exceptions—and the subsequent graceful recovery from such states.

The practice of validating read operations and verifying the integrity of the retrieved data is indispensable, ensuring that the intrinsic properties of the data are preserved across I/O boundaries. This meticulous approach to error handling mitigates the propagation of faults and sustains the reliability of file-driven applications.

Python Code Snippet

```python
import os

def decode_bytes_to_string(byte_data, encoding='utf-8'):
    """
    Decodes a byte sequence to a string using the specified
    ↪ encoding.
    This function implements the conceptual mapping:

        f: B -> C

    where:
      B = set of byte sequences,
      C = set of characters.

    Parameters:
        byte_data (bytes): The incoming byte sequence.
        encoding (str): The text encoding to use (default is
        ↪ 'utf-8').

    Returns:
        str: The decoded string.

    Raises:
        UnicodeDecodeError: If the byte sequence cannot be decoded
        ↪ with the given encoding.
    """
    try:
        decoded_string = byte_data.decode(encoding)
    except UnicodeDecodeError as e:
        raise UnicodeDecodeError(f"Decoding error with encoding
        ↪ '{encoding}': {e}")
    return decoded_string

def read_file_in_chunks(file_path, chunk_size=1024,
↪ encoding='utf-8'):
    """
    Reads a file sequentially in buffered chunks and decodes the
    ↪ content.

    This function demonstrates:
```

160

```
            - Opening a file in binary mode to handle buffering manually.
            - Reading 'chunk_size' bytes per iteration (the block size
            ↪   'b').
            - Decoding the byte chunk, implementing the mapping f: B -> C.
            - Handling errors gracefully when decoding or I/O issues
            ↪   occur.

        Parameters:
            file_path (str): The path to the file to be read.
            chunk_size (int): The number of bytes to read per iteration
            ↪   (default is 1024).
            encoding (str): The encoding used to decode the file content
            ↪   (default is 'utf-8').

        Yields:
            str: A chunk of the file's content decoded into text.
        """
        try:
            with open(file_path, 'rb') as file:
                while True:
                    # Read a block of data; the file pointer
                    ↪   automatically advances.
                    chunk = file.read(chunk_size)
                    if not chunk:
                        # End-of-file reached; exit the loop.
                        break
                    try:
                        # Decode the byte block using the provided
                        ↪   encoding.
                        text = decode_bytes_to_string(chunk, encoding)
                    except UnicodeDecodeError as e:
                        # Error handling: log the error and continue
                        ↪   with the next chunk.
                        print(f"Error decoding chunk: {e}")
                        continue
                    yield text
        except FileNotFoundError:
            print(f"Error: The file '{file_path}' was not found.")
        except PermissionError:
            print(f"Error: Permission denied for file '{file_path}'.")
        except Exception as e:
            print(f"An unexpected error occurred: {e}")


def process_file(file_path, chunk_size=1024, encoding='utf-8'):
    """
    Processes the contents of a file by reading it sequentially in
    ↪   chunks.
    For demonstration purposes, each decoded chunk is simply printed
    ↪   out.

    Parameters:
        file_path (str): The path to the file to be processed.
        chunk_size (int): Number of bytes to read per iteration.
```

```python
        encoding (str): Encoding of the file.
    """
    for chunk in read_file_in_chunks(file_path, chunk_size,
    ↪   encoding):
        # Here, additional processing can be performed on each
        ↪   chunk.
        print(chunk)


if __name__ == '__main__':
    # Set the path to your sample file. Update the filename as
    ↪   necessary.
    sample_file_path = 'sample_text.txt'

    # Specify the block size ('b') used for buffering.
    block_size = 1024   # Adjust this value based on performance
    ↪   requirements.

    print("Starting sequential file reading with buffered I/O...\n")

    # Process the file: reading, decoding, and error handling are
    ↪   performed here.
    process_file(sample_file_path, chunk_size=block_size,
    ↪   encoding='utf-8')

    print("\nFile processing completed successfully.")
```

Chapter 31

File I/O: Writing Files

Fundamental Concepts in File Writing

File output operations constitute a critical component of file-based computing systems, where data generated by a program is transferred to secondary storage. The abstraction of a file as a contiguous block of persistent memory is maintained by a file object that encapsulates the destination for outgoing data. This file object manages an internal pointer that identifies the current position for data insertion. The theoretical model underlying file writing adheres to a clear separation of concerns: the high-level interface provided to application programmers is decoupled from the low-level system calls performed by the operating system. Such a design ensures that complexities related to resource buffering, file system synchronization, and error propagation remain internally administered while a consistent and formalized interface is exposed externally.

Opening Files in Write Mode

The procedure for initiating file output begins with the invocation of an operation that opens a file in an appropriate mode. In this context, the designation of the file mode parameter plays a decisive role in determining the subsequent behavior of file operations. Modes such as w, a, and $w+$ are defined to control the semantics of file creation and modification. For instance, the mode w mandates that an existing file be truncated before new data is written, whereas the mode a ensures that data is appended to the end of the file if it exists, thereby preserving previously stored information. The selection of these modes is governed by considerations of data integrity and access control, thereby providing an unambiguous framework within which file streams are established.

Stream Management and Data Output

Upon successful file opening, the file stream becomes the conduit for the transformation of high-level data representations into a sequence of bytes suitable for storage. The process of outputting data is typically executed by writing to an intermediary buffer that temporarily accumulates data before committing it to permanent storage. This buffer, acting as an abstraction over the slower storage medium, enables the consolidation of multiple discrete write operations into more efficient system calls. The sequential output mechanism is precisely controlled by advancing the file pointer as each batch of data is transferred from the application memory to the file stream. The operational semantics maintain that the integrity of the data is preserved throughout this process, and that the transition from in-memory data structures to a persistent byte stream is executed with formal precision.

Buffering Strategies and System Call Overheads

A central aspect of file writing efficiency is predicated on the buffering strategy employed by the file system. Buffers serve as temporary storage regions that mitigate the overhead associated with frequent system calls by increasing the block size to a designated value, typically expressed as b. This buffering mechanism collects data increments until the buffer reaches capacity, at which point its content is flushed to disk. The algorithmic determination of the optimum buffer size b is driven by trade-offs between latency, throughput, and resource utilization. In environments where write operations are numerous and sporadic, a larger buffer can significantly reduce the frequency of low-level I/O calls, thereby optimizing overall system performance. Conversely, scenarios that demand immediate data persistence may require periodic manual flushing of the buffer to ensure consistency in the event of system failures.

Managing File Streams and Error Handling in File Output

Robust file writing systems incorporate comprehensive error handling to address exceptional conditions that may arise during file operations. Errors in file output can be precipitated by a variety of factors including permission denials, hardware failures, or insufficient storage space. The management of file streams necessitates that errors be detected and processed in a manner that preserves the atomicity and consistency of the file contents. Techniques such as explicitly invoking flush operations or synchronizing file descriptors with the underlying storage hardware play a pivotal role in the detection and mitigation of potential data loss. Furthermore, rigorous validation of each write operation ensures that the number of bytes committed to the file corresponds precisely with expectations, thereby establishing a formal contract between the software and the hardware subsystems. These measures collectively contribute to a resilient file output methodology, where error conditions are addressed systematically and with a high degree of precision.

Python Code Snippet

```
import os

def calculate_optimal_buffer_size(latency, throughput):
    """
    Calculate an optimal buffer size based on latency and
    ↪    throughput.

    Formula:
        b = throughput / latency

    This function ensures that the buffer size is at least 1024
    ↪    bytes.
    It simulates the trade-off between system call overhead and
    ↪    memory usage.
    """
    try:
        # Validate that latency is positive to avoid division by
        ↪    zero.
        if latency <= 0:
            raise ValueError("Latency must be positive and
            ↪    non-zero.")
        buffer_size = throughput / latency  # Compute optimal buffer
        ↪    size
```

```python
        return max(int(buffer_size), 1024)
    except Exception as error:
        print("Error in calculating optimal buffer size:", error)
        return 1024


def write_to_file(filename, data, mode='w', latency=0.1,
↪   throughput=10240):
    """
    Write data to a file using a custom buffering strategy with
    ↪   robust error handling.

    Parameters:
        filename (str): The target file path.
        data (str): The content to write in the file.
        mode (str): File mode for opening the file ('w', 'a', 'w+',
        ↪   etc.).
        latency (float): Estimated system latency (in seconds).
        throughput (int): Assumed throughput in bytes per second.

    The function calculates an optimal buffer size using the
    ↪   equation:
        b = throughput / latency
    and uses the derived buffer size to open the file. Data is
    ↪   written to an
    intermediary buffer and flushed to disk to ensure persistence.
    """
    # Calculate the optimal buffer size based on current conditions.
    buffer_size = calculate_optimal_buffer_size(latency, throughput)
    print(f"Using buffer size: {buffer_size} bytes")

    try:
        # Open the file with the computed buffering size.
        with open(filename, mode, buffering=buffer_size) as file:
            # Write the provided data into the file.
            file.write(data)

            # Flush the in-memory buffer to the OS.
            file.flush()
            # Force the OS to commit the file to disk (synchronous
            ↪   write).
            os.fsync(file.fileno())

            print("Data written and flushed to disk successfully.")
    except Exception as error:
        print("An error occurred while writing to the file:", error)


def main():
    # Sample data includes a demonstration of the optimal buffer
    ↪   size equation.
    data = (
        "File I/O Writing Demonstration\n"
        "-------------------------------\n"
        "Equation for optimal buffer size:\n"
```

166

```
    "   b = throughput / latency\n"
    "\n"
    "Parameters:\n"
    "   throughput (bytes/sec) - The maximum rate at which data
    ↪   is processed.\n"
    "   latency (sec) - The delay before the data transfer
    ↪   begins.\n"
    "\n"
    "Example:\n"
    "   If throughput = 10240 bytes/sec and latency = 0.1 sec
    ↪   then:\n"
    "        b = 10240 / 0.1 = 102400 bytes\n"
    "\n"
    "Using this optimal buffer size minimizes system call
    ↪   overheads by\n"
    "accumulating data in the buffer until a significant amount
    ↪   of data is ready\n"
    "to be flushed to disk, thus improving overall write
    ↪   performance.\n"
    )

    filename = "output.txt"
    write_to_file(filename, data, mode='w', latency=0.1,
    ↪   throughput=10240)

if __name__ == "__main__":
    main()
```

Chapter 32

CSV File Handling

Characteristics of the CSV Format

The Comma Separated Values format represents a lightweight, text-based method for encoding tabular data. Within a CSV file, each record is typically delineated by a newline character, and individual fields within each record are separated by a designated delimiter, most commonly a comma. The simplicity of this structure belies its broad applicability, as CSV files facilitate interoperability across diverse platforms and applications. The standardized arrangement of rows and columns enables the representation of datasets in a form that is simultaneously human-readable and amenable to automated parsing. In many implementations, additional conventions exist to handle fields that contain embedded delimiters or newline characters, such as encapsulating such fields within double quotes.

Parsing Strategies and Error Recovery

Parsing CSV files requires careful consideration of the inherent ambiguities in the format. A robust parser must correctly interpret field boundaries, particularly in cases where fields include extra whitespace, encapsulating quotes, or escaped characters. Techniques for parsing often include tokenization algorithms that identify delimiters while simultaneously managing edge cases such as consecutive delimiters and fields with unescaped line breaks. In scenarios where malformed input is encountered, error recovery strategies become essential. Strategies may involve reverting to default interpretations, skipping over problematic sections, or flagging inconsistencies without terminating the entire parsing process. This layered approach to error handling ensures that the informative structure of the data is preserved despite minor deviations from strict formatting rules.

CSV File Writing Techniques

Writing data to a CSV file demands an inverse process to parsing, wherein structured data must be transformed into a serialized string format that adheres to CSV conventions. This entails the careful construction of records, ensuring that each field is properly delimited and that any characters with special significance, such as commas, newline characters, or quotation marks, are appropriately escaped or encapsulated. The process must account for the possibility of heterogeneous data types by converting each datum into its corresponding string representation. Consistency in the quoting of fields, particularly in the presence of whitespace or reserved characters, is vital to maintain interoperability. The effectiveness of a CSV file writer is measured not only by its correctness but also by its adherence to performance considerations under varied input sizes.

Data Integrity, Encoding, and Type Considerations

In the realm of CSV file handling, preserving data integrity is of paramount importance. This involves ensuring that the conversion of structured data into the CSV format does not result in the loss of semantic meaning or precision. Critical to this process is the recognition of character encoding schemes, with formats such as UTF-8 emerging as the de facto standard to support an extensive range of characters across different languages and scripts. Additionally, numerical values and dates must be rendered in a consistent format to allow for accurate reconstitution during subsequent parsing. The interplay between inherent data types and their string representations necessitates a rigorous approach to normalization and type validation, such that operations on CSV data yield predictable and reproducible outcomes.

Performance and Buffering Considerations in CSV Processing

Efficiency in the reading and writing of CSV files is influenced significantly by the strategies employed for buffering and input/output operations. The transformation of large datasets from textual representation to structured formats, or vice versa, may involve computationally intensive processes if not managed appropriately. Buffering techniques serve to mitigate the overhead associated with frequent system calls by aggregating data in memory prior to performing bulk write operations. Similarly, when parsing, incremental reading strategies can optimize the performance by processing manageable blocks of text, thereby reducing memory footprint and latency. Consideration of buffering parameters, such as block size denoted by b, further contributes to achieving an optimal balance between resource utilization and execution speed. These performance-oriented methodologies are central to the deployment of CSV handling routines in environments that demand high throughput and low latency.

Python Code Snippet

```python
import csv
import sys
import re
from pathlib import Path

def parse_csv_line(line, delimiter=',', quotechar='"'):
    """
    Custom CSV parser that tokenizes a single CSV line.
    It handles quoted fields, escaped quotes, and ignores delimiters
    ↪  within quotes.
    This parser implements a simple state machine:
        - When encountering a quote, toggle the quoted state.
        - When in quoted state, allow embedded quote characters if
        ↪  doubled.
        - When not in quoted state, treat the delimiter as a field
        ↪  separator.
    """
    columns = []
    field = ""
    in_quotes = False
    i = 0
    while i < len(line):
        char = line[i]
```

```python
        if char == quotechar:
            if in_quotes and i + 1 < len(line) and line[i+1] ==
            ↪   quotechar:
                # Escaped quote inside a quoted field: include one
                ↪   quote and skip next
                field += quotechar
                i += 1
            else:
                # Toggle in_quotes state
                in_quotes = not in_quotes
        elif char == delimiter and not in_quotes:
            # End of field reached
            columns.append(field.strip())
            field = ""
        else:
            field += char
        i += 1
    columns.append(field.strip())
    return columns


def write_csv_line(fields, delimiter=',', quotechar='"'):
    """
    Custom CSV writer function that serializes a list of fields into
    ↪   one CSV record.
    It encloses fields in quotes if they contain the delimiter,
    ↪   quotechar, or newlines.
    Embedded quotes are doubled for proper escaping.
    """

    serialized_fields = []

    for field in fields:
        field_str = str(field)
        if (delimiter in field_str) or (quotechar in field_str) or
        ↪   ("\n" in field_str):
            # Double the embedded quote characters
            field_str = field_str.replace(quotechar, quotechar*2)
            # Enclose the field in quotes
            field_str = f'{quotechar}{field_str}{quotechar}'
        serialized_fields.append(field_str)

    return delimiter.join(serialized_fields)


def read_csv_buffered(file_path, buffer_size=1024,
↪   encoding='utf-8'):
    """
    Reads a CSV file using buffered I/O to optimize performance on
    ↪   large files.
    Instead of reading one line at a time, this function reads
    ↪   chunks of text,
    which are then split into lines. Incomplete lines are held over
    ↪   between chunks.

    Parameters:
```

```python
    file_path: path to the CSV file to be read
    buffer_size: block size (denoted as b) for each I/O operation
    encoding: file encoding, default is 'utf-8' for wide character
    ↪   support

    Returns:
     A list of CSV records (each record is a list of fields)
     """
    records = []
    remainder = ""
    try:
        with open(file_path, 'r', encoding=encoding) as f:
            while True:
                chunk = f.read(buffer_size)
                if not chunk:
                    break
                data = remainder + chunk
                # Split into complete lines
                lines = data.split("\n")
                # If the chunk did not end with a newline, preserve
                ↪   last incomplete part
                if data[-1] != "\n":
                    remainder = lines.pop()
                else:
                    remainder = ""
                for line in lines:
                    if line.strip() == "":
                        continue  # Skip empty lines
                    try:
                        record = parse_csv_line(line)
                        records.append(record)
                    except Exception as e:
                        sys.stderr.write(f"Error parsing line:
                        ↪   {line}\nException: {e}\n")
            # Process any remainder left over
            if remainder:
                try:
                    record = parse_csv_line(remainder)
                    records.append(record)
                except Exception as e:
                    sys.stderr.write(f"Error parsing last line:
                    ↪   {remainder}\nException: {e}\n")
    except FileNotFoundError:
        sys.stderr.write(f"File not found: {file_path}\n")
    return records

def write_csv_buffered(records, file_path, buffer_size=1024,
↪   encoding='utf-8'):
    """
    Writes CSV records to a file using a buffering strategy to
    ↪   optimize write operations.
    Each record is converted to a CSV formatted string with the
    ↪   custom writer.
```

172

The entire CSV data is constructed and then written in chunks to
↪ reduce the overhead
from frequent write system calls.

Parameters:
    records: list of CSV records (each record is a list of fields)
    file_path: target file path for the CSV output
    buffer_size: maximum number of characters per I/O write
    ↪ operation
    encoding: output file encoding
    """
    lines = []
    for record in records:
        line = write_csv_line(record)
        lines.append(line)

    csv_data = "\n".join(lines)

    with open(file_path, 'w', encoding=encoding) as f:
        # Write the data in buffered chunks
        for i in range(0, len(csv_data), buffer_size):
            f.write(csv_data[i:i+buffer_size])

def demo_csv_processing():
    """
    Demonstrates the CSV processing workflow:
        - Generates sample CSV data including special cases: embedded
        ↪ delimiters,
        quotes, and multiline fields.
        - Writes the data to a temporary CSV file using buffered I/O.
        - Reads back the data using the custom parser.
        - Prints the parsed records to verify correctness.
    """
    # Sample CSV records, deliberately including special characters
    sample_records = [
        ["Name", "Age", "Occupation", "Comment"],
        ["Alice", "30", "Engineer", 'Loves "technology", especially
        ↪ AI.'],
        ["Bob", "25", "Designer", "Enjoys painting, reading, and,
        ↪ traveling"],
        ["Charlie", "35", "Teacher", 'Quote: "Education is the
        ↪ key"'],
        ["Dana", "40", "Manager", "Multi-line\ncomment with
        ↪ newline"],
    ]

    # Define a temporary file path
    temp_file = Path("temp_sample.csv")

    # Write the CSV data to file
    write_csv_buffered(sample_records, temp_file)
```
```

```python
        print(f"CSV file successfully written to:
        ↪   {temp_file.resolve()}")

        # Read the CSV file back into memory
        parsed_records = read_csv_buffered(temp_file)
        print("Parsed CSV Records:")
        for record in parsed_records:
            print(record)

        # Clean up the temporary file after demonstration
        try:
            temp_file.unlink()
        except Exception as e:
            sys.stderr.write(f"Error deleting temporary file: {e}\n")

if __name__ == "__main__":
    demo_csv_processing()
```

Chapter 33

JSON Data Handling

Fundamental Constructs of JSON Format

JSON, or JavaScript Object Notation, is a lightweight, text-based format for data interchange. It adheres to a simple syntactic design that represents data structures as collections of name/value pairs and ordered lists of values. An object in JSON is delimited by curly braces ({ and }) and encapsulates a series of key-value pairs, wherein keys are strings and values may be strings, numbers, booleans, arrays, objects, or the null literal. Arrays are denoted by square brackets ([and]) and define an ordered sequence of elements. The constraints imposed by the JSON specification ensure that the format remains both human-readable and readily parsed by automated systems, independent of the underlying programming language.

Serialization: Converting Native Structures into JSON

The process of serialization entails the transformation of native in-memory data structures into their JSON textual representation. In this conversion, complex objects, arrays, and primitive data types are systematically encoded following the syntactic rules of the JSON format. The serialization mechanism must ensure that every entity in the original structure is mapped according to predetermined correspondences; for instance, native dictionaries or maps are rendered as JSON objects, while lists and other sequential collections are converted to JSON arrays. Special attention is devoted to preserving the integrity of numerical representations, especially given that numbers must conform to the representation guidelines akin to those outlined in the IEEE 754 standard. The conversion process is methodically designed to eliminate ambiguity, ensuring that the serialized output can be reliably reinterpreted without loss of semantic content.

Deserialization: Reconstructing Data Structures from JSON

Deserialization represents the inverse operation of serialization, wherein a JSON-formatted text is parsed to recreate the original data structures. This transformation is conceptually decomposed into two phases: lexical analysis, wherein the input text is tokenized into elemental symbols based on the JSON grammar, and syntactic analysis, where these tokens are assembled into a hierarchical structure reflective of the original data configuration. During deserialization, the parser must discern the boundaries of objects and arrays, accurately interpret string encodings, and resolve numerical tokens such that they align with the native representations in the host environment. The fidelity of the deserialization process is paramount, as any discrepancy in interpreting the text could lead to misrepresentation of the data, thereby undermining the integrity of subsequent computational operations.

Type Mapping and Data Integrity in JSON Transformation

The transformation between native data types and their JSON counterparts invokes a comprehensive type mapping strategy. Each primitive and composite type is accorded a definitive representation in JSON, necessitating explicit guidelines for conversion. For example, strings are enclosed within double quotes and must properly handle escape sequences, while number types are serialized in a manner that safeguards precision and scale. Boolean values and the null literal maintain their literal representations, ensuring semantic consistency. This mapping is critical not only for the correctness of the transformation but also for the preservation of data

176

integrity. Conformance to these mapping rules ensures that the conversion processes are both deterministic and reversible, thereby preventing the inadvertent loss or alteration of information during serialization or deserialization.

Error Management and Edge Cases in JSON Processing

Robust error management constitutes an integral component of JSON processing. The parser is required to systematically identify and report syntactic anomalies, such as mismatched delimiters, malformed string literals, and the presence of unescaped control characters. Error detection is facilitated by a thorough validation mechanism that scrutinizes the JSON text against the formal specifications of the format. In addition to syntactic errors, semantic inconsistencies—such as numeric overflow or the misinterpretation of data types—are rigorously managed. The handling of edge cases, particularly in the context of irregular whitespace or unexpected token sequences, is accomplished through a combination of defensive parsing techniques and well-defined recovery strategies. This meticulous approach ensures that even in the presence of partial corruption or deviation from strict standards, the data interchange process remains as resilient and predictable as possible.

Performance and Architectural Considerations

The performance of JSON data handling is influenced by both algorithmic strategies and system-level architectural decisions. The computational overhead associated with both serialization and deserialization can be substantial, particularly when processing voluminous datasets. To mitigate these challenges, efficient parsing algorithms are employed that operate in linear time with respect to the size of the input. Architectural designs often incorporate streaming and buffering methodologies that enable incremental processing of JSON text, thus reducing memory consumption and minimizing latency. Furthermore, considerations such as asynchronous processing and parallel parsing are analyzed to accommodate the demands of high-throughput or real-time data exchange environments. The careful orchestration of these performance enhancements ensures that JSON handling remains both scalable and responsive under diverse operational conditions.

Python Code Snippet

```python
import json
import logging
import time

# Configure logging for robust error management
logging.basicConfig(level=logging.ERROR, format="%(asctime)s -
↪  %(levelname)s - %(message)s")

class CustomEncoder(json.JSONEncoder):
    """
    Custom JSON Encoder to handle non-standard objects.
    Converts unknown types to their string representation.
    """
    def default(self, obj):
        try:
            return super().default(obj)
        except TypeError:
            return str(obj)

def serialize_data(data):
    """
    Serializes a Python data structure into a JSON formatted string.
    This function maps native types to their JSON counterparts,
    preserving proper formatting and handling complex objects via
    ↪  CustomEncoder.
    """
    try:
        json_str = json.dumps(data, cls=CustomEncoder, indent=4)
        return json_str
    except (TypeError, ValueError) as e:
        logging.error("Serialization Error: %s", e)
        raise

def deserialize_data(json_str):
    """
    Deserializes a JSON formatted string back into native Python
    ↪  data structures.
    Handles both lexical analysis (tokenizing) and syntactic
    ↪  analysis (structure reconstruction).
    """
    try:
        data = json.loads(json_str)
        return data
    except json.JSONDecodeError as e:
```

```python
        logging.error("Deserialization Error: %s", e)
        raise

def write_json_to_file(data, filename):
    """
    Writes serialized JSON data to a file.
    Demonstrates proper file I/O techniques, ensuring encoding and
    ↪  error management.
    """
    try:
        json_str = serialize_data(data)
        with open(filename, 'w', encoding='utf-8') as f:
            f.write(json_str)
    except Exception as e:
        logging.error("File Writing Error: %s", e)
        raise

def process_json_file(filename):
    """
    Reads a JSON file and deserializes its content.
    Handles file I/O, buffering and uses the deserialization process
    ↪  to ensure data integrity.
    """
    try:
        with open(filename, 'r', encoding='utf-8') as f:
            json_str = f.read()
            data = deserialize_data(json_str)
            return data
    except Exception as e:
        logging.error("File Processing Error: %s", e)
        raise

def stream_json_array(json_str):
    """
    Generator function to yield items from a JSON array one by one.
    This simulates incremental processing and handles edge cases
    ↪  where the JSON may not be a list.
    """
    try:
        data = json.loads(json_str)
        if isinstance(data, list):
            for item in data:
                yield item
        else:
            logging.warning("Provided JSON is not an array. Yielding
            ↪  entire structure.")
            yield data
    except json.JSONDecodeError as e:
        logging.error("Stream Deserialization Error: %s", e)
        raise

if __name__ == "__main__":
    # Sample data structure representing multiple JSON types:
```

```python
# - Strings, numbers, booleans, arrays, nested dictionaries, and
↪   null values.
sample_data = {
    "title": "Introduction to Python Programming",
    "version": 1.0,
    "active": True,
    "chapters": [
        {
            "chapter": 1,
            "title": "JSON Data Handling",
            "sections": [
                "Fundamental Constructs of JSON Format",
                "Serialization: Converting Native Structures
                ↪   into JSON",
                "Deserialization: Reconstructing Data Structures
                ↪   from JSON",
                "Type Mapping and Data Integrity in JSON
                ↪   Transformation",
                "Error Management and Edge Cases in JSON
                ↪   Processing",
                "Performance and Architectural Considerations"
            ]
        },
        {
            "chapter": 2,
            "title": "Advanced Topics",
            "sections": ["Memory Management", "Recursive
            ↪   Algorithms", "OOP Concepts"]
        }
    ],
    "metadata": None
}

# Serialize the sample data structure
print("Serialized JSON Data:")
json_output = serialize_data(sample_data)
print(json_output)

# Measure performance of the serialization process for large
↪   datasets
start_time = time.time()
_ = serialize_data(sample_data)
end_time = time.time()
print(f"\nSerialization Performance: {end_time - start_time}
↪   seconds")

# Deserialize the JSON string back into a Python object to
↪   demonstrate reversibility
try:
    deserialized_data = deserialize_data(json_output)
    print("\nDeserialized Python Object:")
    print(deserialized_data)
except Exception as e:
```

```python
        print("An error occurred during deserialization:", e)

# Demonstrate incremental processing with a streaming generator
↪  on JSON array data
json_array = '[{"id": 1, "value": "A"}, {"id": 2, "value": "B"},
↪  {"id": 3, "value": "C"}]'
print("\nStreaming JSON Array Items:")
for item in stream_json_array(json_array):
    print(item)

# Optional: Write the serialized JSON data to a file and read it
↪  back to test file I/O functions
filename = "sample_data.json"
try:
    write_json_to_file(sample_data, filename)
    file_data = process_json_file(filename)
    print("\nData read from file:")
    print(file_data)
except Exception as e:
    print("File I/O error:", e)
```

Chapter 34

Regular Expressions

Fundamental Constructs of Regular Expression Syntax

Regular expressions are defined as concise patterns that describe sets of strings within the framework of formal language theory. At their core, these expressions are constructed from elementary symbols and combined through operations such as concatenation, alternation (denoted by $|$), and repetition via the Kleene star ($*$). In this formalism, the concatenation of symbols such as a and b produces the pattern ab, which accepts only those strings that sequentially contain a immediately followed by b. The theoretical equivalence between regular expressions and finite automata is well established, with the empty string represented by ϵ serving as a neutral element in concatenative operations. This fundamental basis permits rigorous algebraic manipulation and serves as the foundation for expressive textual pattern definitions.

Theoretical Foundations and Formal Semantics

The semantic underpinnings of regular expressions derive from the theory of regular languages. In this context, any given regular expression corresponds to a set of strings characterized by specific closure properties under union, concatenation, and Kleene closure. The formal definitions are encapsulated by the following operations: the union of two regular expressions R_1 and R_2 is expressed as $R_1 \cup R_2$, their concatenation as $R_1 R_2$, and the Kleene closure of a regular expression R as R^*. These operations guarantee that the resulting language is regular, thereby ensuring its recognizability by finite automata. The precise mapping from expression syntax to the corresponding automata formalism elucidates the limitations and capabilities of pattern matching within this domain.

Character Classes, Quantifiers, and Anchors

The expressive power of regular expressions is significantly enhanced by the utilization of character classes, quantifiers, and anchors. Character classes, denoted by square brackets as in $[AZ]$ or [09], define explicit sets of acceptable characters. Complementary shorthand notations, such as $\backslash d$ for digits, $\backslash s$ for whitespace, and $\backslash w$ for word characters, enable succinct patterns for common character groups. Quantifiers further refine these expressions by specifying the permissible frequency of occurrences; for example, the plus sign (+) indicates one or more occurrences, whereas the question mark (?) designates zero or one occurrence. The notation $\{m, n\}$ restricts an element to appear between m and n times inclusively. Additionally, anchors such as the caret () and the dollar sign ($) assert positional constraints by marking the beginning and end of a line, respectively, thereby confining pattern matches to specific textual positions.

Grouping, Capturing, and Backreferences

Advanced pattern construction in regular expressions often necessitates the segmentation of expressions into logical subcomponents. Grouping is achieved by enclosing subpatterns within parentheses, (), which also provision the mechanism for capturing matches. Capturing groups enable the extraction of specific substrings that conform to the pattern and subsequently facilitate the use of backreferences, typically represented as $\backslash 1$, $\backslash 2$, etc., to enforce consistency across repeated segments. In instances where grouping is solely required for structural or precedence purposes without retaining matched content, non-capturing groups may be utilized, which are denoted by the syntax (? : ...). These constructs are indispensable in the assembly of complex expressions where relational dependencies between substrings must be maintained.

Applications in Pattern Matching and Text Extraction

The application of regular expressions extends to the domain of sophisticated pattern matching and text extraction, thereby serving as an essential tool in the processing of unstructured data. The inherent ability of regular expressions to define intricate matching criteria enables their deployment in tasks such as data validation, lexical analysis, and the extraction of meaningful subcomponents from vast corpora of text. The efficacy of these techniques is anchored in the theoretical properties of finite automata, which underpin the rapid and efficient parsing of input strings. Moreover, the capacity to succinctly specify patterns with a small set of operators renders regular expressions particularly effective in automated text processing systems. The integration of these constructs into larger data manipulation paradigms underscores their critical role in managing both the structural and semantic aspects of textual information within computational frameworks.

Python Code Snippet

```
#!/usr/bin/env python3
"""
This comprehensive Python code snippet demonstrates key regular
↪   expression concepts
as discussed in the chapter on Regular Expressions. The code covers:
    - Concatenation of symbols
    - Union (alternation) using '|'
    - Repetition using the Kleene star '*'
    - Usage of character classes and quantifiers (e.g., \d, \s, +, ?,
↪   {m,n})
    - Anchors (e.g., ^ and $)
    - Grouping with capturing and non-capturing groups
    - Backreferences for matching repeated elements
    - Pattern matching for extracting dates in YYYY-MM-DD format

Each function below illustrates one of these constructs with test
↪   cases.
"""

import re
```

```python
def test_concatenation():
    # Demonstrate concatenation: The pattern 'ab' matches exactly
    ↪ 'a' followed immediately by 'b'.
    pattern = re.compile(r'ab')
    test_strings = ['ab', 'a', 'b', 'abc', 'cab']
    print("Testing concatenation (pattern: 'ab'):")
    for s in test_strings:
        match = pattern.search(s)
        result = match.group(0) if match else None
        print(f"  Input: {s:<10} Match: {result}")


def test_union():
    # Demonstrate union (alternation): 'cat|dog' matches either
    ↪ 'cat' or 'dog'.
    pattern = re.compile(r'cat|dog')
    test_strings = ['cat', 'dog', 'caterpillar', 'dogma', 'mouse']
    print("\nTesting union (pattern: 'cat|dog'):")
    for s in test_strings:
        match = pattern.search(s)
        result = match.group(0) if match else None
        print(f"  Input: {s:<15} Match: {result}")


def test_kleene_star():
    # Demonstrate Kleene star: The pattern '(ab)*' matches zero or
    ↪ more occurrences of 'ab'.
    pattern = re.compile(r'(ab)*')
    test_strings = ['ab', 'abab', 'aba', '', 'a']
    print("\nTesting Kleene star (pattern: '(ab)*'):")
    for s in test_strings:
        # Using fullmatch to ensure the entire string is matched.
        match = pattern.fullmatch(s)
        result = match.group(0) if match else None
        print(f"  Input: {s:<10} Full match: {result}")


def test_quantifiers_and_classes():
    # Demonstrate character classes and quantifiers:
    # The pattern '\d+\s?\w+' requires one or more digits, an
    ↪ optional whitespace, and one or more word characters.
    pattern = re.compile(r'\d+\s?\w+')
    test_strings = ['123abc', '456 abc', 'no match', '789', '12 3']
    print("\nTesting quantifiers and character classes (pattern:
    ↪ '\\d+\\s?\\w+'):")
    for s in test_strings:
        match = pattern.search(s)
        result = match.group(0) if match else None
        print(f"  Input: {s:<10} Match: {result}")


def test_anchors():
    # Demonstrate anchors: The pattern '^start.*end$' ensures the
    ↪ string starts with 'start' and ends with 'end'.
    pattern = re.compile(r'^start.*end$')
```

185

```python
    test_strings = ['start and then some text and finally end',
    ↪   'start middle', 'end start', 'startend']
    print("\nTesting anchors (pattern: '^start.*end$'):")
    for s in test_strings:
        match = pattern.fullmatch(s)
        result = match.group(0) if match else None
        print(f"  Input: {s:<45} Match: {result}")

def test_grouping_and_backreference():
    # Demonstrate grouping and backreferences:
    # The pattern '\b(\w+)\s+\1\b' matches a word followed by one or
    ↪   more spaces and a repetition of the same word.
    pattern = re.compile(r'\b(\w+)\s+\1\b')
    test_strings = ['test test', 'hello world', 'foo foo bar',
    ↪   'repeat repeat, again']
    print("\nTesting grouping and backreferences (pattern:
    ↪   '\\b(\\w+)\\s+\\1\\b'):")
    for s in test_strings:
        match = pattern.search(s)
        result = match.group(0) if match else None
        print(f"  Input: {s:<30} Repeated word: {result}")

def test_non_capturing_group():
    # Demonstrate non-capturing groups:
    # The pattern '(?:abc)+' matches one or more repetitions of
    ↪   'abc' without capturing the group.
    pattern = re.compile(r'(?:abc)+')
    test_strings = ['abc', 'abcabc', 'abcx', 'ab']
    print("\nTesting non-capturing groups (pattern: '(?:abc)+'):")
    for s in test_strings:
        match = pattern.fullmatch(s)
        result = match.group(0) if match else None
        print(f"  Input: {s:<10} Match: {result}")

def test_date_extraction():
    # Demonstrate extraction of dates in the format YYYY-MM-DD.
    # The pattern '\b\d{4}-\d{2}-\d{2}\b' matches dates like
    ↪   '2023-10-12'.
    pattern = re.compile(r'\b\d{4}-\d{2}-\d{2}\b')
    text = ("Important dates are 2023-10-12 and 1999-12-31. "
            "Invalid dates like 2023-1-1 or 99-12-31 will not be
            ↪   matched.")
    matches = pattern.findall(text)
    print("\nTesting date extraction (pattern:
    ↪   '\\b\\d{4}-\\d{2}-\\d{2}\\b'):")
    print(f"  Extracted dates: {matches}")

def main():
    print("----- Regular Expressions Demonstration -----")
    test_concatenation()
    test_union()
    test_kleene_star()
    test_quantifiers_and_classes()
```

```python
    test_anchors()
    test_grouping_and_backreference()
    test_non_capturing_group()
    test_date_extraction()
    print("\nDemonstration completed.")

if __name__ == '__main__':
    main()
```

Chapter 35

Iterators and Iterables

Conceptual Overview of Iteration

Iteration mechanisms in Python are founded upon the notion of progressive element retrieval from a collection without exposing the underlying structure. The concept of an iterator is intrinsically tied to a stateful object that sequentially produces elements from a prescribed sequence. In formal terms, an iterator may be regarded as an abstract machine that, given an initial state, yields a series of outputs through successive state transitions. This mechanism facilitates a deferred evaluation model, wherein elements are computed on demand rather than all at once. Such a mechanism aligns with algorithmic principles that favor minimal memory usage and encapsulation of iteration state, thereby enabling the processing of potentially unbounded sequences.

The Iterator Protocol in Python

In Python, the iterator protocol is implemented through a well-defined interface that mandates the existence of two fundamental methods. The method $_i$ter, when invoked on an iterable object, returns an iterator instance, which is responsible for maintaining the iteration's progress. The method $_n$ext is then employed to retrieve successive elements from the iterator. When no further elements are available, the invocation of $_n$ext must signal termination by raising a StopIteration exception. This formalized protocol ensures that all iterator objects conform to a consistent behavior, thereby permitting the use of iteration constructs—such as for-loops and comprehensions—across diverse object types. The protocol itself is a manifestation of a state transition system, where each call to $_{n}ext$ corresponds to a transition from the current state to a subsequent state until an absorbing state is reached.

Properties and Characteristics of Iterable Objects

An object is classified as iterable if it defines a method $_{i}ter$ that returns an iterator. This property is not confined solely to compound data structures such as lists, tuples, or dictionaries, but extends to any construct that can encapsulate a sequence of values. The central property of an iterable is the capacity to produce fresh iterator instances, which, unlike the iterator obtained from a single traversal, can be independently generated to yield the same sequence of elements. The abstraction of iterability thus decouples the process of element generation from the storage structure itself and enables algorithmic patterns that exploit lazy evaluation. The ability to reinitialize iteration via repeated invocations of $_{i}ter$ distinguishes iterables from iterators, the latter being inherently single-use due to their transient state.

Designing Custom Iterators

The design of custom iterator objects requires a careful implementation of the iterator protocol. An object that is intended to produce a sequence of values must implement $_{i}ter$ such that it returns an iterator—often, the object itself serves in this capacity when accompanied by an appropriate internal state. The $_{n}ext$ method must encapsulate the algorithmic logic necessary to determine the subsequent element as a function of the current state and to update the state accordingly. In scenarios where the sequence is finite, the method must eventually signal the end of iteration by raising StopIteration. The separation of state management from data encapsulation in custom iterator design permits the creation of iterators that operate over both simple and complex data structures, thereby adhering to principled software design constructs such as separation of concerns and modularity.

189

Analytical Perspectives on Iterative Constructs

A rigorous analysis of iterative constructs in Python reveals several critical attributes. The iterator protocol embodies a transition system that is analogous to a finite automaton, with each call to $_{n}$ext effecting a state change. Such a design is amenable to formal reasoning about termination and correctness in algorithmic contexts. The utilization of lazy evaluation inherent to iterators offers significant performance benefits by deferring computation and minimizing memory overhead. Yet, this same property necessitates careful consideration of iterator reuse, as the transient state maintained within an iterator object precludes multiple independent traversals over the same sequence. The theoretical underpinnings of the iterator protocol, when examined through the lens of stateful systems and function composition, provide a robust framework for both the analysis and construction of algorithms that rely on sequential data processing.

Python Code Snippet

```
"""
This script demonstrates various iterator and iterable constructs in
↪ Python,
focusing on the implementation of the iterator protocol using custom
↪ iterator classes,
generator functions, and the distinctions between iterables and
↪ iterators.

Key concepts:
1. The iterator protocol via __iter__ and __next__.
2. Custom iterator for the Fibonacci sequence using the recurrence
↪ relation:
    F(n) = F(n-1) + F(n-2), with F(0) = 0 and F(1) = 1.
3. Lazy evaluation: Elements are computed only on demand.
4. Differences between iterators (single-use) and iterables
↪ (reusable).
"""

# Custom iterator class for generating Fibonacci numbers
class FibonacciIterator:
    def __init__(self, max_steps=None):
        """
        Initialize the Fibonacci iterator.
```

```python
        :param max_steps: Maximum number of Fibonacci numbers to
        ↪ generate.
                          If None, the iterator will generate
                          ↪ numbers indefinitely.
        """
        self.a = 0  # Represents F(0)
        self.b = 1  # Represents F(1)
        self.index = 0
        self.max_steps = max_steps

    def __iter__(self):
        # The object itself is the iterator.
        return self

    def __next__(self):
        # Check if the maximum number of steps has been reached.
        if self.max_steps is not None and self.index >=
        ↪ self.max_steps:
            raise StopIteration

        if self.index == 0:
            # First element of Fibonacci series: F(0)
            result = self.a
        elif self.index == 1:
            # Second element of Fibonacci series: F(1)
            result = self.b
        else:
            # Fibonacci recurrence: F(n) = F(n-1) + F(n-2)
            result = self.a + self.b
            self.a, self.b = self.b, result

        self.index += 1
        return result

# Generator function for Fibonacci sequence
def fibonacci_generator(max_steps=None):
    """
    A generator function that yields Fibonacci numbers.

    This function demonstrates lazy evaluation by yielding values on
    ↪ demand.

    :param max_steps: Maximum number of Fibonacci numbers to yield.
    """
    a, b = 0, 1  # Starting values F(0) and F(1)
    index = 0
    while max_steps is None or index < max_steps:
        yield a
        a, b = b, a + b  # Update using the recurrence relation
        index += 1

# Demonstration of using a custom iterator
def demo_custom_iterator():
```

191

```python
    print("Fibonacci Iterator (first 10 numbers):")
    fib_iter = FibonacciIterator(max_steps=10)
    for number in fib_iter:
        print(number, end=' ')
    print("\n")

# Demonstration of using the generator function
def demo_generator():
    print("Fibonacci Generator (first 10 numbers):")
    for number in fibonacci_generator(max_steps=10):
        print(number, end=' ')
    print("\n")

# Demonstration of properties of iterables vs iterators
def demo_iterable_reusability():
    print("Demonstrating reusability of an iterable (list):")
    numbers = list(range(5))

    # Lists are iterables and can be traversed multiple times.
    for item in numbers:
        print(item, end=' ')
    print("")

    # Using iter() gives an iterator from the iterable.
    num_iterator = iter(numbers)
    print("Single traversal of iterator from list:")
    print(list(num_iterator))

    # The iterator is now exhausted; further traversal yields an
    #  ↪ empty list.
    print("Attempting to traverse the exhausted iterator:")
    print(list(num_iterator))

    # Re-initializing the iterator from the iterable recovers the
    #  ↪ full sequence.
    num_iterator = iter(numbers)
    print("After reinitialization, the iterator yields:")
    print(list(num_iterator))
    print("")

if __name__ == "__main__":
    demo_custom_iterator()
    demo_generator()
    demo_iterable_reusability()
```

Chapter 36

Generators: Using `yield`

Theoretical Foundations of Generator Functions

Generator functions are defined as special subroutines that, upon invocation, establish an internal state capable of producing a sequence of values through successive resumptions. Such functions encapsulate a stateful transformation that, rather than computing an entire sequence and storing it in memory, returns one element at a time. In formal terms, if G represents a generator function, then the process of generation can be modeled by a state transition function δ, where for an initial state s_0, each application of δ produces a pair (v, s') consisting of a yielded value v and an updated state s'. The intrinsic advantage of this design is the deferred computation of sequence elements, wherein only the necessary state components are maintained between successive yield operations.

Internal Mechanism of `yield`

Within the operational semantics of generator functions, the `yield` keyword serves as a control transfer mechanism that both produces a value and suspends the function's execution. At the moment of execution of a `yield` statement, the current evaluation context—including local variable bindings and the remaining sequence of instructions—is preserved. This suspension creates a latent state, denoted by s, that is reactivated upon the subsequent invocation of the generator. The transition from state s to state s' upon yielding a value is analogous to the operation of a finite state automaton, where the saving of the computational context ensures that the generator resumes precisely at the point immediately following the last `yield`. This mechanism establishes a well-defined correspondence between the discontinuous control flow and the sequence of generated outputs.

Memory Efficiency Through Lazy Evaluation

The use of `yield` in generator functions embodies the principle of lazy evaluation, whereby elements of a sequence are computed only as they are required. Instead of precomputing and storing an entire list of values, a generator calculates each element on-the-fly, thereby minimizing memory consumption. Formally, if a generator function is tasked with producing a sequence $\{f(n)\}_{n=0}^{\infty}$, the only state that persists is encapsulated in a state vector s that holds the minimal information necessary to determine the following element. This memory-efficient approach is particularly advantageous when dealing with large or potentially unbounded sequences, as it obviates the need to allocate storage for each element. The deferred evaluation of sequence elements ensures that resources are utilized in a just-in-time fashion, aligning computational effort with actual demand.

Algebraic Representation and Formal Semantics

From an algebraic perspective, the behavior of a generator function can be expressed as a partial function $\pi : S \rightarrow X \times S$, where S denotes the set of possible internal states and X represents the set of outputs. Each invocation of the yield operation applies the mapping π to the current state $s \in S$, producing an output $x \in X$ and transitioning to a new state $s' \in S$. In this formalism, the generator function is considered to be a composition of state transitions that continues until a terminal condition is encountered, at which point the generator ceases to produce further values. This mathematical abstraction not only elucidates the internal workings of generator functions but also provides a framework for rigorously analyzing their correctness and resource allocation properties within a computational model that emphasizes state transitions and lazy evaluation.

Python Code Snippet

```
# The following Python code demonstrates the internal workings of
↪  generator functions,
# modeling their behavior with a state transition function similar
↪  to the algebraic
# mapping : S → X × S described in the chapter. It also compares an
↪  arithmetic progression
# generator with a Fibonacci sequence generator to illustrate lazy
↪  evaluation and internal state management.

def arithmetic_state(s):
    """
    State transition function for an arithmetic progression.

    This function represents the mapping:
        : S → X × S
    where the state S is a tuple (n, step) and:
        - n is the current number (x   X),
        - step is the increment value.

    Given an input state s = (n, step), the function returns:
        (n, (n + step, step))
    where:
        n       -> yielded value,
        n+step -> updated state.
    """
    current_value = s[0]
    new_state = (s[0] + s[1], s[1])
    return current_value, new_state

def pi_generator(s0, pi_func, max_iter=None):
    """
    Generic generator that applies a state transition function
    ↪  repeatedly,
    simulating the algebraic definition of a generator:
        : S → X × S.

    Parameters:
        s0 (tuple): The initial state s.
        pi_func (function): A function implementing the state
        ↪  transition, e.g., arithmetic_state.
        max_iter (int, optional): Maximum number of iterations. If
        ↪  None, the generator is infinite.
```

Yields:
   x: The next value in the sequence defined by the transition
    ↪ *function.*

The generator maintains only the minimal state needed between
  ↪ *yield operations,*
demonstrating the principle of lazy evaluation.
```
"""
s = s0
count = 0
while True:
    x, s = pi_func(s)
    yield x
    count += 1
    if max_iter is not None and count >= max_iter:
        break

def fibonacci_generator(max_iter=None):
    """
```
Generator function for producing the Fibonacci sequence.

This function demonstrates a generator where the internal state
  ↪ *is encapsulated*
by the tuple (a, b), corresponding to consecutive Fibonacci
  ↪ *numbers, and updates*
on each yield. Starting with a = 0 and b = 1, it produces the
  ↪ *sequence:*
    0, 1, 1, 2, 3, 5, 8, ...

Parameters:
   max_iter (int, optional): Maximum number of Fibonacci numbers
    ↪ *to generate.*
                        If None, the generator produces an
                           ↪ *infinite sequence.*

Yields:
   int: The next Fibonacci number in the sequence.
```
    """
    a, b = 0, 1
    count = 0
    while True:
        yield a
        a, b = b, a + b
        count += 1
        if max_iter is not None and count >= max_iter:
            break

if __name__ == "__main__":
```
   # Demonstration using the pi_generator with the arithmetic_state
    ↪ *function.*
   # Initial state: (0, 3) represents starting at 0 with an
    ↪ *increment of 3.*

196

```python
print("Arithmetic progression using pi_generator:")
initial_state = (0, 3)
arithmetic_gen = pi_generator(initial_state, arithmetic_state,
↪  max_iter=10)
for value in arithmetic_gen:
    print(value)

# Demonstration of a Fibonacci sequence generator.
print("\nFibonacci sequence using fibonacci_generator:")
fib_gen = fibonacci_generator(max_iter=10)
for number in fib_gen:
    print(number)
```

Chapter 37

Decorators

Conceptual Foundations of Decorators

Function decorators represent an advanced mechanism to modify or enhance the behavior of functions in a manner that preserves the original semantic structure. In formal terms, a decorator can be regarded as an operator

$$D : \mathcal{F} \to \mathcal{F},$$

where $\mathcal{F}$ is the set of functions under consideration. This operator encapsulates the notion of higher-order functions, as it accepts a function as input and returns a new function whose behavior is augmented by additional operations. The design permits the segregation of auxiliary concerns—such as logging, authentication, or performance evaluation—from the core logic, thereby maintaining a clear separation of concerns. The resulting abstraction introduces a level of modularity that is both expressive and mathematically rigorous.

Mechanisms of Behavioral Modification

The operational mechanism of function decorators involves the interposition of additional behavior during the invocation of a function. When a decorator is applied to a function f, the decorator constructs a new function $D(f)$ which interlaces the execution of f with pre- and post-processing steps. This process is analogous to function composition in the sense that the decorated function can be viewed as the result of a composite mapping

$$(Df)(x) = \phi(f, x),$$

where the mapping ϕ integrates supplementary logic within the call sequence. The execution of $D(f)$ thus commences with an initial phase that may perform validations or resource preparations, followed by the invocation of f, and concludes with final processing steps such as cleanup or result transformation. This layered structure provides an elegant methodology for modifying function behavior dynamically without altering the underlying code of f.

Expressive Syntactic Abstractions

The syntactic design of decorators exploits expressive language constructs to provide a clear and concise means for function augmentation. In many programming languages, the decorator notation offers an elegant shorthand that conceals the underlying mechanism of function wrapping. The application of a decorator is functionally equivalent to the assignment

$$f \leftarrow D(f),$$

which succinctly conveys the notion of behavior enhancement through operator application. The declarative syntax not only improves code readability but also facilitates the consistent extension of function behavior across various components of a software system. This syntactical abstraction is underpinned by fundamental concepts in functional programming, emphasizing the potency of composition over inheritance for behavioral refinement.

Implications for Modularity and Code Reusability

The adoption of decorators as a design construct carries significant implications for modularity and code reusability within software systems. By isolating cross-cutting concerns into dedicated decorator functions, systems achieve a pronounced reduction in code duplication and enhanced separation of logic layers. Each decorator embodies a self-contained module that can be uniformly applied to diverse functions, thereby promoting a high degree of reusability. The modular composition facilitated by decorators ensures that core functionalities remain unencumbered by ancillary operations. This separation not only improves maintainability but also enables the systematic transformation of function behaviors through controlled and independently testable components.

Python Code Snippet

```
import time
import functools

# Decorator that logs function call details, representing the idea
↪  of:
# f ← D(f) where the function f is enhanced with logging behavior.
def log_decorator(func):
    """Decorator that logs entry and exit of a function."""
    @functools.wraps(func)
    def wrapper(*args, **kwargs):
        print(f"Entering '{func.__name__}' with arguments {args} and
        ↪  keyword arguments {kwargs}")
        result = func(*args, **kwargs)
        print(f"Exiting '{func.__name__}' with result {result}")
        return result
    return wrapper

# Decorator that times the execution duration of a function,
# which illustrates inserting pre and post processing steps.
def timer_decorator(func):
    """Decorator that measures the execution time of the
    ↪  function."""
    @functools.wraps(func)
    def wrapper(*args, **kwargs):
        start_time = time.time()  # Pre-processing: record the start
        ↪  time.
        result = func(*args, **kwargs)
        elapsed_time = time.time() - start_time  # Post-processing:
        ↪  calculate elapsed time.
        print(f"Execution time of '{func.__name__}':
        ↪  {elapsed_time:.6f} seconds")
        return result
    return wrapper

# Decorator factory that applies a transformation function to the
↪  output
# of the decorated function. This simulates the equation:
# (D f)(x) = (f, x), where  represents the transformation applied.
def transform_decorator(transformation):
```

```python
    """Factory decorator that transforms the output of the function
    ↪ using a transformation."""
    def decorator(func):
        @functools.wraps(func)
        def wrapper(*args, **kwargs):
            result = func(*args, **kwargs)
            transformed_result = transformation(result)
            print(f"Transformed result of '{func.__name__}' from
            ↪ {result} to {transformed_result}")
            return transformed_result
        return wrapper
    return decorator


# Example transformation function: squares the result.
def square(x):
    return x * x


# The function compute_sum calculates the sum of two numbers.
# The decorators applied enhance this function such that:
# - transform_decorator applies a square transformation () to the
↪ result,
# - timer_decorator measures the execution time,
# - log_decorator logs entry and exit details.
# This layered enhancement is analogous to composing an operator D
↪ with the function f.
@log_decorator
@timer_decorator
@transform_decorator(square)
def compute_sum(a, b):
    """
    Compute the sum of two numbers.
    The decorator chain modifies its behavior:
      - Applying a transformation function to square the sum.
      - Timing the execution.
      - Logging the call details.
    This demonstrates the concept of a decorator as an operator D:
    ↪ → .
    """
    time.sleep(0.5)  # Simulate processing delay.
    return a + b


# Main execution block to test the decorated function.
if __name__ == "__main__":
    result = compute_sum(3, 4)
    print(f"Final output: {result}")
```

Chapter 38

Context Managers

Conceptual Framework of Contextual Resource Management

The mechanism of context managers is grounded in a rigorous conceptual framework that addresses the systematic acquisition and subsequent release of critical resources such as file streams, network connections, and other system-level assets. This framework formulates resource management as a deterministic process whereby the instantiation and finalization of resources occur within clearly defined operational boundaries. When a resource is acquired, it is bound to a well-specified state that guarantees its availability for the duration of its use. The intrinsic property of automatic resource finalization ensures that, regardless of variations in the control flow—including exceptional conditions—the resource is restored to a safe state. This deterministic behavior is essential for maintaining both system stability and the integrity of transient resources.

Operational Mechanism of the with Statement

The operational semantics of the with statement are characterized by a two-phase execution model. In the initial phase, an entry operation is invoked to secure a robust resource binding. This phase may be abstractly represented by an operator E, where $E(R)$

returns a valid resource handle corresponding to the resource R. Once the resource has been successfully acquired, the core operational block executes with the resource held in a defined and stable state. On termination of this block, whether through normal execution or via an abrupt change in control flow due to an error, an exit operation is automatically triggered. This exit operation, denoted by X, is responsible for effectuating the proper release and cleanup of the resource. The automatic invocation of the exit operation ensures that resource sanitization is consistently executed, thereby preserving the environmental contract that governs resource management.

Formal Characterization of Resource Lifecycle Management

Within the theoretical framework of resource management, the lifecycle of a resource is partitioned into discrete stages encompassing initialization, utilization, and finalization. The entry phase may be considered a function I acting upon a target resource T, yielding an operational resource state R, such that $R = I(T)$. Once the resource is actively engaged in operational tasks, its lifecycle is governed by invariant conditions guaranteeing that a corresponding finalization function F will unconditionally execute at the conclusion of the block, formally expressed as $F(R)$. This relationship establishes a bijective association between resource acquisition and release. The explicit decoupling of initialization from finalization under this paradigm is instrumental in enabling precise reasoning about state transitions in environments where resource constraints mandate meticulous control over resource availability and timely deallocation.

Implications on Resource Integrity and System Reliability

The formalization of context managers into the operational semantics of the with statement yields significant implications for both resource integrity and system reliability. By decoupling resource acquisition from its subsequent release, the structural design ensures that resources do not persist in an indeterminate state after their active use—a property critical to averting resource starvation and memory leaks. The invocation of a dedicated finalization operation, irrespective of intervening computational anomalies, fortifies the system against the inadvertent retention of resources. Additionally, the encapsulation of resource management logic into distinct, composable units promotes modularity, enabling both enhanced verification of system properties and optimization of resource utilization. The resultant improvement in reliability is achieved through a methodical enforcement of resource lifecycle invariants, as exemplified by the guaranteed execution of the exit operation upon block termination.

Python Code Snippet

```
#!/usr/bin/env python3

class ResourceManager:
    """
    A context manager that implements deterministic resource
    ↪    acquisition and release,
    demonstrating the formal relationship R = I(T) and F(R) as
    ↪    described in the chapter.

    Attributes:
        resource_name (str): Identifier for the resource.
        resource_state (dict): Dictionary representing the current
        ↪    state of the resource.
    """
    def __init__(self, resource_name):
        self.resource_name = resource_name
        self.resource_state = None

    def __enter__(self):
        # Entry operation: I(T) that initializes and acquires the
        ↪    resource.
        self.resource_state =
        ↪    self.initialize_resource(self.resource_name)
        print(f"Resource '{self.resource_name}' acquired. State:
        ↪    {self.resource_state}")
        return self.resource_state

    def __exit__(self, exc_type, exc_value, traceback):
        # Exit operation: F(R) that finalizes and releases the
        ↪    resource.
        self.finalize_resource(self.resource_state)
        if exc_type:
            print(f"An exception occurred: {exc_type.__name__} -
            ↪    {exc_value}")
```

```python
        print(f"Resource '{self.resource_name}' has been released
        ↪  and finalized.")
        # Return False to propagate any exception that occurred
        ↪  within the block.
        return False

    def initialize_resource(self, resource):
        """
        Simulates the initialization phase I(T): acquires and sets
        ↪  the resource in an 'active' state.
        Returns an initial resource state represented as a
        ↪  dictionary.
        """
        # In practical applications, this could open a file,
        ↪  establish a network connection, etc.
        initial_state = {
            "resource": resource,
            "status": "active",
            "value": 42  # Example attribute; could represent a data
            ↪  buffer or connection parameter.
        }
        return initial_state

    def finalize_resource(self, resource_state):
        """
        Simulates the finalization phase F(R): cleans up or releases
        ↪  the resource.
        Ensures the resource state is reset to 'inactive' regardless
        ↪  of block execution outcome.
        """
        if resource_state:
            resource_state["status"] = "inactive"
            resource_state["value"] = None

def process_resource(resource_state):
    """
    Demonstrates an algorithm that utilizes the resource.

    The processing function applies a sample computation:
        result = resource_state["value"] ** 2
    which reflects the operation E(R) for resource usage, and
    ↪  ensures resource invariants.

    Raises:
        RuntimeError: If the resource is not in an 'active' state.
    """
    try:
        if resource_state["status"] != "active":
            raise RuntimeError("Attempting to process an inactive
            ↪  resource.")
        # Sample computation: square the value associated with the
        ↪  resource.
        result = resource_state["value"] ** 2
```

205

```python
        print(f"Processed resource value squared: {result}")
    except Exception as e:
        print(f"Error during processing: {e}")
        raise


if __name__ == "__main__":
    print("Starting the context-managed resource process...")
    # Using the context manager to ensure acquisition and guaranteed
    ↪ release.
    try:
        with ResourceManager("SampleResource") as resource:
            process_resource(resource)
            # Uncomment the next line to simulate an error during
            ↪ processing.
            # raise ValueError("Simulated processing error")
    except Exception as error:
        print(f"Unhandled exception: {error}")
    print("Resource management process completed successfully.")
```

Chapter 39

Working with Dates and Times

Temporal Data Structures and Representations

Within computational systems, dates and times are encapsulated by structured objects that mirror the inherent complexity of chronometric data. Such objects typically comprise a collection of numerical fields representing the year, month, day, hour, minute, and second, formally described as

$$T = \{Y, M, D, h, m, s\}.$$

This structured representation allows temporal values to be unambiguously defined within a fixed reference framework. The underlying abstraction models the time continuum as a sequence of discrete instants, each characterized by its position within a calendar system. These temporal objects are instantiated to represent both absolute points in time and intervals, thereby establishing a dual capacity for precise event marking and duration measurement.

Chronometric Operations and Arithmetic

Temporal manipulation is grounded in the ability to perform arithmetic operations on date and time objects. The subtraction of two temporal instants, for example, yields a time interval defined as

$$\Delta t = t_2 - t_1,$$

where t_1 and t_2 denote distinct instants. This operation facilitates the computation of durations and the quantification of elapsed time. Moreover, the addition of a time interval to a given instant provides a means to forecast or backtrack through a temporal sequence. The arithmetic operations are designed to observe the invariants dictated by the calendar structure, ensuring that computations such as month transitions, leap years, and daylight saving time adjustments are consistently maintained within the operational semantics.

Formatting and Parsing of Temporal Information

The conversion between structured temporal objects and their textual representations is a critical element of practical date and time manipulation. Formatting mechanisms transform the internal representation into human-readable strings according to predefined or custom-specified patterns, such as

"YYYY-MM-DD HH:MM:SS",

thereby facilitating the display, logging, or serialization of temporal data. Conversely, parsing routines interpret a textual representation, reconstituting the information into a formal object with internal fields mapped in accordance with the designated schema. This bidirectional transformation supports a rigorous consistency between the digital representation of time and its external manifestations, ensuring that discrepancies between formatted output and internal state are minimized.

Time Zone Awareness and Localization

Temporal data inherently involves considerations of universal and local time. The distinction between naive and time zone–aware temporal objects is a critical factor in ensuring that operations remain consistent across disparate geographical regions. A time zone–aware object is augmented with an offset field, which memorializes its deviation from Coordinated Universal Time (UTC), thus enabling arithmetic operations to account for regional differences and the complexities of daylight saving time. Such augmentation can be formally expressed as an extension of the base temporal tuple,

$$T_{aware} = \{Y, M, D, h, m, s, \delta\},$$

where δ represents the time zone offset. The integration of time zone information is pivotal in ensuring that subsequent temporal computations, comparisons, and conversions yield correct and context-sensitive results.

Theoretical Considerations in Temporal Computation

The study of temporal computation necessitates a rigorous theoretical framework that encapsulates both the continuous and discrete aspects of time. Temporal objects must adhere to a set of invariants that guarantee consistency in the face of arithmetic manipulations and formatting transformations. For instance, the conversion function

$$f : T \to S,$$

which maps a temporal object to its string representation, is required to be bijective over the domain of permissible dates and times, thus preserving uniqueness and reversibility. Additionally, the properties of temporal intervals and their additive behavior must align with the axioms of real number arithmetic, modulo the constraints imposed by calendar-specific adjustments. In this context, the interplay between formal definitions and practical implementations is of paramount significance, ensuring that temporal data remains both mathematically sound and operationally robust.

Python Code Snippet

```python
from datetime import datetime, timedelta, timezone

# For time zone handling, attempt to use zoneinfo (available in
↪   Python 3.9+)
try:
    from zoneinfo import ZoneInfo
except ImportError:
    # Fallback: for older Python versions, one might install and use
    ↪   pytz.
```

```python
from pytz import timezone as ZoneInfo

# ------------------------------------------------------------
# 1. Temporal Data Structures and Representations
#
# Representing a temporal object T as:
#     T = {Y, M, D, h, m, s}
#
# Here we define two datetime objects t1 and t2 based on the tuple
# ↪  above.
# ------------------------------------------------------------
t1 = datetime(2023, 10, 1, 12, 0, 0)     # T1: 2023-10-01 12:00:00
t2 = datetime(2023, 10, 2, 15, 30, 45)   # T2: 2023-10-02 15:30:45

print("T1 =", t1)
print("T2 =", t2)


# ------------------------------------------------------------
# 2. Chronometric Operations and Arithmetic
#
# The subtraction of two temporal instants yields a time interval:
#     t = t2 - t1
# ------------------------------------------------------------
delta_t = t2 - t1
print("Delta t =", delta_t)  # Shows the duration between T1 and T2

# Addition of a time interval to a temporal object:
#     t3 = t1 + t
t3 = t1 + delta_t
print("T1 + Delta t =", t3)


# ------------------------------------------------------------
# 3. Formatting and Parsing of Temporal Information
#
# Define a format for the textual representation:
#     "YYYY-MM-DD HH:MM:SS"
# ------------------------------------------------------------
format_str = "%Y-%m-%d %H:%M:%S"

# Formatting: Convert a datetime object (T) to its string
# ↪  representation (S)
t1_str = t1.strftime(format_str)
print("Formatted T1:", t1_str)

# Parsing: Convert a formatted string back to a datetime object
parsed_t1 = datetime.strptime(t1_str, format_str)
print("Parsed T1:", parsed_t1)


# ------------------------------------------------------------
# 4. Time Zone Awareness and Localization
#
# A time zone aware temporal object can be seen as an extension:
#     T_aware = {Y, M, D, h, m, s, }
```

```python
#
# Here,  represents the time zone offset.
# ------------------------------------------------------------
# Create a UTC time zone aware datetime object from t1.
t1_aware = t1.replace(tzinfo=timezone.utc)
print("T1 with UTC timezone:", t1_aware)

# Convert the UTC-based time to a specific timezone (e.g.,
↪   America/New_York)
try:
    ny_zone = ZoneInfo("America/New_York")
except Exception as e:
    print("ZoneInfo not available, defaulting to UTC")
    ny_zone = timezone.utc

t1_ny = t1_aware.astimezone(ny_zone)
print("T1 in New York timezone:", t1_ny)

# ------------------------------------------------------------
# 5. Mapping Functions and Invertibility
#
# Define a bijective mapping function f: T → S,
# where T is a datetime object and S is its string representation.
# ------------------------------------------------------------
def datetime_to_string(dt):
    """Convert a datetime object to a formatted string."""
    return dt.strftime(format_str)

def string_to_datetime(s):
    """Parse a formatted string back to a datetime object."""
    return datetime.strptime(s, format_str)

# Demonstrate the mapping and its invertibility:
original_dt = t2
string_repr = datetime_to_string(original_dt)
inverted_dt = string_to_datetime(string_repr)
print("Original T2:", original_dt)
print("String representation of T2:", string_repr)
print("Inverted datetime from string:", inverted_dt)

# ------------------------------------------------------------
# 6. Additional Example: Scheduling with Time Intervals
#
# Calculate a meeting's end time by adding a time interval to a
↪   start time.
# ------------------------------------------------------------
meeting_start = datetime(2023, 10, 1, 9, 0, 0)
meeting_duration = timedelta(minutes=90)   # 90-minute meeting
↪   duration
meeting_end = meeting_start + meeting_duration
print("Meeting Start:", meeting_start)
print("Meeting End (after 90 minutes):", meeting_end)
```

```python
# ----------------------------------------------------------
# 7. Handling Special Cases: Leap Year Adjustments
#
# When adding one year to a date, special care is required for dates
# ↪  like Feb 29.
# This function adds one year; if the resulting date is invalid
# ↪  (e.g., Feb 29 on
# a non-leap year), it adjusts to Feb 28.
# ----------------------------------------------------------
def add_one_year(dt):
    """
    Add one year to the given datetime object.
    If dt is Feb 29 and the following year is not a leap year,
    ↪  adjust to Feb 28.
    """
    try:
        return dt.replace(year=dt.year + 1)
    except ValueError:
        # Adjust for Feb 29 when next year is not a leap year.
        return dt.replace(month=2, day=28, year=dt.year + 1)

# Example with a leap day date
leap_date = datetime(2020, 2, 29)
one_year_later = add_one_year(leap_date)
print("Original Leap Date:", leap_date)
print("One Year Later (adjusted for leap year):", one_year_later)
```

Chapter 40

Slicing Techniques for Data Structures

Conceptual Foundations of Slicing Operations

A slicing operation is defined on an ordered sequence $S = (s_0, s_1, \ldots, s_{n-1})$ and is formally regarded as an extraction function that selects and rearranges a contiguous or noncontiguous subsequence from S. The canonical notation, $S[i : j : k]$, denotes a slicing operation that begins at an index i, terminates before reaching an index j, and advances in increments of k. Formally, this operation yields a new sequence

$$S' = \left(s_i,\ s_{i+k},\ s_{i+2k},\ \ldots,\ s_{i+m \cdot k}\right)$$

where the integer m is the largest nonnegative value such that the index $i + m \cdot k$ satisfies the bounds imposed by j. This formulation implicitly assumes that default values are adopted when the parameters i, j, or k are unspecified, as determined by the inherent boundaries of the sequence.

Slicing Applied to Linear Data Structures

Fundamental data structures such as lists and strings are inherently sequential, and the slicing operator provides a mechanism for their systematic segmentation. When applied to a list or a string,

$S[i:j:k]$ selects elements based on the progression defined by the indices. In the case of a list, with elements of potentially heterogeneous types, the slicing operation maintains the list structure in the resulting subset, preserving the order and the intrinsic properties of the original list. Similarly, for strings, slicing produces substrings that are themselves valid sequences of characters. The semantic consistency of this operator is crucial; for example, if $k > 0$, the iteration continues while $i + m \cdot k < j$, and conversely, for $k < 0$, the iteration is performed while $i + m \cdot k > j$.

Indexing Notation and Boundary Conditions

The indices used in slicing operations often permit negative values, which correspond to offsets measured from the end of the sequence. Given a sequence S of length n, an index i is interpreted such that for $i < 0$, the effective index is $n + i$. The extension of the slicing operator to accommodate arbitrary step values k, including negative increments, introduces a level of generality that requires careful consideration of boundary conditions. The slicing operation may be regarded as a function

$$\sigma : S \times \mathbb{Z} \times \mathbb{Z} \times \mathbb{Z} \to S',$$

subject to the constraints that for sequential consistency i, j, and k are chosen to ensure all produced indices lie within the interval $[0, n)$. This perspective allows one to formalize the extraction of subsequences as the restriction of the identity mapping on S to a properly defined index set.

Advanced Perspectives on Slicing in Arbitrary Sequences

Beyond the elementary applications to lists and strings, slicing techniques extend naturally to a broader class of sequence-like data structures. For any sequence that adheres to a uniform indexing protocol, the operator $S[i:j:k]$ provides a powerful abstraction for data manipulation. Rendering the slicing operation as an algebraic transformation, one may interpret it as applying a projection to the domain of S. This projection, denoted by a characteristic function χ, selects an index p from the set $\{0, 1, \ldots, n-1\}$ if and only if there exists an integer m such that

$$p = i + m \cdot k \quad \text{and} \quad p \in [\min(i,j), \max(i,j)).$$

In this manner, slicing is viewed as a specialized form of function restriction, where the step parameter k enforces a periodic sampling of the original sequence. The mathematical rigor inherent in this formulation ensures that the operation is deterministic, invertible under appropriate conditions, and adaptable to sequences that may not be stored contiguously in memory.

Python Code Snippet

```python
def custom_slice(seq, start=None, stop=None, step=1):
    """
    Custom slicing function that mimics Python's sequence slicing
    ↪  operation:

        S' = ( seq[start], seq[start+step], seq[start+2*step], ... )

    The function computes the sliced subsequence by iteratively
    ↪  adding 'step' to the
    starting index until the boundary condition determined by 'stop'
    ↪  is met.

    Parameters:
        seq (sequence): The input sequence (e.g., list, string).
        start (int, optional): The starting index. If None, defaults
        ↪  to 0 for step > 0,
                               or to len(seq)-1 for step < 0.
        stop (int, optional): The stopping index. If None, defaults
        ↪  to len(seq) for step > 0,
                               or to -1 for step < 0.
        step (int): The step increment (must be nonzero).

    Returns:
        list: A list containing the sliced elements.
    """
    n = len(seq)
    if step == 0:
        raise ValueError("slice step cannot be zero")

    # Set default values based on the direction of slicing
    if start is None:
        start = 0 if step > 0 else n - 1
    if stop is None:
        stop = n if step > 0 else -1
```

```python
    # Adjust negative indices to their positive equivalents
    if start < 0:
        start = n + start
    if stop < 0:
        stop = n + stop

    result = []
    index = start
    if step > 0:
        while index < stop and index < n:
            result.append(seq[index])
            index += step
    else:  # step < 0
        while index > stop and index >= 0:
            result.append(seq[index])
            index += step
    return result

def compute_slice_indices(seq, start=None, stop=None, step=1):
    """
    Compute the list of indices for the slicing operation based on
    ↪   the formula:

        p = start + m * step     where m is the largest nonnegative
        ↪   integer such that
        the index satisfies the condition defined by 'stop'.

    This aligns with the mathematical formulation:

        S' = ( s_{start}, s_{start+step}, s_{start+2*step}, ... )

    Parameters:
        seq (sequence): The input sequence.
        start (int, optional): The starting index.
        stop (int, optional): The stopping index.
        step (int): The step increment.

    Returns:
        list: A list of computed indices that would be selected by
        ↪   the slicing.
    """
    n = len(seq)
    if step == 0:
        raise ValueError("slice step cannot be zero")

    if start is None:
        start = 0 if step > 0 else n - 1
    if stop is None:
        stop = n if step > 0 else -1

    if start < 0:
        start = n + start
    if stop < 0:
```

```
            stop = n + stop

        indices = []
        index = start
        if step > 0:
            while index < stop and index < n:
                indices.append(index)
                index += step
        else:  # step < 0
            while index > stop and index >= 0:
                indices.append(index)
                index += step
        return indices


if __name__ == "__main__":
    # Example with a list
    lst = list(range(10))
    print("Original list:", lst)

    # Slicing using a positive step:
    # For lst[2:9:2], the expected output is [2, 4, 6, 8]
    pos_slice_custom = custom_slice(lst, 2, 9, 2)
    pos_slice_builtin = lst[2:9:2]
    print("custom_slice(lst, 2, 9, 2):", pos_slice_custom)
    print("Built-in slicing lst[2:9:2]:", pos_slice_builtin)
    print("Computed indices for lst[2:9:2]:",
     ↪ compute_slice_indices(lst, 2, 9, 2))

    # Example with a string
    s = "Hello, Python!"
    # Slicing the string from index 7 onwards, expected to return
     ↪ "Python!"
    str_slice_custom = custom_slice(s, 7, None, 1)
    str_slice_builtin = s[7:]
    print("\nOriginal string:", s)
    print("custom_slice(s, 7, None, 1):", "".join(str_slice_custom))
    print("Built-in slicing s[7:]:", str_slice_builtin)

    # Example with negative step:
    # For lst[8:1:-2], the expected output is [8, 6, 4, 2]
    neg_slice_custom = custom_slice(lst, 8, 1, -2)
    neg_slice_builtin = lst[8:1:-2]
    print("\nNegative step slicing for list:")
    print("custom_slice(lst, 8, 1, -2):", neg_slice_custom)
    print("Built-in slicing lst[8:1:-2]:", neg_slice_builtin)
    print("Computed indices for lst[8:1:-2]:",
     ↪ compute_slice_indices(lst, 8, 1, -2))
```

217

Chapter 41

Mutable vs Immutable Objects

Definition and Classification

Objects are categorized based on their capacity for internal state modification. An object is defined as mutable if its state can be altered after creation, thereby allowing modifications to be performed in-place. Conversely, an object is deemed immutable when its state, once established, remains constant throughout its lifetime. In the immutable case, any operation that aims to alter the state does not modify the object itself but rather produces a distinct object encapsulating the new state. This dichotomy is central to understanding object behavior and the resultant ramifications in computational systems.

Memory Model and Object Identity

The allocation of objects in memory exhibits marked differences contingent upon their mutability. Mutable objects are structured so that every modification changes the object at its original memory location. If a mutable object M undergoes an operation f that alters its state, then the memory identity satisfies

$$\mathrm{Id}(M) = \mathrm{Id}(f(M)).$$

In contrast, operations on immutable objects necessarily result in a new object. For an immutable object I, if an operation g is applied such that a modified version is required,

$$\text{Id}(I) \neq \text{Id}(g(I)).$$

This property delineates a clear separation in the handling of in-place updates and the creation of new instances, thereby affecting both memory management and the semantics of variable assignment.

Implications on Program Behavior

The mutable or immutable nature of an object directly influences program behavior. Mutable objects, due to their in-place modification characteristic, can lead to side effects if multiple variables reference the same object. This shared reference phenomenon underscores the necessity for rigorous control of state changes within a system. Immutable objects, by contrast, inherently preclude such side effects; any operation that would change their apparent state results in the generation of a new object. Thus, the use of immutability can simplify reasoning about program behavior, reduce the likelihood of unintentional state interference, and facilitate certain optimizations such as object caching or interning.

Comparative Analysis

A comparative framework can be established by considering a mutable object M and an immutable object I under similar operations. For a mutable object, an operation f leading to an update yields

$$f(M) = M',$$

where M' represents the same object as M with an updated state, and the identity remains unchanged. For an immutable object, an analogous operation g produces a new object,

$$g(I) = I',$$

with the stipulation that
$$I' \neq I.$$

This distinction is not merely academic; it influences strategies for managing aliasing, synchronization in concurrent environments, and the overall design of data structures. The in-place update mechanism of mutable objects can lead to variable aliasing, whereby multiple identifiers refer to a single stateful entity. Immutable objects, on the other hand, eliminate these hazards by ensuring that any state-altering transformation implicitly results in a separate instance.

Formal Perspective on Object Immutability

From a formal standpoint, immutability can be described using a mapping of objects under transformation functions. Let X denote an object and let $f: X \to Y$ represent an operation applied to X. The object X is immutable if, for any operation f, the following condition holds:

$$
f(X) = \begin{cases} X, & \text{if the operation is a no-op,} \\ X', & \text{if the operation results in state change, with } X' \neq X. \end{cases}
$$

This formulation implies that immutable objects strictly prohibit in-place modifications. Instead, any function that conceptually "modifies" an object must return an object that is distinct from the original, reinforcing the notion that immutability is maintained via object replacement rather than state alteration.

Effects on Functional and Imperative Paradigms

The influence of mutability extends deeply into programming paradigms. In the realm of functional programming, immutability is a foundational principle that ensures referential transparency. Since immutable objects cannot be altered after creation, functions operating on them are side-effect free, which simplifies reasoning about program correctness and enables more robust optimization techniques. Conversely, imperative programming paradigms frequently leverage mutable objects to facilitate efficient in-place updates, thereby streamlining state management. However, this approach introduces complexity in tracking state changes and controlling side effects. The contrasting use of mutability in these paradigms underscores the trade-offs between state transparency and operational efficiency in software system design.

Python Code Snippet

```python
# This Python code demonstrates key concepts from the chapter on
↪  "Mutable vs Immutable Objects".
# It shows how operations on mutable objects result in in-place
↪  updates (same memory id)
# while operations on immutable objects create new objects
↪  (different memory id).

def mutable_operation(m):
    """
    Demonstrates in-place modification of a mutable object.
    Equation Representation: id(M) == id(f(M))

    For a mutable object 'm', any operation that changes its state
    ↪  (e.g., appending an element)
    will not alter its memory identity.
    """
    print("Inside mutable_operation:")
    print("Before modification -> Object:", m, "ID:", id(m))
    m.append(99)  # In-place modification
    print("After modification  -> Object:", m, "ID:", id(m))
    return m

def immutable_operation(t):
    """
    Demonstrates transformation of an immutable object.
    Equation Representation: id(I) != id(g(I))

    For an immutable object 't' (such as a tuple), applying an
    ↪  operation (like concatenation)
    will produce a new object with a different memory id.
    """
    print("Inside immutable_operation:")
    print("Before transformation -> Object:", t, "ID:", id(t))
    new_t = t + (99,)  # Returns a new tuple
    print("After transformation  -> Object:", new_t, "ID:",
    ↪  id(new_t))
    return new_t

def formal_update(x, operation="update"):
    """
    Formal update function reflecting the chapter's discussion:
      - If the operation is a no-op, return the same object.
      - For a mutable object, perform an in-place update.
      - For an immutable object, return a completely new object.

    This mirrors the formal perspective:
      f(X) = X for no state change (no-op)
      f(X) = X' for state change with X' != X.
    """
    if operation == "noop":
```

221

```python
            return x
    else:
        if isinstance(x, list):
            # In-place update for mutable objects (list)
            x.append(100)
            return x
        elif isinstance(x, tuple):
            # Immutable update: return a new tuple
            return x + (100,)
        else:
            # For immutable built-in types like int or str, use
            ↪   arithmetic or concatenation.
            return x + 100

# Demonstrating aliasing with mutable objects:
print("=== Mutable Object Aliasing Demonstration ===")
list_a = [10, 20, 30]
list_b = list_a  # Both list_a and list_b reference the same object
print("Before modification:")
print("  list_a:", list_a, "ID:", id(list_a))
print("  list_b:", list_b, "ID:", id(list_b))
list_a[0] = 99  # Modify the list in-place
print("After modification:")
print("  list_a:", list_a, "ID:", id(list_a))
print("  list_b:", list_b, "ID:", id(list_b))
print()


# Testing mutable_operation on a list
print("=== Testing mutable_operation with a list ===")
my_list = [1, 2, 3]
print("Before calling mutable_operation:")
print("  my_list:", my_list, "ID:", id(my_list))
result_mutable = mutable_operation(my_list)
print("After calling mutable_operation:")
print("  Result:", result_mutable, "ID:", id(result_mutable))
print("Verification: id(my_list) == id(result_mutable):",
↪   id(my_list) == id(result_mutable))
print()


# Testing immutable_operation on a tuple
print("=== Testing immutable_operation with a tuple ===")
my_tuple = (1, 2, 3)
print("Before calling immutable_operation:")
print("  my_tuple:", my_tuple, "ID:", id(my_tuple))
result_immutable = immutable_operation(my_tuple)
print("After calling immutable_operation:")
print("  Result:", result_immutable, "ID:", id(result_immutable))
print("Verification: id(my_tuple) != id(result_immutable):",
↪   id(my_tuple) != id(result_immutable))
print()


# Demonstrating the formal_update function on mutable and immutable
↪   objects:
```

222

```python
print("=== Demonstrating formal_update Function ===")
mutable_obj = [4, 5, 6]
immutable_obj = (4, 5, 6)
print("Before formal_update:")
print("  mutable_obj:", mutable_obj, "ID:", id(mutable_obj))
print("  immutable_obj:", immutable_obj, "ID:", id(immutable_obj))
updated_mutable = formal_update(mutable_obj, operation="update")
updated_immutable = formal_update(immutable_obj, operation="update")
print("After formal_update:")
print("  updated_mutable:", updated_mutable, "ID:",
↪  id(updated_mutable))
print("  updated_immutable:", updated_immutable, "ID:",
↪  id(updated_immutable))
print("Verification:")
print("  For mutable object: id remains same?", id(mutable_obj) ==
↪  id(updated_mutable))
print("  For immutable object: id changes?", id(immutable_obj) !=
↪  id(updated_immutable))
print()

# Demonstrating usage of lambda for an immutable update on a tuple:
print("=== Lambda Function Demonstration for Immutable Tuple Update
↪  ===")
immutable_lambda = (7, 8, 9)
print("Before lambda update:")
print("  immutable_lambda:", immutable_lambda, "ID:",
↪  id(immutable_lambda))
# Lambda function creates a new tuple by adding an element.
lambda_update = lambda x: x + (10,)
updated_lambda = lambda_update(immutable_lambda)
print("After lambda update:")
print("  updated_lambda:", updated_lambda, "ID:",
↪  id(updated_lambda))
print("Verification: id(immutable_lambda) != id(updated_lambda):",
↪  id(immutable_lambda) != id(updated_lambda))
```

Chapter 42

Copying Objects: Shallow and Deep Copy

Conceptual Foundations of Object Copying

An object in a programming environment is frequently composed of one or more nested sub-objects, each of which may be mutable or immutable. The process of duplicating such objects can be characterized by two distinct paradigms: shallow copying and deep copying. A shallow copy, denoted here as $S(x)$ for an object x, replicates only the top-level structure of x while retaining references to the same sub-objects. In contrast, a deep copy, denoted as $D(x)$, recursively duplicates every component of x, such that for every nested element $x_i \in x$, the corresponding element in the duplicated object satisfies

$$D(x)_i = D(x_i)$$

with the inherent guarantee that

$$\mathrm{Id}(D(x)_i) \neq \mathrm{Id}(x_i).$$

This fundamental difference serves as the basis for managing object duplication and is critical in preventing unintended side effects deriving from aliasing of mutable sub-structures.

Mechanisms and Memory Considerations

The operational distinction between shallow and deep copying is intimately linked to the underlying memory model and the management of object identities. In the case of a shallow copy, the outer container is duplicated; however, each nested object is not independently replicated. Mathematically, if an object x comprises elements $\{x_1, x_2, \ldots, x_n\}$, then a shallow copy is expressed as

$$S(x) = \{x_1, x_2, \ldots, x_n\},$$

where for any index i, the invariant

$$\mathrm{Id}(S(x)_i) = \mathrm{Id}(x_i)$$

holds. This mechanism, while providing computational efficiency in terms of memory and processing time, allows modifications applied via one reference to inadvertently affect all aliases of the underlying sub-objects.

Conversely, deep copying entails the traversal of the complete object graph associated with x, ensuring that each individual sub-object is independently duplicated. Hence, for a composite object,

$$D(x) = \{D(x_1), D(x_2), \ldots, D(x_n)\},$$

and for all indices i, the condition

$$\mathrm{Id}(D(x)_i) \neq \mathrm{Id}(x_i)$$

is strictly maintained. The recursive nature of deep copying, particularly in the presence of nested or cyclic references, typically necessitates the use of auxiliary mechanisms to track and manage already copied objects. Such approaches ensure that infinite recursion is avoided and that the integrity of the entire duplication process is preserved.

Formal Modeling of Copying Semantics

To provide a formal perspective, let $\mathcal{O}$ denote the set of all objects under consideration and let $C : \mathcal{O} \to \mathcal{O}$ represent an arbitrary copy operation. The shallow copy operator S and the deep copy operator D are defined with the following properties. For any primitive object o that does not admit internal structure, the identities

$$S(o) = o \quad \text{and} \quad D(o) = o$$

225

apply. For any composite object $x \in \mathcal{O}$ with an internal structure expressible as

$$x = \{x_1, x_2, \ldots, x_n\},$$

the shallow copy is defined by

$$S(x) = \{x_1, x_2, \ldots, x_n\},$$

and the deep copy is obtained via the recursive definition

$$D(x) = \{D(x_1), D(x_2), \ldots, D(x_n)\}.$$

This formalism underscores the distinction between non-recursive replication and a comprehensive traversal of the nested object space. The conditions imposed by deep copying ensure that for every element of x, the relation

$$\forall i, \quad \text{Id}(D(x)_i) \neq \text{Id}(x_i)$$

remains valid, thereby eliminating any possibility of aliasing between the original and the copied structure.

Practical Implications for Object Duplication

Within systems that accommodate mutable data structures, the choice between employing a shallow or a deep copy is of paramount importance when managing object duplication. Shallow copy techniques are often favored in scenarios where performance optimization is critical and where the modifications are restricted to the top-level structure of an object. However, when sub-objects are subject to alteration, the preservation of reference identity inherent in shallow copies can propagate changes throughout all aliases of the object. This side effect is captured by the equivalence

$$\exists x_i \in x : \quad \Delta(x_i) \Rightarrow \Delta(S(x)_i)$$

where $\Delta(x_i)$ denotes a state change in the sub-object x_i.

Deep copy, by enforcing a strict separation of the entire object graph, precludes any inadvertent sharing of mutable components. The complete replication provided by deep copying ensures that subsequent modifications to $D(x)$ remain isolated from x, as encapsulated by

$$\forall i, \quad \Delta(D(x)_i)\Delta(x_i).$$

This isolation is particularly beneficial in multi-threaded environments or in any circumstance where the preservation of the original state is critical amid concurrent operations. Notwithstanding, the computational overhead associated with deep copying—both in terms of additional memory allocation and the recursive computational cost—necessitates a judicious evaluation of the trade-offs between efficiency and safety.

Comparative Theoretical Considerations

The dichotomy between shallow and deep copying can be further elucidated by considering the effects of update operations on duplicated objects. Let u be an update function that modifies an object's state. When applied to a shallow copy $S(x)$, the function u may act upon shared references, yielding a scenario where

$$u(S(x)_i) = u(x_i)$$

for one or more indices i, thereby causing modifications that propagate back to the original object x. In contrast, for a deep copy $D(x)$, the same update function satisfies the condition

$$u(D(x)_i) \quad \text{is independent of} \quad u(x_i)$$

for all constituent elements. This theoretical comparison serves to reinforce the principle that deep copying is the more robust mechanism in the context of mutable object graphs, as it guarantees complete structural disassociation between the source and the duplicate. The choice of copying strategy, therefore, becomes a function of the requirements for isolation versus computational expediency, a trade-off that is central to the design of reliable software systems.

Memory Efficiency and Computational Trade-offs

Shallow copying offers a significant advantage in terms of memory efficiency by replicating only the outer container without delving into the nested structure. Formally, if an object x exhibits a depth of d, then the computational cost associated with shallow copying may be approximated by a constant factor, denoted as $O(1)$

for the top-level container, assuming that each reference copy is performed in constant time. Conversely, deep copying necessitates a full traversal of an object graph, incurring a computational cost that grows with the overall complexity of the structure. If the total number of nested elements is represented by N, then the cost of deep copying may be approximated by $O(N)$.

The efficiency trade-off is further complicated by the potential presence of cyclic references. Deep copying in such cases requires the implementation of mechanisms to recognize previously encountered objects, thereby preventing infinite recursion. The use of such mechanisms often implies additional memory overhead and increased algorithmic complexity. This interplay between memory efficiency and computational resource allocation accentuates the need for a rigorous assessment when selecting an appropriate copying strategy in the design and implementation of systems that manage dynamic, mutable objects.

Python Code Snippet

```
import copy

def shallow_copy(obj):
    """
    Create a shallow copy of the object.
    This corresponds to the mathematical representation:
        S(x) = {x_1, x_2, ..., x_n}
    where for every element x_i in x:
        id(S(x)_i) == id(x_i)
    """
    return copy.copy(obj)

def deep_copy(obj):
    """
    Create a deep copy of the object.
    This corresponds to the recursive formulation:
        D(x) = {D(x_1), D(x_2), ..., D(x_n)}
    ensuring for each x_i in x:
        id(D(x)_i) != id(x_i)
    """
    return copy.deepcopy(obj)

def print_structure_and_ids(obj, label):
    """
    Print the structure of the object and the id() values of the
    ↪   object itself
    and its immediate sub-objects (if any).
    """
```

```python
    print(f"{label} (id: {id(obj)}):")
    if isinstance(obj, list):
        for index, item in enumerate(obj):
            print(f"  Element {index} (id: {id(item)}) -> {item}")
    elif isinstance(obj, dict):
        for key, value in obj.items():
            print(f"  Key {key} -> Value (id: {id(value)}) ->
            ↪ {value}")
    else:
        print(f"  Value: {obj}")
    print()

# Demonstration with a composite object: a list of lists
original = [[1, 2, 3], [4, 5, 6]]

print("=== Initial State ===")
print_structure_and_ids(original, "Original Object")

# Create shallow and deep copies
shallow = shallow_copy(original)
deep = deep_copy(original)

print("=== After Copying ===")
print_structure_and_ids(shallow, "Shallow Copy")
print_structure_and_ids(deep, "Deep Copy")

# Modify a nested element in the original object
print("=== After Modifying Original Object ===")
original[0][0] = 'modified'

print("Original Object after modification:")
print_structure_and_ids(original, "Original Object")

print("Shallow Copy after original modification (shares
↪ sub-objects):")
print_structure_and_ids(shallow, "Shallow Copy")

print("Deep Copy after original modification (independent copy):")
print_structure_and_ids(deep, "Deep Copy")

#
↪ -------------------------------------------------------------------------
# Additional simulation of shallow and deep copy using recursive
↪ functions

def S(x):
    """
    Simulate the shallow copy operation.
    For composite objects like lists, the outer container is
    ↪ replicated,
    but the inner elements remain the same objects.
    """

    if isinstance(x, list):
```

229

```python
        return [item for item in x]
    elif isinstance(x, dict):
        return {k: v for k, v in x.items()}
    else:
        return x

def D(x):
    """
    Simulate the deep copy operation recursively.
    For composite objects like lists or dicts, replicate each
    ↪ element recursively
    ensuring that for every element x_i in x, id(D(x)_i) != id(x_i).
    """
    if isinstance(x, list):
        return [D(item) for item in x]
    elif isinstance(x, dict):
        return {k: D(v) for k, v in x.items()}
    else:
        return x

# Using the simulation functions
original_sim = [[1, 2], [3, 4]]
s_copy = S(original_sim)
d_copy = D(original_sim)

print("=== Simulation of Recursive Copying ===")
print("Original (Simulation):")
print_structure_and_ids(original_sim, "Original Simulated Object")
print("Shallow Simulation S(x):")
print_structure_and_ids(s_copy, "S(x)")
print("Deep Simulation D(x):")
print_structure_and_ids(d_copy, "D(x)")

#
↪  --------------------------------------------------------------------------
# Demonstration of cyclic reference handling in deep copy

print("=== Handling Cyclic References ===")
cyclic_list = []
# Create a cycle: the list contains itself
cyclic_list.append(cyclic_list)

try:
    shallow_cyclic = shallow_copy(cyclic_list)
    deep_cyclic = deep_copy(cyclic_list)
    print("Cyclic list shallow copy (outer container duplicated,
    ↪  inner reference unchanged):")
    print(f"  id(cyclic_list): {id(cyclic_list)},
    ↪  id(cyclic_list[0]): {id(cyclic_list[0])}")
    print(f"  id(shallow_cyclic): {id(shallow_cyclic)},
    ↪  id(shallow_cyclic[0]): {id(shallow_cyclic[0])}")
```

```
    print("Cyclic list deep copy (handled via memoization to avoid
    ↪   infinite recursion):")
    print(f"  id(deep_cyclic): {id(deep_cyclic)}")
    # For deep copies, the inner cyclic reference should point to
    ↪   deep_cyclic itself
    print(f"  id(deep_cyclic[0]): {id(deep_cyclic[0])}")
except Exception as e:
    print("Error occurred while copying cyclic references:", e)
```

Chapter 43

Memory Management and Garbage Collection

Memory Allocation in Python's Runtime Environment

Memory allocation in Python is governed by an internal memory manager that abstracts platform-dependent allocation details and provides uniform allocation, management, and reclamation of memory for objects. The runtime segregates memory into segments called arenas, each of which is subdivided into smaller blocks that are allocated to objects. In this model, the operation of allocating memory for a new object relies on the efficient subdivision of these arenas, thereby minimizing the latency associated with repeated system calls. The allocation process can be conceptually modeled by defining an arena A and a set of blocks $\{b_1, b_2, \ldots, b_n\}$ such that each object o allocates a block $b_i \subset A$, where the size and alignment of b_i satisfy the requirements imposed by the underlying hardware. This stratification of memory not only improves the performance of individual allocations but also facilitates the overall management of transient objects in a dynamic execution environment.

Reference Counting Mechanism

At the core of Python's memory management lies a reference counting mechanism that embeds a counter with each object. Denote by ref(o) the reference count of an object o. Upon creation, an object is assigned an initial reference count, typically 1, and this count is incremented or decremented as additional references to the object are made or removed, respectively. An invariant maintained by the system is that when ref(o) = 0, the object becomes eligible for immediate reclamation, and its memory is returned to the pool of available memory. Formally, the deallocation is triggered by the condition

$$\text{ref}(o) = 0 \quad \Longrightarrow \quad \text{deallocate}(o).$$

This mechanism ensures that objects no longer in use are promptly cleaned up; however, its inability to detect and handle cyclic references necessitates supplementary strategies for comprehensive memory reclamation.

Generational Garbage Collection

Complementing the reference counting strategy, Python employs a generational garbage collection subsystem designed to detect and reclaim cyclic garbage. In this approach, objects are organized into multiple generations, typically labeled as G_0, G_1, and G_2, reflecting the age of the objects in terms of the number of collection cycles they have survived. New objects are allocated in the youngest generation, G_0, and are promoted to older generations if they persist beyond predetermined thresholds. The rationale for this design is based on empirical observations that most objects are short-lived; hence, immediate reclamation via reference counting is effective for temporary objects, while periodic scans of older generations, where cyclic references are more prevalent, help to recover memory that would otherwise remain inaccessible. The garbage collection process involves a three-phase traversal of the object graph, verifying the reachability of objects and ensuring that even in the presence of cyclic dependencies, memory is reclaimed. Mathematically, if an object o in generation G_i is determined to be unreachable by the roots of the object graph, then it satisfies the condition

$$\forall r \in \mathcal{R}, \quad o \notin \text{reach}(r),$$

where $\mathcal{R}$ denotes the set of root objects and reach(r) represents the set of objects reachable from r. Such objects are then collected, and their associated memory is safely deallocated.

Interactions Between Allocation and Reclamation

The synergy between immediate deallocation via reference counting and the periodic full-scale reclamation of cyclic garbage engenders a robust memory management model. In scenarios where objects do not participate in reference cycles, the decrement of $ref(o)$ to zero triggers instant deallocation, thus minimizing the memory footprint of transient objects. In contrast, objects involved in cyclic structures may maintain nonzero reference counts despite being unreachable from any active root. The generational garbage collector periodically inspects these structures, using heuristic thresholds based on allocation frequency and object survival rates to balance efficiency and thoroughness. The model operates under the assumption that by segmenting objects into generations and by employing both immediate and deferred reclamation techniques, the overall performance is optimized with respect to both memory utilization and computational overhead. The interplay between these strategies ensures that memory is managed in a self-regulating, coherent manner, where the rapid turnover of short-lived objects is complemented by a systematic removal of intractable cyclic dependencies, thereby maintaining the integrity and responsiveness of the runtime environment.

Python Code Snippet

```
# This code simulates key elements of Python's memory management:
# - Immediate deallocation when reference count reaches 0:
#       if ref(o) == 0 then deallocate(o)
# - A simple generational garbage collection mechanism that collects
#   objects unreachable from the set of root objects.
#
# Note: This is a simulation and does not reflect Python's actual
↪  internal
# memory handling.

class MyObject:
    def __init__(self, name):
        self.name = name
        self.ref_count = 1  # initial reference count: ref(o) = 1
        self.references = []  # list of objects referenced by this
        ↪  object
        self.generation = 0  # Starting generation for GC simulation
```

```python
    def __hash__(self):
        return id(self)

    def __eq__(self, other):
        return id(self) == id(other)

    def add_ref(self):
        # Increase reference count to simulate adding a reference.
        self.ref_count += 1
        print(f"{self.name}: add_ref -> {self.ref_count}")

    def remove_ref(self):
        # Decrease reference count to simulate removing a reference.
        self.ref_count -= 1
        print(f"{self.name}: remove_ref -> {self.ref_count}")
        # Invariant: if ref(o) == 0 then deallocate(o)
        if self.ref_count == 0:
            self.deallocate()

    def add_reference(self, obj):
        # Establish a reference from this object to another.
        self.references.append(obj)
        obj.add_ref()
        print(f"{self.name} now references {obj.name}")

    def deallocate(self):
        # Deallocate this object and release its references.
        print(f"Deallocating {self.name} as ref_count == 0")
        # Remove references held by this object.
        while self.references:
            ref_obj = self.references.pop()
            ref_obj.remove_ref()

class MemoryManager:
    def __init__(self):
        # Maintain three generations to simulate generational GC.
        self.generations = {0: set(), 1: set(), 2: set()}
        self.objects = set()   # All allocated objects.
        self.roots = set()     # Root objects from which reachability
        ↪   is determined.

    def allocate(self, name):
        # Allocate a new object and add it to Generation 0.
        obj = MyObject(name)
        self.objects.add(obj)
        self.generations[0].add(obj)
        print(f"Allocated object {obj.name} in Generation 0")
        return obj

    def add_root(self, obj):
        # Add an external reference (root) to the object.
        self.roots.add(obj)
        obj.add_ref()   # Extra reference for root status.
```

235

```python
            print(f"Added {obj.name} to roots")

    def remove_root(self, obj):
        # Remove an external root reference.
        if obj in self.roots:
            self.roots.remove(obj)
            obj.remove_ref()
            print(f"Removed {obj.name} from roots")

    def promote(self, obj):
        # Promote an object to an older generation if suitable.
        current_gen = obj.generation
        if current_gen < 2:
            self.generations[current_gen].discard(obj)
            obj.generation += 1
            self.generations[obj.generation].add(obj)
            print(f"Promoted {obj.name} to Generation
              ↪  {obj.generation}")

    def _dfs(self, obj, visited):
        # Depth-first search to collect all objects reachable from
          ↪  obj.
        if obj in visited:
            return
        visited.add(obj)
        for ref in obj.references:
            self._dfs(ref, visited)

    def generational_gc(self):
        # Compute the set of all reachable objects from the roots.
        reachable = set()
        for root in self.roots:
            self._dfs(root, reachable)
        # Identify and collect unreachable objects.
        for obj in list(self.objects):
            if obj not in reachable:
                print(f"GC: Collecting unreachable object
                  ↪  {obj.name}")
                # Force deallocation regardless of cyclic
                  ↪  references.
                while obj.ref_count > 0:
                    obj.remove_ref()
                self.objects.remove(obj)
                # Remove the object from its generation.
                for gen in self.generations.values():
                    gen.discard(obj)

def simulation_demo():
    mm = MemoryManager()

    print("\n--- Creating objects and forming a cycle ---")
    # Allocate objects A, B, C
    a = mm.allocate("A")
```

```python
    b = mm.allocate("B")
    c = mm.allocate("C")

    # Form a cyclic reference: A -> B -> C -> A
    a.add_reference(b)
    b.add_reference(c)
    c.add_reference(a)

    # Add external roots to A and B.
    mm.add_root(a)
    mm.add_root(b)

    print("\n--- Removing roots to simulate unreachable cycle ---")
    # Remove roots to simulate loss of external references.
    mm.remove_root(a)
    mm.remove_root(b)

    # At this point, A, B, and C form a cycle and still have nonzero
    ↪   ref_count.
    # Run generational garbage collection to collect cyclic garbage.
    print("\n--- Running Generational Garbage Collection ---")
    mm.generational_gc()

    print("\n--- Simulating object promotion ---")
    # Allocate another object D and promote it to an older
    ↪   generation.
    d = mm.allocate("D")
    mm.add_root(d)
    mm.promote(d)    # Promote D to Generation 1.
    mm.remove_root(d)
    mm.generational_gc()

if __name__ == "__main__":
    simulation_demo()
```

Chapter 44

String Encoding and Decoding

Foundations of String Representation

In formal terms, a string is defined as a finite sequence of abstract characters taken from a specified alphabet, where each character is a member of a set denoted by $\mathcal{C}$. The transformation from these abstract entities to a tangible sequence of bits is achieved via an encoding process. This process involves the association of each character with a unique numerical code, often referred to as a code point, that belongs to a structured set such as the Unicode set $\mathcal{U}$. The encoding function is typically represented as a mapping

$$E : \mathcal{C} \to \{0,1\}^*,$$

where $\{0,1\}^*$ stands for the set of all finite-length binary sequences. This mapping provides the foundation upon which textual data, spanning multiple languages and dialects, is represented in digital systems. The inherent abstraction facilitates discussions regarding the efficiency of storage, the ease of manipulation, and the interplay between display and internal representation.

Character Set Standards and Encoding Schemes

A wide array of character set standards has been developed to accommodate the representation of varied linguistic symbols and technical glyphs. Historically, systems such as the American Standard Code for Information Interchange (ASCII) were sufficient for basic text; however, the emergence of global communication demanded a more inclusive approach. Modern encoding schemes, including but not limited to UTF-8, UTF-16, and UTF-32, have thereby been adopted to satisfy this requirement. These encoding schemes determine the specific manner in which code points are translated into sequences of bits. For instance, in variable-length encoding schemes such as UTF-8, characters are represented using sequences that may vary in length, a property that optimizes storage for texts predominantly based on smaller code points while retaining the capability to represent a vast array of symbols. Conversely, fixed-length encodings allocate an invariant number of bits per character, simplifying certain algorithmic operations at the cost of potential space inefficiency. The formal description of an encoding scheme can be expressed as a function from the character set $\mathcal{C}$ to the collection of possible bit strings, a mapping that is subject both to the constraints imposed by hardware and to the theoretical characteristics of the scheme itself.

Techniques in Encoding: Fixed-Length and Variable-Length Mappings

The methodology underlying the encoding process can be categorized into fixed-length and variable-length mappings. In fixed-length encoding, every character in $\mathcal{C}$ is associated with a bit string of constant length, n, where n is determined by the cardinality of the character set. This mapping, denoted by

$$E_f : \mathcal{C} \to \{0,1\}^n,$$

ensures that the extraction of any individual character is achieved in constant time, thus rendering operations such as random access efficient. In contrast, variable-length encoding, described by the function

$$E_v : \mathcal{C} \to \bigcup_{k=1}^{m} \{0,1\}^k,$$

utilizes bit strings of differing lengths. An essential property of these schemes is the prefix condition, which requires that no encoded character's bit string is the prefix of another, thereby ensuring self-synchronization during decoding. The design of variable-length encodings reflects a trade-off between space conservation and the complexity of bit-stream segmentation, with practical implementations balancing these factors in scenarios where storage and bandwidth constraints are paramount.

Decoding Mechanisms and Error Handling

Decoding constitutes the inverse process of encoding; it recovers the original string from a continuous sequence of bits. The decoding function

$$D : \{0,1\}^* \to \mathcal{C}^*$$

must effectively partition the bit stream into discrete segments according to the rules defined by the encoding scheme. The process is inherently more intricate in the context of variable-length encoding due to the absence of uniformity in segment sizes. Consequently, algorithms are employed to recognize valid bit patterns and to handle borderline cases where the input stream may not conform to the anticipated structure. Error handling during decoding is of paramount importance; when an unrecognized or malformed sequence is encountered, the decoding process resorts to predetermined strategies such as substituting invalid segments with a replacement symbol or flagging the occurrence for further processing. The robustness of the decoding operation is measured by its ability to maintain the invariant

$$D(E(c)) = c \quad \text{for all } c \in \mathcal{C},$$

under ideal conditions, thereby ensuring that the reversible transformation preserves the integrity of the original textual information even in the face of transmission errors and data corruption.

Python Code Snippet

```python
# This Python code snippet demonstrates the key encoding and
↪   decoding mechanisms
# discussed in the chapter "String Encoding and Decoding".
#
# The chapter introduces two types of encoding:
# 1. Fixed-length encoding:
#       E_f:  → {0,1}, where every character in the character set ()
↪   is represented
#       by a binary string of constant length 'n' (e.g., 7 bits for
↪   ASCII characters).
#
# 2. Variable-length encoding:
#       E_v:  →  {0,1}, where the binary representation may vary in
↪   length.
#       These encodings must satisfy the prefix property (i.e., no
↪   valid code is a prefix of another)
#       to ensure correct segmentation during the decoding step.
#
# The decoding functions D_f and D_v are defined so that the
↪   invariant holds:
#       D(E(c)) = c   for all c in
#
# Below, we implement:
#   - fixed_length_encode and fixed_length_decode for fixed-length
↪   encoding.
#   - variable_length_encode and variable_length_decode for
↪   variable-length encoding.
#   - Error handling in the variable-length decoding process,
↪   substituting invalid segments
#     with a replacement symbol '?'.
#
# Note: Although real-world encodings (e.g., UTF-8) are more
↪   complex, this snippet
# serves as an educative demonstration of the underlying principles.

def fixed_length_encode(text, bit_length=7):
    """
    Encodes the given text using fixed-length binary encoding.
    Each character is converted to its ordinal value and then
    ↪   represented in a binary string
    of fixed length, following the mapping:
        E_f:  → {0,1}.
    For example, the character 'A' is transformed into its 7-bit
    ↪   binary form.
    """
    encoded = ""
    for char in text:
        # Convert the character to its binary representation, padded
        ↪   to 'bit_length' bits.
        binary_str = format(ord(char), '0{}b'.format(bit_length))
```

241

```
        encoded += binary_str
    return encoded

def fixed_length_decode(encoded, bit_length=7):
    """
    Decodes a fixed-length encoded binary string back into text.
    The function processes the stream in fixed-size chunks (of
    ↪   length 'bit_length'),
    each representing one character, thus acting as:
        D_f: {0,1}* → *.
    """
    text = ""
    for i in range(0, len(encoded), bit_length):
        binary_str = encoded[i:i+bit_length]
        text += chr(int(binary_str, 2))
    return text


# Example variable-length encoding mapping (Huffman-like scheme)
# This mapping ensures the prefix property: no code in the mapping
↪  is a prefix of another.
# The mapping represents:
#      E_v:  →  {0,1}.
variable_length_mapping = {
    'a': '0',
    'b': '101',
    'c': '100',
    'd': '111',
    'e': '1101',
    'f': '1100'
}


def variable_length_encode(text, mapping):
    """
    Encodes the text using a variable-length encoding scheme.
    Each character in the text is replaced by its corresponding
    ↪   binary code from the provided mapping.
    If a character does not exist in the mapping, an error pattern
    ↪   ('???') is inserted as a placeholder.
    """
    encoded = ""
    for char in text:
        if char in mapping:
            encoded += mapping[char]
        else:
            # Error handling: if the character is unmapped, insert
            ↪   an error sequence.
            encoded += "???"
    return encoded

def variable_length_decode(encoded, mapping):
    """
    Decodes a variable-length encoded binary string back to text.
```

242

```python
    The function uses the prefix condition to correctly segment the
    ↪   bit-stream.
    It also handles errors: if an error sequence ('???') is
    ↪   encountered (or no valid segment is found),
    a replacement character '?' is inserted.

    This function implements:
        D_v: {0,1}* → *
    """
    # Create a reverse mapping for efficient lookup: binary code ->
    ↪   character.
    reverse_mapping = {v: k for k, v in mapping.items()}
    decoded = ""
    i = 0
    while i < len(encoded):
        # Check for the error placeholder.
        if encoded[i:i+3] == "???":
            decoded += "?"
            i += 3
            continue

        match_found = False
        # Try lengths from 1 to an upper bound (here, 5 bits) for a
        ↪   valid code.
        for length in range(1, 6):
            if i + length <= len(encoded):
                segment = encoded[i:i+length]
                if segment in reverse_mapping:
                    decoded += reverse_mapping[segment]
                    i += length
                    match_found = True
                    break
        if not match_found:
            # If no valid segment is found, treat as error and move
            ↪   forward by one bit.
            decoded += "?"
            i += 1
    return decoded

# Demonstration and invariant testing.

# Fixed-length Encoding Demonstration:
original_text_fixed = "Hello"
encoded_fixed = fixed_length_encode(original_text_fixed)
decoded_fixed = fixed_length_decode(encoded_fixed)
print("Fixed-length Encoding:")
print("Original:", original_text_fixed)
print("Encoded :", encoded_fixed)
print("Decoded :", decoded_fixed)
print("Invariant Check (Fixed-length):", original_text_fixed ==
↪   decoded_fixed)

# Variable-length Encoding Demonstration:
```

```python
original_text_variable = "abcdef"
encoded_variable = variable_length_encode(original_text_variable,
↪    variable_length_mapping)
decoded_variable = variable_length_decode(encoded_variable,
↪    variable_length_mapping)
print("\nVariable-length Encoding:")
print("Original:", original_text_variable)
print("Encoded :", encoded_variable)
print("Decoded :", decoded_variable)
print("Invariant Check (Variable-length):", original_text_variable
↪    == decoded_variable)

# Demonstration with error handling in variable-length encoding:
original_text_with_error = "abcx"  # 'x' is not present in our
↪    variable_length_mapping.
encoded_error = variable_length_encode(original_text_with_error,
↪    variable_length_mapping)
decoded_error = variable_length_decode(encoded_error,
↪    variable_length_mapping)
print("\nVariable-length Encoding with Error Handling:")
print("Original:", original_text_with_error)
print("Encoded :", encoded_error)
print("Decoded :", decoded_error)
```

Chapter 45

Docstrings and Code Documentation

Foundations of Docstrings

Docstrings constitute a formalized mechanism for embedding descriptive metadata within source code. They serve to elucidate the purpose, parameters, and expected outcomes of modules, functions, and classes. In many programming languages, notably in Python, a docstring is a string literal that appears as the first statement in a definition and is subsequently associated with the object. This convention allows the creation of a concise yet comprehensive narrative that maps the implementation to its intended semantics. The practice can be formalized by considering a mapping

$$\Psi : \mathcal{C} \to \mathcal{D},$$

where $\mathcal{C}$ represents the set of code constructs and $\mathcal{D}$ the set of corresponding descriptive narratives. Such an abstraction promotes not only clarity but also the systematic generation of external documentation through automated tools. The literature emphasizes that the precision of these narrative elements directly influences the long-term maintainability and understandability of the code base.

In-line Commentary and Annotations

In-line documentation refers to the strategically placed textual annotations interwoven with source code. These annotations provide granular insights into the logic of code blocks, elucidating non-obvious steps, algorithmic decisions, and exceptional case handling. It is common to observe that in a well-documented code base, in-line remarks offer a layer of localized explanation that augments the broader narrative given by docstrings. When one examines a complex algorithm or a nuanced control flow, the immediate presence of in-line documentation alleviates cognitive load by succinctly translating abstract logic into an easily digestible form. In this context, the annotation process can be modeled as the transformation

$$\Phi : \mathcal{I} \to \mathcal{A},$$

where $\mathcal{I}$ represents logical segments of code and $\mathcal{A}$ the annotations that clarify the intent behind each segment. Such a structural approach ensures that the interplay between the code and its annotations remains coherent and directly facilitates both peer review and systematic debugging.

Implications for Code Maintainability

The integration of clear docstrings with meticulous in-line documentation forms a robust framework that underpins code maintainability. Comprehensive documentation functions as an inherent form of self-description within the software, reducing ambiguity and fostering a shared understanding of the design rationale among developers. The consistency and clarity offered by high-quality documentation are particularly significant in large-scale systems, where code evolution and refactoring are routine. When documentation is precise, it enables the identification of potential discrepancies between the intended system behavior and its actual implementation. In formal terms, if E denotes the execution of a code segment and D its associated documentation, then the invariant

$$D(E(c)) \approx c,$$

for a code construct c, reflects the alignment between functionality and its narrative. This alignment streamlines maintenance activities, aids in the onboarding of new contributors, and ultimately contributes to the resilience and longevity of software systems.

Python Code Snippet

```
"""
This Python script illustrates key ideas from the chapter:
  1. The mapping :  →  , which extracts documentation (docstrings)
  ↪   from code constructs.
  2. The mapping :  →  , which associates code segments with inline
  ↪   annotations.
  3. The invariant D(E(c))   c, showing that the documentation (D) of
  ↪   the executed code (E) reflects the original construct (c).

The script includes:
  - A function 'psi' to retrieve the docstring of a given function
  ↪   or class.
  - A function 'phi' to map a code segment (represented as a string)
  ↪   to an inline annotation.
  - An 'invariant_check' function to verify that the output of a
  ↪   function matches an expected behavior.
  - A sample algorithm (factorial function) with comprehensive
  ↪   docstrings and inline commentary.
"""


def psi(code_construct):
    """
    Mimics the mapping :  →  by retrieving the docstring associated
    ↪   with a code construct.

    Parameters:
        code_construct (object): A function, class, or any object
        ↪   that supports a __doc__ attribute.

    Returns:
        str: The docstring of the provided object, or 'No docstring
        ↪   available' if none exists.
    """
    return code_construct.__doc__ or "No docstring available"


def phi(code_segment, annotation):
    """
    Simulates the mapping :  →  by linking a code segment to an
    ↪   inline annotation.

    Parameters:
        code_segment (str): A textual representation of a code
        ↪   segment.
        annotation (str): A description or comment explaining the
        ↪   purpose or logic of the code segment.

    Returns:
        dict: A dictionary mapping the provided code segment to its
        ↪   annotation.
    """
```

```python
    return {code_segment: annotation}

def invariant_check(func, expected_behavior, input_val):
    """
    Checks the invariant D(E(c))   c, where:
      - D is the documentation extraction via psi,
      - E is the execution of the function,
      - c is the code construct (function).

    Parameters:
        func (function): The function to be tested.
        expected_behavior (any): The (expected) return value when
        ↪  func is executed with input_val.
        input_val (any): The input value for the function call.

    Returns:
        bool: True if the function's output equals the expected
        ↪  behavior; False otherwise.
    """
    # Execute the function with the given input.
    output = func(input_val)
    # The approximation check here is a strict equality test.
    return output == expected_behavior

def factorial(n):
    """
    Computes the factorial of a non-negative integer n.

    The factorial is defined as:
        n! = n * (n-1) * ... * 2 * 1, with 0! defined as 1.

    Parameters:
        n (int): A non-negative integer whose factorial is to be
        ↪  computed.

    Returns:
        int: The factorial of n.

    Example:
        factorial(5) returns 120.
    """
    # Base case: if n is 0 or 1, return 1.
    if n <= 1:
        return 1
    # Recursive case: multiply n by the factorial of (n - 1).
    return n * factorial(n - 1)

if __name__ == "__main__":
    # Demonstrate the  mapping: retrieving docstring from the
    ↪  'factorial' function.
    doc_for_factorial = psi(factorial)
    print("Docstring for 'factorial':")
    print(doc_for_factorial)
```

248

```python
# Demonstrate the  mapping: linking a code segment with an
↪   annotation.
sample_code = "if n <= 1: return 1"
comment = "Checks the base condition for the factorial
↪   function."
annotation_mapping = phi(sample_code, comment)
print("\nInline Annotation Mapping:")
print(annotation_mapping)

# Use invariant_check to verify that the factorial function
↪   works as expected.
test_input = 5
expected_output = 120
if invariant_check(factorial, expected_output, test_input):
    print("\nInvariant check passed: factorial({}) ==
    ↪   {}".format(test_input, expected_output))
else:
    print("\nInvariant check failed: factorial({}) !=
    ↪   {}".format(test_input, expected_output))

# Additional verification: output the function's docstring and
↪   execution result to reflect D(E(c))  c.
print("\nVerifying Documentation-Execution Invariant:")
print("Function Documentation:\n", psi(factorial))
print("Execution Result:\n factorial({}) =
↪   {}".format(test_input, factorial(test_input)))
```

Chapter 46

Code Organization and Modularity

Function Decomposition and Semantic Integrity

The partitioning of computational tasks into discrete functions is a core principle of structured programming. Each function may be regarded as a self-contained unit, analogous to a mathematical mapping $f\colon X \to Y$, where the domain X comprises valid input parameters and the codomain Y represents the corresponding output. Such decomposition fosters enhanced readability by isolating logical fragments of the code, thereby allowing individual elements to be understood, maintained, and tested in isolation. The practice of encapsulating a single responsibility within a function promotes semantic integrity and mitigates the risks of side effects that occur in more entangled code bases. High cohesion within functions and low coupling between them are essential attributes that facilitate both code reuse and error localization. The design of functions involves careful consideration of input validation, preconditions, and postconditions, all of which contribute to a well-defined and robust interface.

Module Abstractions and the Hierarchy of Implementation

The abstraction provided by modules introduces an intermediate organizational layer that groups related functions, data structures, and class definitions. A module serves as a container that encapsulates a coherent subset of functionality, enabling a logical partitioning of the code base that aligns with conceptual boundaries present in the underlying problem domain. This hierarchical arrangement allows for a reduction in cognitive complexity, as each module can be understood as a mini-application with clearly delineated responsibilities. The internal structure of a module should be organized in such a manner as to ensure that dependencies are minimized and that the public interface is kept as succinct as possible. By adhering to principled naming conventions and modular design, the aggregation of related functionality within a module facilitates both collaborative development and the incremental evolution of the software.

Package Design and Structural Scalability

At a higher level of abstraction, the organization of modules into packages forms the backbone of scalable code architecture. A package is a structured collection of modules, arranged to reflect the architecture of the application or library. This layered organization not only enhances the maintainability of complex systems but also serves to promote extensive reuse across different projects. The relational structure can be formalized by considering a set $\mathcal{M}$ of modules such that each module $m \in \mathcal{M}$ contributes a distinct aspect of functionality, with the interconnection of these modules governed by well-defined interfaces. When organized into packages, the resulting hierarchy ensures that changes localized to a particular package do not inadvertently propagate to unrelated areas of the system. Furthermore, deliberate compartmentalization into packages facilitates the application of modular testing strategies and supports the seamless integration of version control practices. The deliberate design choices made at the package level are instrumental in achieving a balance between granularity and abstraction, ultimately promoting both clarity and systematic code reuse in large-scale software projects.

Python Code Snippet

```
#!/usr/bin/env python
"""
A comprehensive Python script demonstrating:
1. Function Decomposition and Semantic Integrity:
   - Input validation via preconditions.
   - A mathematical mapping f: X -> Y using a quadratic function.
2. Module Abstractions and Hierarchical Implementation:
   - Encapsulation of related functionalities within a class.
   - Use of decorators to log function execution.
3. Package Design and Structural Scalability:
   - Simulated modular testing and integration using a main
   ↪   function.
"""

import math
import logging
from functools import wraps

# Configure logging to display debug statements.
logging.basicConfig(level=logging.DEBUG, format='%(levelname)s:
↪   %(message)s')

def validate_input(x):
    """
    Validates that the input x is a numeric value (int or float) and
    ↪   non-negative.

    Preconditions:
        - x must be of type int or float.
        - x must be greater than or equal to 0.

    Postconditions:
        - Returns True if the input is valid.
        - Raises ValueError if the input is invalid.
    """
    if not isinstance(x, (int, float)):
        raise ValueError("Input must be a numeric type (int or
        ↪   float).")
    if x < 0:
        raise ValueError("Input must be non-negative.")
    return True

def log_function(func):
    """
    Decorator to log the entry, exit, and result of a function call.
```

It provides insight into the function's input parameters and its
↪ output,
aiding in debugging and maintaining semantic clarity.
"""

```python
@wraps(func)
def wrapper(*args, **kwargs):
    logging.debug("Calling function '%s' with args=%s
    ↪ kwargs=%s", func.__name__, args, kwargs)
    result = func(*args, **kwargs)
    logging.debug("Function '%s' returned %s", func.__name__,
    ↪ result)
    return result
return wrapper


@log_function
def compute_quadratic(x):
    """
    Computes the quadratic mapping f(x) = x^2 + 2x + 1.

    This function demonstrates a mathematical function mapping f: X
    ↪ -> Y.

    Preconditions:
        - The input x is validated as a non-negative number.

    Postconditions:
        - Returns the result of the quadratic equation.
    """
    validate_input(x)
    result = x**2 + 2 * x + 1
    return result


class FunctionLibrary:
    """
    A collection of static methods that encapsulate mathematical and
    utility functions to demonstrate module abstraction and
    ↪ hierarchical organization.
    """

    @staticmethod
    @log_function
    def compute_mapping(x, func):
        """
        Applies a provided mathematical mapping (function) to input
        ↪ x.

        This method represents the abstraction f: X -> Y by
        ↪ delegating the computation to func.

        Preconditions:
            - x is validated by the called function (if applicable).
            - func must be a callable.
```

```
    Postconditions:
        - Returns the output of func(x).
    """
    if not callable(func):
        raise ValueError("The provided mapper must be
        ↪   callable.")
    return func(x)

@staticmethod
@log_function
def compute_square_root(x):
    """
    Computes the square root of x using Python's math module.

    Preconditions:
        - Input x must be a non-negative number (validated by
        ↪   validate_input).

    Postconditions:
        - Returns the square root value of x.
    """
    validate_input(x)
    return math.sqrt(x)

def main():
    """
    Main entry point of the script.

    It demonstrates:
    - The application of the quadratic mapping function.
    - A subsequent transformation (square root computation) on the
    ↪   function output.
    - Error handling when invalid input is provided.
    """
    # Sample input values
    x_values = [0, 1, 2, 3, 4]
    quadratic_results = []
    sqrt_results = []

    # Process each input value using the defined functional
    ↪   mappings.
    for x in x_values:
        # Compute the quadratic mapping f(x) = x^2 + 2x + 1
        quad_val = FunctionLibrary.compute_mapping(x,
        ↪   compute_quadratic)
        quadratic_results.append(quad_val)

        # Compute the square root of the result from the quadratic
        ↪   function
        sqrt_val = FunctionLibrary.compute_square_root(quad_val)
        sqrt_results.append(sqrt_val)

    # Log the computed results for inspection
```

```python
    logging.info("Input Values          : %s", x_values)
    logging.info("Quadratic Function Results: %s",
    ↪  quadratic_results)
    logging.info("Square Root of Quadratic Results: %s",
    ↪  sqrt_results)

    # Demonstrate error handling with invalid input
    try:
        FunctionLibrary.compute_mapping(-1, compute_quadratic)
    except ValueError as error:
        logging.error("Error encountered: %s", error)

if __name__ == '__main__':
    main()
```

Chapter 47

Using Assertions for Basic Testing

Foundations of Assertion-Based Testing

Assertions function as integral logical checkpoints within a program, encapsulating the expectation that specific conditions should always hold true during execution. An assertion typically comprises a Boolean expression that, under normal operation, evaluates to *True*. In scenarios where the condition evaluates to *False*, the assertion mechanism triggers an immediate exception, thereby preventing further execution under erroneous states. This method of embedding logical safeguards directly into the code serves as a rudimentary form of proof, ensuring that assumed invariants and preconditions remain valid throughout the computational process. Within the realm of software verification, these built-in validity checks provide an automated mechanism for detecting deviations from the intended design, contributing to a clearer understanding of the program's internal consistency.

Operational Semantics of Assert Statements

The implementation of assertions involves the evaluation of logical predicates that represent assumptions about program state at designated checkpoints. The operational semantics dictate that when an assertion evaluates to a non-affirmative Boolean value, a runtime exception is generated, thereby flagging the anomaly immediately. This behavior not only interrupts the normal flow of execution but also aids in the precise localization of defects by providing contextual information at the moment of failure. In many programming environments, assertion evaluation can be disabled during production runs to optimize performance, while remaining essential during the development and testing phases. Such conditional evaluation is governed by the underlying semantics of the execution environment and is central to the philosophy that assertions should capture only those conditions deemed logically indispensable.

Assertions as a Lightweight Testing Mechanism

Assertions offer a succinct method for verifying that code adheres to expected behavior without the overhead of a dedicated testing framework. By embedding testable conditions within the functional logic, assertions serve as both documentation of the intended behavior and as real-time checks that validate the correctness of intermediate computations. This approach aligns with the principle of design by contract, where preconditions, postconditions, and invariants articulate the mutual obligations between various software components. The effectiveness of assertions in this capacity lies in their ability to integrate verification directly within the execution path, thereby facilitating prompt detection of inconsistencies or violations of the established contract. Their utility is particularly pronounced in complex systems where the interdependency of components necessitates robust, yet lightweight, internal testing strategies.

Considerations and Limitations

While assertions constitute a powerful tool for basic testing, their application must be circumscribed within appropriate contexts. The deliberate use of assertions is best suited for capturing conditions that are fundamentally assumed to be invariant, rather than for routine error handling or input validation in environments where external error management is preferable. Moreover, the potential deactivation of assertions in performance-critical deployments underscores the importance of not relying solely on them for comprehensive error detection. It is crucial to distinguish between conditions that warrant an immediate assertion failure and those that are better managed by separate error-handling mechanisms. The judicious application of assertion-based testing, therefore, depends on an in-depth analysis of the program's logical structure and an understanding of the operational semantics that govern the execution environment.

Python Code Snippet

```python
import math

def quadratic_roots(a, b, c):
    """
    Compute the real roots of the quadratic equation: a*x^2 + b*x +
    ↪  c = 0.

    Preconditions:
      - Coefficient 'a' must not be zero.
      - The discriminant (b*b - 4*a*c) must be non-negative to yield
    ↪    real roots.

    Postconditions:
      - Each computed root should satisfy the quadratic equation
    ↪    within a small tolerance.

    Parameters:
      a (float): Coefficient of x^2 (must be non-zero).
      b (float): Coefficient of x.
      c (float): Constant term.

    Returns:
      tuple: A tuple containing the two real roots (root1, root2).
    """
    # Verify precondition: 'a' must not be zero.
    assert a != 0, "Coefficient 'a' must not be zero for a quadratic
    ↪    equation."

    # Compute discriminant and check for non-negative value.
    discriminant = b * b - 4 * a * c
    assert discriminant >= 0, "Negative discriminant encountered.
    ↪    Complex roots are not handled."

    # Calculate roots using the quadratic formula.
    sqrt_disc = math.sqrt(discriminant)
    root1 = (-b + sqrt_disc) / (2 * a)
    root2 = (-b - sqrt_disc) / (2 * a)
```

```
        # Verify postconditions: The roots should nearly satisfy the
        ↪ original equation.
        tolerance = 1e-6
        assert abs(a * root1**2 + b * root1 + c) < tolerance, "Root1
        ↪ does not satisfy the equation within tolerance."
        assert abs(a * root2**2 + b * root2 + c) < tolerance, "Root2
        ↪ does not satisfy the equation within tolerance."

        return root1, root2

def factorial(n):
    """
    Compute the factorial of a non-negative integer n using
    ↪ recursion.

    Preconditions:
        - n must be an integer greater than or equal to 0.

    Postconditions:
        - The result is an integer representing n! (the product of all
        ↪ positive integers up to n).

    Parameters:
        n (int): A non-negative integer.

    Returns:
        int: The factorial of n.
    """
    # Precondition: Input must be a non-negative integer.
    assert isinstance(n, int) and n >= 0, "n must be a non-negative
    ↪ integer."

    if n == 0:
        return 1

    result = n * factorial(n - 1)

    # Simple postcondition: For n > 0, result should be at least n.
    if n > 0:
        assert result >= n, "Computed factorial appears incorrect."
    return result

def fibonacci(n):
    """
    Compute the nth Fibonacci number using an iterative approach.

    Preconditions:
        - n must be a non-negative integer.

    Loop Invariant:
        - At each iteration, 'a' holds Fibonacci(k) and 'b' holds
        ↪ Fibonacci(k+1),
        where k starts from 0.
```

259

```python
Parameters:
    n (int): The index in the Fibonacci sequence (starting from
    ↪  0).

Returns:
    int: The nth Fibonacci number.
"""
# Precondition: n should be a non-negative integer.
assert isinstance(n, int) and n >= 0, "n must be a non-negative
↪  integer."

if n == 0:
    return 0
elif n == 1:
    return 1

a, b = 0, 1
# Iteratively compute Fibonacci numbers up to index n.
for k in range(2, n + 1):
    a, b = b, a + b
    # Loop Invariant check: b should be greater than or equal to
    ↪  a.
    assert b >= a, "Loop invariant error: Next Fibonacci term is
    ↪  not greater or equal to the previous term."
# Postcondition: b is the nth Fibonacci number.
return b


if __name__ == "__main__":
    # Demonstration of quadratic_roots with a valid quadratic
    ↪  equation: x^2 - 3x + 2 = 0
    a, b, c = 1, -3, 2
    roots = quadratic_roots(a, b, c)
    print("Quadratic Equation: {}x^2 + {}x + {} = 0".format(a, b,
    ↪  c))
    print("Computed roots:", roots)

    # Demonstration of factorial computation.
    test_values = [0, 1, 5, 10]
    for val in test_values:
        fact = factorial(val)
        print("Factorial of {} is {}".format(val, fact))

    # Demonstration of Fibonacci sequence computation.
    fib_index = 10
    fib_number = fibonacci(fib_index)
    print("Fibonacci number at index {} is {}".format(fib_index,
    ↪  fib_number))

    # Uncomment the following lines one at a time to see assertion
    ↪  failures:
    # 1. This will trigger an assertion since 'a' is zero.
    # quadratic_roots(0, 2, 1)
```

260

```
# 2. This will trigger an assertion due to negative input in
↪   factorial.
# factorial(-5)

# 3. This will trigger an assertion in fibonacci due to the
↪   wrong type.
# fibonacci(3.5)
```

Chapter 48

The itertools Module: Efficient Iteration Tools

Foundations of Iterator-Based Paradigms

Iteration, as an abstract computational paradigm, is formulated upon the principles of lazy evaluation and sequential data consumption. Python's iterator protocol defines a uniform interface that facilitates on-demand generation of elements without necessitating the retention of an entire collection in memory. The itertools module encapsulates a suite of such iterator-based tools, ensuring that looping constructs are assembled with both efficiency and elegance. In this context, an iterator is conceptualized as an entity that yields successive values via an internal state transition, ultimately mirroring the mathematical framework of sequences where each term is generated by a deterministic algorithm.

Infinite Iterators and Controlled Termination

A significant component of the module is the provision of infinite iterators, which are designed to produce unbounded series of elements. These iterators generate values according to predefined recurrent relations or arithmetic progressions, thereby offering a stream of data that can, in theory, extend indefinitely. The practical utilization of such iterators necessitates the imposition of bounds through external mechanisms, such as slicing or predicate-based termination. This controlled consumption aligns with the formal definition of an infinite sequence, where the nth term is defined according to a specific recurrence relation, yet only a finite subset is realized during execution.

Finite Iterators and Compositional Constructs

Complementary to infinite iterators are those constructs that inherently impose finite bounds on the sequence of values produced. These iterators are characterized by their ability to dynamically halt iteration upon satisfying a particular condition, a feature grounded in the logic of predicate evaluation. The design of such constructs emphasizes computational efficiency by ensuring that only the requisite data elements are generated and processed. Moreover, the compositional nature of these iterators permits the assembly of complex iteration pipelines through the chaining of multiple finite sequences, thereby enabling a modular approach to data processing that conforms to principles of both memory efficiency and clarity in execution flow.

Combinatorial Iterators and Structural Variability

Within the itertools module lies a set of tools dedicated to the systematic generation of combinatorial constructs. These iterators facilitate the exploration of multidimensional arrangement spaces by generating Cartesian products, permutations, and combinations from one or more input sequences. The underlying mathematics is rooted in combinatorial theory, where the enumeration of possible arrangements is closely related to factorial and binomial computations. By leveraging these iterators, complex combinatorial problems can be addressed without resorting to the explicit creation of large intermediate data structures. Instead, each potential combination or permutation is generated on demand, thereby achieving an optimal balance between computational load and memory utilization.

Utilities for Iterator Manipulation and Data Structuring

The module further extends its functionality with utilities designed for the manipulation and structural transformation of iterators. Functions that concatenate disparate iterators allow for the creation of a singular, continuous stream from multiple sources. Additionally, grouping utilities enable the aggregative organization of data based on intrinsic properties, thereby affording a high degree of flexibility in iterative data processing. These tools exploit advanced principles of functional composition and set theory, ensuring that complex iterative constructs can be restructured or segmented with minimal overhead. Such utilities underscore the module's commitment to delivering performance-enhanced solutions while adhering to strict principles of modular design and abstraction.

Python Code Snippet

```python
import itertools

def main():
    # 1. Foundations of Iterator-Based Paradigms
    # Using an infinite iterator to generate an arithmetic
    ↪    progression (even numbers).
    print("Infinite iterator example (first 10 even numbers):")
    even_numbers = itertools.count(start=0, step=2)  # Infinite
    ↪    sequence: 0, 2, 4, ...
    first_ten = list(itertools.islice(even_numbers, 10))
    print(first_ten)

    # 2. Infinite Iterators and Controlled Termination
    # Cycle through a finite sequence indefinitely and slice the
    ↪    first 10 values.
    print("\nCycle iterator example (cycling through 'A', 'B',
    ↪    'C'):")
    cyclic = itertools.cycle(['A', 'B', 'C'])
    cyclic_values = list(itertools.islice(cyclic, 10))
    print(cyclic_values)

    # 3. Finite Iterators and Compositional Constructs
    # Repeat a string a fixed number of times, then chain with
    ↪    another iterator.
    print("\nRepeat and chain iterators example:")
    repeated = itertools.repeat("hello", 5)
    extra = ["world", "python", "code"]
    chained = itertools.chain(repeated, extra)
```

```python
print(list(chained))

# 4. Combinatorial Iterators and Structural Variability
data = [1, 2, 3]
print("\nCombinatorial iterators examples:")
# Cartesian product (all ordered pairs with repetition from
↪ data)
cartesian = list(itertools.product(data, repeat=2))
print("Cartesian product (repeat=2):", cartesian)
# All possible permutations of the list
perms = list(itertools.permutations(data))
print("Permutations:", perms)
# All combinations of 2 elements from the list
combs = list(itertools.combinations(data, 2))
print("Combinations (r=2):", combs)

# 5. Utilities for Iterator Manipulation and Data Structuring
# Group elements based on their remainder modulo 3
print("\nGroupby example (grouping numbers by modulo 3):")
numbers = [0, 1, 2, 3, 4, 5, 6, 7, 8, 9]
# It is important to sort with the same key used for grouping.
numbers_sorted = sorted(numbers, key=lambda x: x % 3)
for key, group in itertools.groupby(numbers_sorted, key=lambda
↪ x: x % 3):
    print(f"Remainder {key}: {list(group)}")

# Additional: Fibonacci sequence generator
print("\nFibonacci generator using yield and islice:")
def fibonacci():
    a, b = 0, 1
    while True:
        yield a
        a, b = b, a + b
fib_gen = fibonacci()
first_10_fib = list(itertools.islice(fib_gen, 10))
print("First 10 Fibonacci numbers:", first_10_fib)

# Additional: Using a recurrence relation to generate a custom
↪ sequence.
# Recurrence relation: a_n = 2 * a_(n-1) + 1 with a starting
↪ value.
print("\nRecurrence relation sequence (a_n = 2 * a_(n-1) + 1):")
def recurrence_relation(a0, n):
    a = a0
    for _ in range(n):
        yield a
        a = 2 * a + 1
sequence = list(recurrence_relation(1, 10))
print("Generated sequence:", sequence)

# Custom iterator demonstration using a class with __iter__ and
↪ __next__.
```

```python
    print("\nCustom iterator class example (iterating from 5 to
↪    12):")
    class CustomIterator:
        def __init__(self, start, limit):
            self.current = start
            self.limit = limit
        def __iter__(self):
            return self
        def __next__(self):
            if self.current > self.limit:
                raise StopIteration
            value = self.current
            self.current += 1
            return value
    custom_iter = CustomIterator(5, 12)
    print("Custom iterator values:", list(custom_iter))

if __name__ == "__main__":
    main()
```

Chapter 49

Functional Programming Tools: map, filter, reduce

Foundations of Functional Abstractions

The functional paradigm in computer science is characterized by an emphasis on the use of higher-order functions and immutable data structures. Central to this paradigm is the notion that computation may be expressed as the evaluation of mathematical functions, often devoid of side effects. This perspective enables the construction of programs in which functions are first-class citizens, meaning they can be passed as arguments to other functions, returned as values from other functions, and composed to form more complex operations. Consequently, the design of functional programming tools is deeply informed by theoretical constructs derived from lambda calculus and category theory. In this framework, the operations `map`, `filter`, and `reduce` provide succinct mechanisms to express data transformations and aggregations, thereby promoting a declarative style of programming that emphasizes the "what" rather than the "how" in data manipulation. Formally, these operations enable expressions of computation that are mathematically rigorous and facilitate reasoning about program correctness and optimization.

The map Operation: Element-wise Transformation

The map function embodies the principle of element-wise transformation. Given a set of elements $D = \{d_1, d_2, \ldots, d_n\}$ and a unary function $f : D \to E$, the operation produces a new sequence by applying f to each element, yielding the sequence $\langle f(d_1), f(d_2), \ldots, f(d_n) \rangle$. This operation can be perceived as a morphism that preserves the structure of the data set while effecting the desired conversion of each element within an immutable context. The formal property of homomorphism here is emphasized by the preservation of order and the independence of each transformation step. By abstracting the process of iterative transformation into a single declarative expression, the use of map minimizes the cognitive load associated with managing explicit loops and mutable state, thereby aligning computational logic with mathematical clarity.

The filter Operation: Predicate-Driven Selection

The filter function serves as a mechanism for selectively extracting elements from a collection based on a Boolean predicate. For a given predicate $p : D \to \{\text{True}, \text{False}\}$ and a domain D, the filter operation yields a subsequence

$$\{d \in D \mid p(d) = \text{True}\},$$

thereby partitioning the original set into elements that satisfy the predicate and those that do not. The operation is inherently non-destructive; it preserves the order of elements that meet the specified criterion while eliminating those that do not. This selective process is pivotal in scenarios requiring the isolation of relevant data from noise or extraneous information. The theoretical underpinning of filter is captured by its alignment with set comprehension in mathematics, where a domain is refined by a Boolean condition, ensuring that the resulting subset adheres to clearly defined properties.

The reduce Operation: Aggregative Folding of Data

In contrast to the element-wise transformation effected by `map` and the selective extraction accomplished by `filter`, the `reduce` operation integrates the sequence of elements into a single accumulated value. Formally, given an associative binary function $g : E \times D \to E$ and an initial accumulator value $a_0 \in E$, `reduce` transforms a sequence $\{d_1, d_2, \ldots, d_n\}$ into a singular result through a recursive process defined by

$$a_n = g(g(\ldots g(a_0, d_1), d_2) \ldots, d_n).$$

The requirement of associativity for the function g is critical, as it ensures that the order of application does not affect the final outcome, thereby enabling parallelization and optimization of the folding process. This operation is instrumental when collapsing a data set into an aggregate measure—such as a sum, product, or other cumulative statistics—while retaining the inherent structure of the transformation through a well-defined folding mechanism.

Compositional Dynamics and Interoperation

The interplay among `map`, `filter`, and `reduce` epitomizes the essence of compositional programming in a functional context. Each of these tools addresses a distinct facet of data manipulation: transformation, selection, and aggregation, respectively. When combined, they enable the construction of powerful pipelines that process data in a concise and declarative manner. Mathematically, the composition can be conceptualized as a compound function

$$h = \mathtt{reduce} \circ \mathtt{filter} \circ \mathtt{map},$$

where the successive application of these operations results in a transformation from an initial data set to a final aggregated value. This sequential application not only simplifies the representation of complex processing tasks but also facilitates formal reasoning about the correctness and efficiency of the computation. The careful orchestration of these operations illustrates the synergy that arises from embracing immutability and higher-order functions, thereby

269

reinforcing the theoretical foundations that support modern functional programming practices.

Python Code Snippet

```python
# Import the reduce function from the functools module
from functools import reduce

# Define a unary function for the map operation.
# This function represents f: D -> E, where for each input d in D,
# it returns f(d) = d^2.
def square(x):
    return x ** 2

# Define a predicate function for the filter operation.
# This function represents p: D -> {True, False}.
# Here, it checks if a number is even.
def is_even(x):
    return x % 2 == 0

# Define a binary function for the reduce operation.
# This function represents g: E x D -> E, used to aggregate values.
# In this example, it sums two numbers.
def add(x, y):
    return x + y

# Original data set, D = {1, 2, 3, 4, 5, 6}
data = [1, 2, 3, 4, 5, 6]

#
↪   ----------------------------------------------------------------------
# Map Operation: Apply the square function to each element in data.
# Mathematically:
#    mapped_data = <f(d1), f(d2), ..., f(dn)>
mapped_data = list(map(square, data))
print("Mapped Data (Square each element):", mapped_data)
# Expected output: [1, 4, 9, 16, 25, 36]

#
↪   ----------------------------------------------------------------------
# Filter Operation: Select only the even elements from mapped_data.
# Mathematically:
#    filtered_data = { d in mapped_data | is_even(d) == True }
filtered_data = list(filter(is_even, mapped_data))
print("Filtered Data (Keep only even numbers):", filtered_data)
# Expected output: [4, 16, 36]

#
↪   ----------------------------------------------------------------------
```

```python
# Reduce Operation: Aggregate the filtered data using the add
↪   function.
# Mathematically, for an initial value a0:
#    a_n = g(g(...g(a0, d1), d2), ..., d_n)
# Here, a0 is chosen as 0.
reduced_value = reduce(add, filtered_data, 0)
print("Reduced Value (Sum of filtered numbers):", reduced_value)
# Expected output: 56


#
↪   ----------------------------------------------------------------------
# Composite Pipeline: Combine map, filter, and reduce operations.
# This corresponds to the composition:
#    h = reduce  filter  map
composite_result = reduce(add, list(filter(is_even, map(square,
↪   data))), 0)
print("Composite Pipeline Result:", composite_result)
# Expected output: 56


#
↪   ----------------------------------------------------------------------
# Additional demonstration using lambda functions to inline the
↪   operations.
result_lambda = reduce(lambda acc, x: acc + x,
                       list(filter(lambda x: x % 2 == 0,
                                   map(lambda x: x**2, data))),
                       0)
print("Composite Pipeline with Lambda:", result_lambda)
# Expected output: 56


#
↪   ----------------------------------------------------------------------
# Summary of operations:
# 1. Mapping: Transform each element d in data using f(x)=x^2,
#    resulting in: [d^2 for d in data].
# 2. Filtering: Select elements from the mapped data that satisfy
↪   is_even,
#    resulting in: [d for d in mapped_data if d % 2 == 0].
# 3. Reducing: Aggregate the filtered data using addition to obtain
↪   a single value,
#    computed as: reduce(add, filtered_data, 0).
# This code snippet demonstrates the functional programming tools in
↪   Python
# that embody the mathematical expressions and algorithms discussed
↪   in the chapter.
```

Chapter 50

The functools Module: Partial and Caching

Partial Function Application

Partial function application is a mechanism that transforms a function of several arguments into a function with fewer arguments by fixing a subset of its parameters. Consider a function

$$f : A \times B \to C.$$

By designating a particular value $a_0 \in A$ as fixed, one derives a new function

$$g : B \to C$$

defined by

$$g(b) = f(a_0, b)$$

for every $b \in B$. This operation, while reminiscent of currying, preserves a more general arity and provides a controlled means to bind specific arguments. The formal abstraction achieved through partial application enables intricate function composition, as the act of pre-binding parameters simplifies subsequent function calls and enhances modularity within complex functional constructs.

Within the framework of mathematical function theory, partial application corresponds to the restriction of the domain of a multivariate function. The implementation of such an abstraction not only reduces redundancy by obviating the need to repeatedly specify invariant arguments, but also reinforces the principle of

272

referential transparency. This invariance guarantees that, once an argument is fixed, the behavior of the resulting function remains independent of external mutable state. As a consequence, the process aligns with the theoretical underpinnings of lambda calculus, where functions are treated as first-class citizens and transformations occur solely by substitution.

The adoption of partial function application within the functools module affords a rigorous methodology for decomposing functions into simpler, reusable components. By encapsulating fixed parameters within a newly constructed function, the subsequent expression of computational pipelines becomes more succinct and mathematically coherent. Such an approach is instrumental in mitigating the cognitive overhead associated with handling repetitious argument passing, thereby streamlining the development of functionally composed algorithms.

Caching Decorators

Caching decorators constitute a sophisticated utility designed to optimize function calls through the preservation of computed results. Let

$$f : X \to Y$$

represent a function whose evaluation may entail significant computational resources. A caching decorator transforms f into a new function $\hat{f}$ such that for every input $x \in X$, the value $\hat{f}(x)$ is derived by first inspecting a cache. If the result corresponding to x is present, it is retrieved directly; otherwise, $f(x)$ is computed and stored. This behavior can be summarized as

$$\hat{f}(x) = \begin{cases} \text{cache}(x) & \text{if } x \in \text{dom(cache)}, \\ f(x) & \text{otherwise.} \end{cases}$$

The caching mechanism, often identified with memoization, leverages the deterministic nature of pure functions by ensuring that for any fixed input, the output remains invariant and hence eligible for reuse.

The theoretical foundation underlying caching decorators is deeply intertwined with concepts from dynamic programming and combinatorial optimization. The strategy effectively reduces redundant computations by capitalizing on the existence of a bijective mapping between inputs and their computed outputs. In formal terms, if the mapping

$$m : X \to Y$$

encapsulates the cache, then for all $x \in X$ the relation

$$m(x) = f(x)$$

holds after the initial evaluation. This functional equivalence ensures that repeated invocations of $\hat{f}$ do not incur additional computational overhead beyond the initial calculation, provided the cached result is available.

Furthermore, the implementation of caching within the functools module is executed with careful attention to the principles of immutability and referential transparency. The caching decorator abstracts the state management inherent in cache utilization, enforcing a separation between the immutable computational result and the transient mechanism of retrieval. The design may also incorporate policies for cache eviction and size limitations, which, although primarily of practical concern, are conceptually connected to the broader theory of resource bounded computation.

The integration of caching decorators stands as a testament to the utility of mathematical abstraction in optimizing algorithmic performance. By ensuring that functions exhibit consistent behavior regardless of repeated invocations with the same inputs, caching reinforces the deterministic paradigm essential to both theoretical inquiry and practical application within the realm of functional programming.

Python Code Snippet

```python
import functools

# ---------------------------
# Partial Function Application
# ---------------------------
def multiply(a, b):
    """
    Returns the product of two numbers.

    Mathematical representation:
        f: A x B -> C, where f(a, b) = a * b.
    """
    return a * b

# Using functools.partial to fix the first argument.
```

```python
# By fixing a = 5, we create a new function g such that:
#   g(b) = f(5, b)
multiply_by_5 = functools.partial(multiply, 5)

# Demonstration of partial function application.
print("Partial Function Application Example:")
print("multiply_by_5(10) =", multiply_by_5(10))   # Expected output:
↪  50


# ---------------------------
# Caching Decorators using lru_cache
# ---------------------------
@functools.lru_cache(maxsize=None)
def fibonacci(n):
    """
    Computes the nth Fibonacci number using recursion with caching.

    Mathematical Formula:
        fibonacci(n) = {
                        0                               if n == 0,
                        1                               if n == 1,
                        fibonacci(n-1) + fibonacci(n-2)   otherwise.
                       }
    """
    if n < 2:
        return n
    return fibonacci(n - 1) + fibonacci(n - 2)

print("\nCaching Decorator Example using lru_cache (Fibonacci):")
for i in range(10):
    print(f"Fibonacci({i}) =", fibonacci(i))


# ---------------------------
# Manual Caching Decorator Implementation
# ---------------------------
def manual_cache_decorator(func):
    """
    A simple caching decorator that stores computed results in a
    ↪  dictionary.

    For a function f: X -> Y, the decorator transforms it to a
    ↪  function \hat{f} such that:

        \hat{f}(x) =
          { cache(x) if x is in cache,
            f(x)     otherwise (and then cache the result) }.
    """
    cache = {}

    @functools.wraps(func)
    def wrapper(*args):
        if args in cache:
```

275

```python
            print(f"Retrieving cached result for arguments: {args}")
            return cache[args]
        result = func(*args)
        cache[args] = result
        print(f"Caching result for arguments: {args}")
        return result
    return wrapper


@manual_cache_decorator
def power(a, b):
    """
    Computes the exponentiation operation a^b.
    """
    return a ** b


print("\nManual Caching Decorator Example:")
print("power(2, 3) =", power(2, 3))
print("power(2, 3) =", power(2, 3))  # This call should retrieve the
↪    result from cache
```

Chapter 51

Working with Recursion in Python

Conceptual Foundations of Recursion

Recursion is a method of defining functions in which the solution to a problem is expressed in terms of solutions to smaller instances of the same problem. In this framework, a function f is defined on a domain D by appealing to its own evaluation on elements of a reduced subset of D. Formally, a recursive definition may be expressed as

$$f(x) = \begin{cases} g(x) & \text{if } x \in B, \\ h\Big(x,\, f(x_1),\, f(x_2),\, \ldots,\, f(x_k)\Big) & \text{if } x \in D \setminus B, \end{cases}$$

where B is a nonempty subset of D known as the base case, g is a function that provides a direct evaluation for inputs in B, and h is an operator that combines the value of x with the results of one or more recursive calls on properly reduced instances $x_1, x_2, \ldots, x_k \in D$. This self-referential construction embodies the essence of recursive computation and aligns with principles of well-foundedness, ensuring that every chain of recursive calls terminates in an element of B.

Structural Design of Recursive Functions

The design of a recursive function is intrinsically tied to the precise identification of two critical components: the base case and the recursive case. The base case, defined by a predicate $C(x)$, guarantees termination by handling the simplest instances for which the answer can be returned directly without further recursion. Concurrently, the recursive case defines a relationship whereby the function $f(x)$ is articulated in terms of one or more evaluations of itself on arguments that are strictly simpler than x. Mathematically, for an element $x \in D$, the recursive definition takes the form

$$f(x) = h\Big(x, \ \{f(x') \mid x' \in R(x)\}\Big),$$

where $R(x)$ is a set of values derived from x that satisfies $R(x) \subset D$ and is chosen such that iterative application of R eventually leads to an element in the base case B. Ensuring that the recursive call progresses towards a base case is analogous to establishing a well-founded ordering on D, thereby precluding infinite descent. This duality of structure is fundamental for maintaining both the logical correctness and the computational feasibility of recursive procedures.

Analytical Considerations of Recursive Computation

The evaluation of recursive functions frequently necessitates an analysis based on recurrence relations, which serve to quantify the computational resources—such as time and memory—utilized in the process of self-invocation. A typical recurrence relation may be expressed in the form

$$T(n) = a\,T\left(\frac{n}{b}\right) + f(n),$$

where $T(n)$ denotes the total computational cost for an input of size n, a represents the number of recursive calls in the recursive branch, b is the factor by which the input size is reduced, and $f(n)$ accounts for the cost of operations performed at the current level of recursion. Such relations provide insight into the asymptotic behavior of recursive algorithms and facilitate the classification of their efficiency via established techniques of recurrence solving.

Furthermore, the conceptual parallelism between recursion and mathematical induction is noteworthy. The correctness of a recursive function is typically ascertained by verifying that the base case holds and that, assuming correctness for an arbitrary element in the domain, the recursive step preserves this correctness for a more complex input. This inductive reasoning underpins the theoretical robustness of recursive definitions and reinforces the reliability of self-referential computational models.

In the context of Python, the recursive paradigm is implemented by allowing functions to invoke themselves, subject to the constraints of the language's call stack and memory management. The linear nature of the call stack implies that each recursive call incurs additional overhead, thus necessitating a judicious design of recursion depth and structure. The interplay between theoretical guarantees, as provided by well-founded recursive definitions, and the practical limitations imposed by runtime environments underscores the nuanced balance required in crafting recursive solutions.

Python Code Snippet

```
# This Python code snippet illustrates key recursive concepts,
# algorithms, and recurrence relations discussed in the chapter.
#
# It demonstrates:
#    - A recursive function for factorial computation
#        f(n) = { 1,                    if n == 0  (base case)
#               { n * f(n - 1),         if n > 0   (recursive case)
#
#    - A naive recursive implementation for the Fibonacci sequence,
#      following:
#        f(n) = f(n - 1) + f(n - 2) with f(0)=0, f(1)=1
#
#    - A memoized version of Fibonacci to optimize recursive calls.
#
#    - The Merge Sort algorithm, which embodies a recurrence of the
# ↪  form:
#        T(n) = 2 * T(n/2) + O(n)
#
#    - A generic recursive function template illustrating the
# ↪  structure:
#        f(x) = g(x)                          if x in base case B,
#             = h(x, {f(x') for x' in R(x)}) if x is not in B.
#
# Each function is fully implemented and includes inline comments
# ↪  referencing
# the theoretical foundations of recursion and recurrence relations.
```

```python
# Example 1: Recursive computation of factorial
def factorial(n):
    """
    Compute the factorial of n recursively.

    Follows:
        f(n) = 1                    if n == 0 (base case)
             = n * f(n-1)           if n > 0  (recursive case)

    This is analogous to the recurrence:
        T(n) = T(n-1) + O(1)
    """
    if n < 0:
        raise ValueError("Negative values are not allowed")
    if n == 0:
        return 1  # Base case: f(0) = 1
    return n * factorial(n - 1)  # Recursive call: f(n) = n * f(n-1)

# Example 2: Naive recursive Fibonacci sequence
def fibonacci(n):
    """
    Compute the nth Fibonacci number using a naive recursive
    ↪ approach.

    The recursive definition is:
        f(0) = 0
        f(1) = 1
        f(n) = f(n-1) + f(n-2)    for n >= 2

    Its cost recurrence is:
        T(n) = T(n-1) + T(n-2) + O(1)
    """
    if n < 0:
        raise ValueError("Negative values are not allowed")
    if n == 0:
        return 0  # Base case: f(0) = 0
    if n == 1:
        return 1  # Base case: f(1) = 1
    return fibonacci(n - 1) + fibonacci(n - 2)  # Recursive calls

# Example 3: Optimized recursive Fibonacci with memoization
def fibonacci_memo(n, memo=None):
    """
    Compute the nth Fibonacci number using recursion with
    ↪ memoization.

    Memoization caches intermediate results to improve efficiency.
    """
    if memo is None:
        memo = {}
    if n in memo:
        return memo[n]
```

280

```python
    if n < 0:
        raise ValueError("Negative values are not allowed")
    if n == 0:
        return 0  # Base case
    if n == 1:
        return 1  # Base case
    memo[n] = fibonacci_memo(n - 1, memo) + fibonacci_memo(n - 2,
    ↪   memo)
    return memo[n]


# Example 4: Merge Sort Algorithm (Divide and Conquer Recursion)
def merge_sort(arr):
    """
    Sort an array using the merge sort algorithm.

    The recurrence relation for merge sort is:
        T(n) = 2 * T(n/2) + O(n)

    - Divide: Split the array into two halves.
    - Conquer: Recursively sort each half.
    - Combine: Merge the two sorted halves.
    """
    if len(arr) <= 1:
        return arr  # Base case: arrays of length 0 or 1 are already
        ↪   sorted

    mid = len(arr) // 2
    left = merge_sort(arr[:mid])
    right = merge_sort(arr[mid:])

    return merge(left, right)

def merge(left, right):
    """
    Merge two sorted lists into a single sorted list.
    """
    merged = []
    i = j = 0

    # Merge the two lists until one is exhausted
    while i < len(left) and j < len(right):
        if left[i] <= right[j]:
            merged.append(left[i])
            i += 1
        else:
            merged.append(right[j])
            j += 1

    # Append any remaining elements
    merged.extend(left[i:])
    merged.extend(right[j:])

    return merged
```

```python
# Example 5: Generic Recursive Function Template
def recursive_function(x):
    """

    A generic recursive function following the structure:

        f(x) = g(x)                          if x is in the base case
        ↪    (B)
             = h(x, {f(x') for x' in R(x)}) if x is not in B

    In this template:
      - is_base_case(x) defines whether x meets the condition for
      ↪    termination.
      - direct_evaluation(x) computes g(x) for the base case.
      - reduction(x) defines the set R(x) of reduced instances.
      - combine(x, results) computes h(x, {f(x') for x' in R(x)}).
    """
    if is_base_case(x):
        return direct_evaluation(x)   # g(x)

    # Recursively invoke on all reduced instances from x's reduction
    ↪    set R(x)
    results = [recursive_function(x_prime) for x_prime in
    ↪    reduction(x)]
    return combine(x, results)   # h(x, {f(x') for x' in R(x)})

def is_base_case(x):
    # For example: x is in the base case if x is less than or equal
    ↪    to 1.
    return x <= 1

def direct_evaluation(x):
    # For the base case, simply return x.
    return x

def reduction(x):
    # For demonstration, reduce x by subtracting 1.
    # In general, this function should return a list of "simpler"
    ↪    inputs.
    return [x - 1]

def combine(x, results):
    # Combines the results from the recursive calls.
    # Here we add x to the sum of all recursive results.
    return x + sum(results)

# Main block to test the recursive implementations
if __name__ == "__main__":
    # Test Factorial
    num = 5
    print("Factorial of", num, "is", factorial(num))

    # Test Naive Recursive Fibonacci
```

```
fib_index = 10
print("Fibonacci number at index", fib_index, "is",
↪   fibonacci(fib_index))

# Test Memoized Fibonacci for efficiency
print("Memoized Fibonacci number at index", fib_index, "is",
↪   fibonacci_memo(fib_index))

# Test Merge Sort algorithm
unsorted_list = [38, 27, 43, 3, 9, 82, 10]
print("Original list:", unsorted_list)
print("Sorted list:", merge_sort(unsorted_list))

# Test Generic Recursive Function Template
x_value = 4
print("Result of the generic recursive function for", x_value,
↪   "is", recursive_function(x_value))
```

Chapter 52

Recursive Algorithms and Tail Recursion

Recursive Algorithm Paradigms

Recursion has emerged as a fundamental methodology in the design and analysis of algorithms, wherein complex problems are decomposed into simpler, self-similar subproblems. This paradigm is characterized by the definition of a function in terms of smaller instances of itself, yielding inherently expressive formulations of numerous computational tasks. Many classical algorithms, such as those employed in divide-and-conquer strategies, traversals of hierarchical data structures, and backtracking search procedures, leverage recursion to provide elegant and succinct problem solutions. A typical recursive formulation is encapsulated by a recurrence relation of the form

$$T(n) = a\,T\!\left(\frac{n}{b}\right) + f(n),$$

where the constants a and b characterize the branching factor and the reduction in problem size, respectively, and $f(n)$ quantifies the cost of combining the results of subproblems. Such relations afford a rigorous framework for asymptotic analysis and enable the derivation of tight bounds on algorithmic performance. The self-referential nature of recursive algorithms not only simplifies conceptualization but also permits the application of mathematical induction to establish correctness and to elucidate the structural properties of the solution space.

Tail Recursion and its Optimization

Tail recursion represents a specialized subset of recursive algorithms in which the recursive invocation constitutes the final computational act of the function. In this formulation, no additional processing remains to be performed after the recursive call returns, thereby allowing the current computational context to be replaced by that of the subsequent call. Formally, a function f is tail recursive if it can be expressed in the following manner:

$$f(x) = \begin{cases} g(x), & \text{if } C(x) \text{ holds,} \\ f\big(h(x)\big), & \text{otherwise,} \end{cases}$$

where $C(x)$ characterizes the base condition, $g(x)$ defines the direct evaluation for instances satisfying $C(x)$, and $h(x)$ delineates the transformation leading to a simpler instance. The absence of further operations post-recursion enables optimization techniques such as tail call elimination, wherein the runtime environment reuses the current stack frame for successive calls. This optimization effectively transforms the recursive process into an iterative one, thus ensuring that the space complexity remains bounded by a constant rather than scaling with the depth of recursive invocations.

The optimization provided by tail recursion stems from its structural property that obviates the need for maintaining an elaborate call stack. In a conventional recursive algorithm, each invocation accumulates additional state information, which may lead to significant memory overhead. In contrast, tail recursive functions leverage a control flow that permits immediate substitution of the current execution context with that of the recursive call. When augmented with accumulator parameters, tail recursion can capture the intermediate results in a manner that facilitates both efficient recombination and seamless translation to an iterative loop. This interplay between recursion and iteration is of particular interest in the domain of compiler design and runtime systems, where the ability to automatically transform tail recursive calls into efficient loops can yield substantial performance improvements.

In theoretical analyses, tail recursion is often juxtaposed with non-tail recursive counterparts to emphasize the minimal overhead in function invocation. When the recursive call is the final operation, the function's execution can be perceived as adhering to a linear iterative process mathematically equivalent to a while loop.

The resulting transformation not only reduces stack utilization but also simplifies reasoning about the functional behavior. Consequently, tail recursive algorithms serve as a bridge between the expressive clarity of recursive definitions and the resource efficiency typically ascribed to iterative solutions.

Python Code Snippet

```python
import sys

# Increase recursion limit for deep recursive calls (if necessary)
sys.setrecursionlimit(10000)

#
↪    --------------------------------------------------------------------
# Example 1: Recursive Algorithm Paradigm using Merge Sort
#
# The merge sort algorithm is a classic example of a
↪    divide-and-conquer
# strategy that follows the recurrence relation:
#    T(n) = 2 * T(n/2) + O(n)
# where the input list is recursively split into halves until
↪    trivial,
# and then merged back together in sorted order.

def merge_sort(arr):
    if len(arr) <= 1:
        return arr
    mid = len(arr) // 2
    left = merge_sort(arr[:mid])
    right = merge_sort(arr[mid:])
    return merge(left, right)

def merge(left, right):
    merged = []
    i = j = 0
    # Merge two sorted sublists
    while i < len(left) and j < len(right):
        if left[i] <= right[j]:
            merged.append(left[i])
            i += 1
        else:
            merged.append(right[j])
            j += 1
    merged.extend(left[i:])
    merged.extend(right[j:])
    return merged

#
↪    --------------------------------------------------------------------
```

```python
# Example 2: Recursive vs Tail Recursive implementations.
#
# We demonstrate the classic recursive formulation with a standard
# factorial function, and then show a tail recursive version that
# ↪   uses
# an accumulator to hold intermediate results.
#
# Standard recursive factorial (non-tail recursive):
def factorial(n):
    if n <= 1:
        return 1
    else:
        return n * factorial(n - 1)


# Tail recursive factorial using an accumulator:
def tail_recursive_factorial(n, acc=1):
    if n <= 1:
        return acc
    else:
        # The recursive call is in tail position (no further
        # ↪   computation after it)
        return tail_recursive_factorial(n - 1, n * acc)


#
# ↪   -------------------------------------------------------------------
# Example 3: Tail Recursion Optimization via a Decorator
#
# Python does not automatically optimize tail-recursive calls.
# ↪   However,
# we can simulate tail call elimination using a decorator that
# ↪   replaces
# recursion with iteration. This utilizes an exception-based
# ↪   trampoline.
#
# Exception class to signal a tail call:
class TailCallException(Exception):
    def __init__(self, func, args, kwargs):
        self.func = func
        self.args = args
        self.kwargs = kwargs


# Decorator to optimize tail recursive functions:
def tail_call_optimized(func):
    """
    This decorator simulates tail call optimization by repeatedly
    ↪   handling
    tail calls in a loop rather than consuming additional stack
    ↪   frames.
    """
    def wrapper(*args, **kwargs):
        f = func
        while True:
            try:
```

287

```python
            return f(*args, **kwargs)
        except TailCallException as e:
            f = e.func
            args = e.args
            kwargs = e.kwargs
    return wrapper

# Tail recursive Fibonacci function using the TailCallException
↪   mechanism:
@tail_call_optimized
def tail_recursive_fibonacci(n, a=0, b=1):
    if n == 0:
        return a
    # Instead of calling tail_recursive_fibonacci directly, we raise
    ↪   an exception
    # to simulate a tail call that the decorator will handle
    ↪   iteratively.
    raise TailCallException(tail_recursive_fibonacci, (n - 1, b, a +
    ↪   b), {})

#
↪   -----------------------------------------------------------------------
# Driver code to demonstrate the algorithms
if __name__ == "__main__":
    # Demonstrate Merge Sort
    unsorted_list = [38, 27, 43, 3, 9, 82, 10]
    sorted_list = merge_sort(unsorted_list)
    print("Merge Sort Example:")
    print("Original List:", unsorted_list)
    print("Sorted List  :", sorted_list)
    print()

    # Test the Factorial functions
    num = 5
    print("Factorial Examples:")
    print("Non-tail recursive factorial of", num, ":",
    ↪   factorial(num))
    print("Tail recursive factorial of", num, "    :",
    ↪   tail_recursive_factorial(num))
    print()

    # Test the Tail Recursive Fibonacci function
    fib_index = 10
    print("Tail Recursive Fibonacci Example:")
    print("Fibonacci number at index", fib_index, ":",
    ↪   tail_recursive_fibonacci(fib_index))
```

Chapter 53

List Sorting and Custom Sorting Techniques

Fundamental Concepts in Sorting

The discipline of sorting encompasses the systematic rearrangement of elements within a list according to a prescribed order. The underlying objective is to establish a sequence in which, for any two elements x and y, the relation $x \leq y$ holds under a binary ordering relation that is required to be total, transitive, and antisymmetric. Such an ordering is formalized by the definition of a comparability function that assigns an unambiguous position to every element. The mathematical foundation of this task is rooted in order theory, whereby the set of all elements is structured into a partially or totally ordered set that fulfills these axiomatic properties.

1 Definition and Ordering Properties

Within the context of sorting algorithms, an ordering predicate is typically denoted by the relation $<$. For any elements x, y, and z from the set being sorted, the predicate must satisfy the conditions of totality (for every distinct pair of elements, a comparison can be made), transitivity (if $x < y$ and $y < z$, then $x < z$), and antisymmetry (if both $x < y$ and $y < x$ hold, then it must follow that $x = y$). These properties ensure that the sorting process yields a unique arrangement when a stable sorting method is applied. In addition, the notion of stability in sorting maintains that equivalent elements—those for which neither $x < y$ nor $y < x$ holds—preserve their pre-sorted relative order.

2 Computational Complexity and Theoretical Analysis

Considerable effort has been expended in analyzing the computational complexities associated with sorting algorithms. In the realm of comparison-based sorting, lower bounds have been established proving that any algorithm conforming to this paradigm requires at least $\Omega(n \log n)$ comparisons in the worst-case scenario. Algorithms such as merge sort and heap sort asymptotically approach these bounds by effectively balancing the number of comparisons and the overhead required for merging or heap maintenance. A rigorous examination of the decision tree model elucidates that the number of leaves in the tree, which represents all possible sorted orders, grows factorially with the number of elements n, thereby mandating a logarithmic depth that manifests as the lower bound on computational complexity.

Custom Sorting Methodologies

Customization in sorting is necessitated by scenarios in which the natural order of elements does not directly correspond to the domain-specific criteria imposed by the problem space. The need for non-standard ordering emerges when elements possess multidimensional attributes or when the inherent structure of the data demands a specialized treatment. Custom sorting methodologies are underpinned by the introduction of auxiliary functions that either extract keys from complex elements or perform direct pairwise comparisons through comparator functions.

1 Comparator Functions and Key Transformations

A prevalent approach to customizing sorting behavior lies in the utilization of key transformations. By defining a function $k : X \to Y$, where X is the set of elements to be sorted and Y is an auxiliary ordered set, the sorting process can be recast such that the condition for ordering is established as $x \leq y$ if and only if $k(x) \leq k(y)$. This transformation effectively reduces a potentially intricate ordering problem into one that leverages the natural order of a simpler domain. Alternatively, a comparator function $C : X \times X \to \{-1, 0, 1\}$ can be specified to directly ascertain the order between any two elements. The design of such functions is critical; they must be constructed in a manner that guarantees a total order while being computationally efficient enough to avoid unduly impacting the overall runtime of the sorting algorithm.

2 Architectural Considerations in Custom Sorting

The integration of custom logic into sorting algorithms often introduces additional architectural considerations. Primary among these is the balance between flexibility and performance. The invocation of user-defined key or comparator functions introduces an overhead that must be carefully evaluated, particularly in scenarios where the sorting process is applied to large datasets. Further, the criterion for stability plays an essential role when sorting complex objects. Stability ensures that when elements are equivalent according to the custom criteria, their relative order remains consistent with their sequence in the original unsorted list. This property is especially pertinent when sequential sorting operations are employed to impose multiple layers of ordering based on various attributes.

3 Comparative Analysis of Custom Sorting Approaches

A critical analysis of custom sorting techniques reveals a spectrum of trade-offs between the direct use of comparator functions and the indirect approach of key extraction followed by standard sorting routines. The key transformation method is particularly advantageous in cases where the preprocessing of elements into a comparable form can be efficiently accomplished, as it leverages highly optimized base sorting algorithms. In contrast, comparator-based approaches afford a greater degree of control, allowing for dynamic evaluation of order during the sorting process. However, such flexibility may come at the expense of increased computational complexity if the comparator function is non-trivial. The selection of a custom sorting strategy is therefore contingent on the specific requirements of the application, the structure of the data, and the performance constraints imposed by the operating environment.

Python Code Snippet

```
import functools

#
↪    ---------------------------------------------------------------------
# This comprehensive Python code snippet illustrates various sorting
# techniques and algorithms as discussed in the chapter. It
↪    demonstrates:
#
# 1. Custom sorting using key transformations.
#      - Implements sorting of a dataset with multiple attributes by
↪    applying
#        a key function that enforces a custom total order. This
↪    mirrors the
#        mathematical formulation: for elements x and y, x <= y if
↪    k(x) <= k(y).
#
# 2. Custom sorting using comparator functions.
#      - Uses a comparator function to directly compare elements,
↪    ensuring
#        properties of totality, transitivity, and antisymmetry are
↪    maintained.
#        The function returns -1, 0, or 1 for less than, equal to, or
↪    greater than.
#
# 3. Merge sort algorithm implementation.
#      - Provides a classical divide-and-conquer merge sort algorithm
↪    that
#        performs O(n log n) comparisons in the worst-case scenario,
↪    reflecting
#        the lower bound for any comparison-based sorting algorithm.
#
# 4. Stability demonstration in sorting.
#      - Shows how Python's sorted() function maintains the relative
↪    order
#        of equal elements (stability), which is critical when
↪    multiple layers
#        of sorting criteria are applied.
#
#
↪    ---------------------------------------------------------------------

# Helper function: prints a header followed by the list content.
def print_list(header, lst):
    print(header, lst)
```

```
#
↪   -----------------------------------------------------------------------
# 1. Custom Sorting using Key Transformations
#
# Given a list of tuples representing (name, age, score), we aim to
↪   sort
# the data such that it is ordered by descending score and, among
↪   equal
# scores, by ascending age. This is achieved by transforming each
↪   element
# using a key function that computes (-score, age).
#
↪   -----------------------------------------------------------------------
data = [
    ("Alice", 30, 88.5),
    ("Bob", 25, 91.0),
    ("Charlie", 35, 88.5),
    ("David", 30, 91.0),
    ("Eve", 28, 85.0)
]

# Sorting using a lambda function as key:
#    - Negative score (-x[2]) converts descending order into
↪   ascending order.
#    - Age (x[1]) is used as a secondary criterion.
data_sorted_key = sorted(data, key=lambda x: (-x[2], x[1]))
print_list("Sorted using key transformation:", data_sorted_key)


#
↪   -----------------------------------------------------------------------
# 2. Custom Sorting using a Comparator Function
#
# Alternatively, a comparator function can be defined to directly
↪   compare two
# elements. Python's sorted() function does not take comparator
↪   functions
# directly; instead, we use functools.cmp_to_key to convert the
↪   comparator
# into a key function.
#
# The comparator 'custom_comparator' enforces:
#    - Primary ordering by score (descending),
#    - Secondary ordering by age (ascending),
# ensuring a total order.
#
↪   -----------------------------------------------------------------------
def custom_comparator(a, b):
    # Compare by score in descending order.
    if a[2] > b[2]:
        return -1
    elif a[2] < b[2]:
        return 1
```

293

```
        else:
            # If scores are equal, compare by age in ascending order.
            if a[1] < b[1]:
                return -1
            elif a[1] > b[1]:
                return 1
            else:
                return 0

data_sorted_cmp = sorted(data,
↪ key=functools.cmp_to_key(custom_comparator))
print_list("Sorted using comparator function:", data_sorted_cmp)


#
↪ --------------------------------------------------------------------------
# 3. Merge Sort Implementation demonstrating O(n log n) Complexity
#
# Merge sort is a classic comparison-based sorting algorithm that
↪ achieves
# the theoretical lower bound of Omega(n log n) comparisons. It
↪ recursively
# divides the list into halves and merges the sorted halves.
#
↪ --------------------------------------------------------------------------
def merge_sort(lst):
    """
    Recursively sorts the list using the merge sort algorithm.
    Returns a new sorted list.
    """
    if len(lst) <= 1:
        return lst
    mid = len(lst) // 2
    left = merge_sort(lst[:mid])
    right = merge_sort(lst[mid:])
    return merge(left, right)

def merge(left, right):
    """
    Merges two pre-sorted lists into a single sorted list.
    Maintains the order properties required for stable sorting.
    """
    merged = []
    i = j = 0
    while i < len(left) and j < len(right):
        # Assuming a simple numerical order (x <= y) is defined.
        if left[i] <= right[j]:
            merged.append(left[i])
            i += 1
        else:
            merged.append(right[j])
            j += 1
    merged.extend(left[i:])
```

294

```
        merged.extend(right[j:])
        return merged

# Example unsorted numeric list.
unsorted_list = [38, 27, 43, 3, 9, 82, 10]
sorted_list = merge_sort(unsorted_list)
print_list("Sorted using merge sort:", sorted_list)


#
↪   ------------------------------------------------------------------------
# 4. Demonstration of Stable Sorting
#
# Stability in sorting ensures that when two elements compare equal,
# their original order is preserved. This is important when sorting
↪   on
# primary and secondary keys.
#
↪   ------------------------------------------------------------------------
records = [
    {"name": "Alice", "score": 88},
    {"name": "Charlie", "score": 88},
    {"name": "Bob", "score": 91},
    {"name": "David", "score": 91},
]

# Sorting by score only. Since Python's built-in sorted() is stable,
# Alice remains before Charlie, and Bob remains before David.
sorted_records = sorted(records, key=lambda x: x["score"])
print_list("Stable sorted records by score:", sorted_records)


#
↪   ------------------------------------------------------------------------
# Note:
# The merge_sort algorithm herein reflects the mathematical
↪   underpinning
# of sorting outlined in the chapter, particularly the concept that
↪   any
# comparison-based sorting algorithm must perform at least (n log n)
# comparisons in the worst-case scenario.
#
↪   ------------------------------------------------------------------------
```

Chapter 54

Using the sorted() and sort() Methods

Conceptual Framework and Semantic Distinctions

The Python programming language provides two primary mechanisms for achieving ordered sequences from collections of data: the built-in sorted() function and the list.sort() method. The sorted() function is defined as a global operation that accepts any iterable and produces a new list containing the sorted elements. In contrast, the sort() method is an intrinsic operation available exclusively to list objects that rearranges the elements within the original list in place. These distinct operational paradigms have profound implications in terms of side effects, mutability, and the functional programming style. In the case of sorted(), the original iterable remains unchanged, thereby preserving data integrity when immutability is a concern. Conversely, list.sort() modifies the original sequence, a behavior that is preferable when memory efficiency and in-place data transformation are the primary objectives.

Algorithmic Foundations and Stability

Both sorted() and list.sort() are underpinned by the Timsort algorithm, a hybrid sorting technique derived from merge sort and insertion sort. The algorithm is designed to exploit existing order within data, thereby providing substantial performance gains on partially ordered inputs. Central to Timsort is the guarantee of stability; that is, for any pair of elements x and y such that $x = y$, the pre-sorted relative order is maintained after the sorting process. This stability is essential in scenarios where data objects contain multiple attributes and the sort is performed on a specific attribute while preserving the order determined by a previously applied criterion. Timsort's worst-case performance is $O(n \log n)$, a bound that provides theoretical assurances for its efficiency across a broad spectrum of input distributions.

Performance Characteristics and Memory Considerations

A critical evaluation of the sorted() function and the list.sort() method necessitates an examination of their performance characteristics and memory usage. The list.sort() method is optimized for in-place sorting, meaning it rearranges the items without requiring an allocation of additional lists. This quality minimizes memory overhead and can lead to improved performance when the original list is no longer required in its unsorted state. On the other hand, sorted() inherently produces a new list, incurring both time and memory costs associated with the creation and copying of the data. Consequently, in applications where preserving the original iterable is nonessential and resource constraints are stringent, the use of list.sort() is often more advantageous. It is also noteworthy that both methods share common optional parameters, such as the key function and reverse flag, which allow for extensive customization of the sorting criteria while uniformly leveraging the underlying Timsort implementation.

Contextual Applicability and Usage Paradigms

The choice between employing the sorted() function and the list.sort() method is contingent upon the specific requirements of the computing context. In scenarios emphasizing a declarative programming style or needing to maintain the original data sequence for further operations, the non-destructive behavior of sorted() is of critical importance. Conversely, when data transformation is intended to be performed locally within a list object and the preservation of memory allocation is paramount, list.sort() serves as the more efficient approach. Additionally, the capability of sorted() to process any iterable makes it a versatile tool in diverse application paradigms where the conversion of data types is frequent. The strategic deployment of these methods, informed by considerations of algorithmic stability, computational complexity, and memory efficiency, forms an integral component of effective data manipulation within Python's broader ecosystem.

Python Code Snippet

```python
# Comprehensive demonstration of the sorted() function and
↪    list.sort() method,
# including stability aspects of Timsort, performance
↪    characteristics, and various optional parameters.

import random
import time

def demonstrate_sorted_vs_inplace_sort():
    """
    Demonstrates two primary sorting methods in Python:
    1. sorted() - a global function that returns a new sorted list
    ↪    without modifying the original.
    2. list.sort() - a method that sorts the list in place.

    Also illustrates the stability property of Timsort:
    When elements have equal sort keys, their original relative
    ↪    order is preserved.
    """
    # Sample data: a list of tuples in the format (Category, Value,
    ↪    ID)
    # 'ID' is used to track the original order of items.
    data = [
        ("A", 10, 1),
        ("B", 20, 2),
        ("A", 10, 3),
        ("B", 15, 4),
        ("A", 5, 5),
        ("B", 20, 6),
        ("A", 10, 7)
    ]

    print("Original Data:")
    for item in data:
        print(item)
```

```python
    # Use sorted() to sort by the 'Value' (second element of the
    ↪  tuple)
    # This does not alter the original data list.
    sorted_data = sorted(data, key=lambda x: x[1])
    print("\nData after sorted() by value (non-destructive):")
    for item in sorted_data:
        print(item)

    # Confirm that the original list remains unmodified.
    print("\nOriginal Data remains unchanged:")
    for item in data:
        print(item)

    # In-place sorting using list.sort() with the same key.
    data.sort(key=lambda x: x[1])
    print("\nData after in-place sort() by value (original list
    ↪  modified):")
    for item in data:
        print(item)

    # The stability of Timsort is evident here:
    # For elements with equal 'Value' (e.g., (A,10,1), (A,10,3),
    ↪  (A,10,7)),
    # the order (1, 3, 7) is preserved post-sort.


def performance_comparison():
    """
    Compares the performance of sorted() and list.sort() on a large
    ↪  list.
    Both utilize Timsort with a worst-case performance of O(n log
    ↪  n), yet they differ
    in memory usage and minor time overhead due to the creation of a
    ↪  new list in sorted().
    """
    # Generate a large random list of integers.
    large_list = [random.randint(0, 100000) for _ in range(10000)]

    # Measure execution time for sorted() function.
    start_time = time.time()
    new_sorted_list = sorted(large_list)
    sorted_time = time.time() - start_time

    # Measure execution time for list.sort() method (operates
    ↪  in-place).
    list_copy = large_list.copy()   # Ensure identical unsorted
    ↪  input.
    start_time = time.time()
    list_copy.sort()
    inplace_sorted_time = time.time() - start_time

    print("\nPerformance Comparison on a list of 10,000 integers:")
```

```python
    print("Time taken by sorted() function: {:.6f}
    ↪    seconds".format(sorted_time))
    print("Time taken by list.sort() method: {:.6f}
    ↪    seconds".format(inplace_sorted_time))

    # Both methods share the Timsort algorithm, but sorted() creates
    ↪    a new list,
    # resulting in additional memory allocation compared to the
    ↪    in-place sort.


def additional_sorting_examples():
    """
    Provides further examples of sorting:
    - Simple numeric list sorting in ascending and descending order.
    - Using lambda functions with key and reverse parameters.
    - Sorting a list of strings by their length.
    """
    # Simple list of numbers.
    sample = [5, 3, 9, 1, 4]
    print("\nOriginal sample list:", sample)

    ascending = sorted(sample)
    descending = sorted(sample, reverse=True)
    print("Sorted in ascending order:", ascending)
    print("Sorted in descending order:", descending)

    # Sorting using key: sort words by their length.
    words = ["banana", "apple", "cherry", "date"]
    sorted_words = sorted(words, key=lambda word: len(word))
    print("\nOriginal words list:", words)
    print("Words sorted by length:", sorted_words)

    # The examples reinforce that both sorted() and list.sort()
    ↪    accept optional parameters
    # (such as key and reverse) and rely on the stable and efficient
    ↪    Timsort algorithm.


if __name__ == "__main__":
    print("---- Demonstration of sorted() vs. list.sort() Methods
    ↪    ----")
    demonstrate_sorted_vs_inplace_sort()
    performance_comparison()
    additional_sorting_examples()
```

Chapter 55

Understanding and Using the zip() Function

Overview of the zip() Function

The zip() function is a built-in operation that serves as a mechanism for aggregating elements from multiple iterables. Formally, this function accepts a collection of iterables and returns an iterator that produces tuples. Each tuple is constructed by pairing the first element from each provided iterable, then the second element from each, proceeding in this parallel fashion. The intrinsic nature of zip() can be characterized as a mapping over the input iterables whereby the i-th aggregated tuple is given by

$$(z_1, z_2, \ldots, z_k) = (\text{iterable}_1[i], \text{iterable}_2[i], \ldots, \text{iterable}_k[i]).$$

It is essential to note that the operation terminates upon reaching the end of the shortest iterable, thereby ensuring that each tuple is complete and consistent in terms of element composition.

Aggregation Mechanism and Iterative Process

The aggregation performed by zip() is underpinned by the iterator protocol inherent in Python. Each input iterable is first trans-

301

formed into an iterator, and the aggregation process then occurs in a lockstep fashion. This synchronous traversal ensures that elements are sampled concurrently from each source. Mathematically, if the lengths of the iterables are represented by $n_1, n_2, \ldots, n_k$, then the number of tuples generated is

$$n = \min(n_1, n_2, \ldots, n_k),$$

which governs the termination of the iteration. The lazy evaluation model, employed by zip(), implies that tuples are generated on demand rather than materialized en masse. This characteristic contributes notably to memory efficiency, as the complete result is not instantiated until explicitly iterated over.

Parallel Iteration and Synchronized Traversal

A central application of the zip() function lies in its facilitation of parallel iteration. Parallel iteration is realized by the synchronized extraction of elements from disparate iterables in a manner that preserves a consistent relationship across sequences. In this context, zip() constructs an aggregated sequence in which each element encapsulates corresponding positions from each iterable. This enables analyses and transformations that depend on the simultaneous presence of related data points extracted from multiple sources. The function's design ensures that the integrity of positional correspondence is maintained during iteration, effectively creating a new perspective on the original data as an ensemble of coordinated tuples.

Theoretical and Computational Insights

From an algorithmic standpoint, the operational complexity of the zip() function is directly related to the minimum size among the involved iterables, that is, of order $O(n)$ where

$$n = \min(n_1, n_2, \ldots, n_k).$$

This linear complexity arises because the function performs a constant amount of work for each of the n tuples generated. In addition, due to the lazy nature of tuple creation, the memory overhead is minimal, as no intermediate list is formed unless explicitly converted. The design of zip() exemplifies a balance between computational efficiency and functional expressiveness, rendering it a powerful abstraction for data aggregation. Moreover, the operation of zip() embodies key concepts in parallel computation and iterator design, reinforcing principles such as data immutability during traversal and the preservation of element positionality across diverse input streams.

Python Code Snippet

```python
def custom_zip(*iterables):
    """
    Custom implementation of the built-in zip function.

    This function aggregates elements from each provided iterable in
    ↪  lockstep.
    It stops when the shortest iterable is exhausted.

    Mathematically, for iterables:
        iterable_1, iterable_2, ..., iterable_k
    the i-th tuple produced is:
        (iterable_1[i], iterable_2[i], ..., iterable_k[i])
    and the number of tuples is given by:
        n = min(len(iterable_1), len(iterable_2), ...,
        ↪  len(iterable_k))
    """
    # First, convert each iterable into its corresponding iterator
    iterators = [iter(it) for it in iterables]
    while True:
        current_tuple = []
        # Attempt to retrieve the next element from each iterator
        for it in iterators:
            try:
                current_tuple.append(next(it))
            except StopIteration:
                # One of the iterators is exhausted: end the
                ↪  iteration.
                return
        yield tuple(current_tuple)


if __name__ == "__main__":
    # Example iterables with varying lengths
    numbers = [10, 20, 30, 40]
    letters = ['a', 'b', 'c']
    flags = [True, False, True, False, True]

    # Using the built-in zip() function
    print("Built-in zip() output:")
```

```python
zipped_builtin = list(zip(numbers, letters, flags))
print(zipped_builtin)

# Using the custom_zip() implementation defined above
print("\nCustom zip() output:")
zipped_custom = list(custom_zip(numbers, letters, flags))
print(zipped_custom)

# Verify the termination condition:
# The number of aggregated tuples should equal the minimum
↪   length of the iterables.
min_length = min(len(numbers), len(letters), len(flags))
print("\nExpected number of tuples (min length):", min_length)
print("Actual number of tuples from zip():",
↪   len(zipped_builtin))

# Demonstrating parallel iteration over the aggregated tuples
print("\nParallel Iteration Demonstration:")
for idx, (num, char, flag) in enumerate(zip(numbers, letters,
↪   flags)):
    print(f"Tuple {idx}: ({num}, {char}, {flag})")

# Additional example: Processing the aggregated data
# Here we sum the numbers and concatenate the letters from the
↪   tuples.
total_sum = 0
concatenated_letters = ""
for num, char, flag in zip(numbers, letters, flags):
    total_sum += num
    concatenated_letters += char
print("\nSum of numbers:", total_sum)
print("Concatenated letters:", concatenated_letters)

# Demonstrating lazy evaluation with generators: elements are
↪   generated on-demand.
def lazy_generator(n):
    """Yield numbers from 0 to n-1 lazily while indicating
    ↪   generation."""
    for i in range(n):
        print(f"Generating value: {i}")
        yield i

print("\nUsing zip() with lazy generators:")
gen1 = lazy_generator(4)
gen2 = lazy_generator(3)
for a, b in zip(gen1, gen2):
    print(f"Received pair: ({a}, {b})")
```

Chapter 56

Enumerate and Looping with Indices

Fundamental Mechanisms of Enumerative Iteration

Within the realm of iterative processes over ordered collections, the enumerate() function furnishes a mechanism for automatic association between positional indices and their corresponding elements. At each discrete step of the iteration, the function produces a tuple of the form (i, a_i), where i stands for the zero-based index and a_i denotes the element at that particular index in the sequence. This implicit pairing obviates the necessity of external counter variables, thereby reducing the likelihood of indexing errors while streamlining the construct of sequential traversal. The abstraction provided by enumerate() encapsulates the underlying iterator protocol, ensuring that each element is accessed systematically and in lockstep with its numerical identifier, thus establishing a clear one-to-one correspondence that is both mathematically precise and computationally robust.

Mathematical Formulation and Algorithmic Efficiency

Consider an ordered sequence $A = \{a_0, a_1, \ldots, a_{n-1}\}$. The operation executed by enumerate() can be formally conceptualized as a mapping

$$\phi : \{0, 1, \ldots, n-1\} \to \{(0, a_0), (1, a_1), \ldots, (n-1, a_{n-1})\},$$

where for each index i, the correspondence is established via $\phi(i) = (i, a_i)$. This formulation ensures an isomorphic relationship between the index set and the set of produced tuples. The lazy evaluation property inherent in enumerate() guarantees that each tuple is generated on demand, thereby maintaining a constant time and space overhead per iteration, formally characterized as $O(1)$. For a sequence of length n, the complete traversal adheres to an overall time complexity of $O(n)$, ensuring that resource allocation remains optimal even when applied to large-scale data structures.

Contextual Applications and Conceptual Implications

The integration of enumerate() within iterative paradigms yields significant enhancements in algorithm design and cognitive clarity. By simultaneously extracting the index and the associated element, this function facilitates operations that inherently depend on positional information, such as conditional processing, indexed modifications, and structural verifications. The duality of information—composed of a numerical index coupled with its corresponding data element—serves as a powerful paradigm for reconciling the structural attributes of a sequence with its semantic content. This approach not only simplifies the logical flow of iterative constructs but also provides an intrinsic mechanism to validate assumptions about data ordering and integrity. The systematic pairing realized through enumerate() is particularly advantageous in contexts where the positional context is crucial, thereby supporting refined analytical operations as well as complex traversal routines without incurring additional syntactic overhead.

Python Code Snippet

```
# This script demonstrates the fundamental mathematical and
↪    algorithmic concepts
# of enumerative iteration as discussed in this chapter.
#
# Key objectives:
# 1. Use the built-in enumerate() function to automatically pair
↪    indices with elements.
# 2. Implement a custom function that mimics the mapping : {0, 1,
↪    ..., n-1} → {(0, a), (1, a), ..., (n-1, a)}.
# 3. Validate that both implementations produce identical enumerated
↪    mappings.
# 4. Illustrate the lazy evaluation property of enumerate() by
↪    retrieving elements one-by-one.
#
# The mapping  is realized implicitly by:
#     (i) = (i, a_i)
# where i is the zero-based index and a_i is the element at the i-th
↪    position.
#
# Time Complexity:
#    - Each call to next() on the enumerate iterator takes O(1) time.
#    - The overall traversal of a sequence with n elements is O(n).


def demonstrate_enumerate(sequence):
    """
    Demonstrates the use of the built-in enumerate() function.

    Parameters:
        sequence (iterable): An ordered collection of elements.

    Returns:
        list of tuples: A list where each tuple is (index, element),
        ↪    reflecting the mapping (i) = (i, a_i).
    """
    print("Enumerating using built-in enumerate():")
    enumerated_result = []
    for i, a_i in enumerate(sequence):
        # At each iteration, (i, a_i) is produced where:
        # i: current index (0-based)
        # a_i: element at position i
        print(f"Index: {i}, Element: {a_i}")
        enumerated_result.append((i, a_i))
    return enumerated_result

def custom_enumerate(sequence):
    """
    Custom implementation of enumerative mapping to replicate the
    ↪    operation of enumerate().
```

```
    This function constructs the mapping  such that for each index
↪   i:
        (i) = (i, a_i)

    Parameters:
        sequence (iterable): An ordered collection of elements.

    Returns:
        list of tuples: A list containing (index, element) pairs.
    """
    print("Enumerating using custom implementation:")
    enumerated_result = []
    for i in range(len(sequence)):
        a_i = sequence[i]
        print(f"Index: {i}, Element: {a_i}")
        enumerated_result.append((i, a_i))
    return enumerated_result


def demonstrate_lazy_evaluation(sequence):
    """
    Demonstrates the lazy evaluation property of enumerate().

    Instead of generating all (index, element) tuples at once,
    the enumerate object produces tuples on-demand using the
↪   iterator protocol.

    Parameters:
        sequence (iterable): An ordered collection of elements.
    """
    print("Demonstrating lazy evaluation with enumerate():")
    lazy_enum = enumerate(sequence)
    print("Created lazy enumerator. Using next() to retrieve tuples
↪   on demand:")
    try:
        while True:
            # Each call to next() fetches the next tuple (i, a_i)
            i, a_i = next(lazy_enum)
            print(f"Lazy Evaluation - Index: {i}, Element: {a_i}")
    except StopIteration:
        print("All elements have been enumerated using lazy
↪   evaluation.")


def main():
    # Define an ordered sequence A = { a, a, ..., a }
    A = ["apple", "banana", "cherry", "date", "elderberry"]
    print("Original Sequence A:")
    print(A)
    print("\n--- Using built-in enumerate() ---\n")
    result_builtin = demonstrate_enumerate(A)

    print("\n--- Using custom enumerate implementation ---\n")
    result_custom = custom_enumerate(A)
```

```python
    # Validate that both methods produce an isomorphic mapping of
    ↪   index to element.
    if result_builtin == result_custom:
        print("\nValidation: Both methods yield identical enumerated
        ↪   mappings.")
    else:
        print("\nValidation: There is a discrepancy between the two
        ↪   implementations.")

    print("\n--- Demonstrating Lazy Evaluation Property ---\n")
    demonstrate_lazy_evaluation(A)

if __name__ == "__main__":
    main()
```

Chapter 57

Using Command-line Arguments in Python

Fundamentals of Command-line Argument Processing

Command-line argument processing constitutes a pivotal mechanism in enabling parameterized script execution. The construct originates from a raw sequence of strings supplied by the operating system at invocation, thereby permitting the specification of variable inputs to modulate program behavior. In the Python paradigm, the sequence is typically accessed as an ordered collection, wherein the initial element represents the script identifier and subsequent tokens embody the parameters intended for dynamic execution. This mechanism facilitates an abstraction whereby the numerical order of input tokens corresponds directly to their functional roles within the application.

Structure and Representation of Argument Data

Internally, command-line arguments are represented as an ordered list

$$A = \{a_0, a_1, \ldots, a_{n-1}\},$$

where each element a_i is a string token extracted from the input interface. The convention assigns a_0 to denote the executable or script name, while indices $i \geq 1$ contain the substantive parameters that influence the program's operational configuration. Subsequent processing is required to convert these default string representations into contextually appropriate data types. This conversion process is instrumental in validating the input and enforcing a coherent mapping between the raw tokens and the program's configurational schema.

Frameworks and Approaches for Argument Parsing

The abstraction of raw command-line inputs necessitates robust frameworks that translate string sequences into structured parameter sets. Fundamentally, this translation is characterized by a mapping

$$\phi : S \rightarrow P,$$

where $S = \{s_0, s_1, \ldots, s_{n-1}\}$ represents the input token sequence and P denotes the set of processed parameters. Advanced parser configurations, as implemented in various Python modules, support both positional and optional arguments. The parsing process involves the systematic examination of each token, its classification according to predefined syntactic rules, and the subsequent assignment of semantic meaning. This approach not only enhances error detection but also abstracts the complexity of manual input handling, thereby optimally aligning the raw input stream with the program's dynamic configuration requirements.

Dynamic Parameterization and Execution Modulation

The capacity to modulate program behavior based on runtime parameters exemplifies an advanced feature of dynamic software systems. Through the processing of command-line arguments, a Python script imbues its operational logic with the flexibility to adapt to diverse execution contexts without source code modification. The arguments serve as external variables that influence conditional branches, algorithmic pathways, and functional parameters. In formal terms, the program's execution state can be expressed as a function

$$f : P \to E,$$

where P encapsulates the set of validated parameters and E represents the potential execution outcomes. This dynamic parameterization permits a detailed and responsive configuration strategy, ensuring that the program's behavior is both context-sensitive and inherently adaptable to varying operational demands.

Parser Configuration and Argument Semantics

The rigorous configuration of an argument parser involves the precise delineation of parameter semantics. This encompasses the discrimination between mandatory and optional parameters, the specification of flags and switches, and the establishment of conventions for positional dependencies. The parser operationalizes a series of validation protocols to ensure that the incoming token sequence adheres to the expected schema. Error handling mechanisms are integrated to manage inconsistencies and typographical anomalies in the input data. The resulting mapping from raw tokens to semantically enriched parameters is critical in maintaining the integrity of the program's operational configuration, thereby reinforcing the underlying architecture with a coherent and resilient input processing framework.

Python Code Snippet

```
#!/usr/bin/env python3
""" 

This script demonstrates the processing of command-line arguments in
↪    Python.
It is based on the concepts discussed in the chapter, including:

1. The raw argument list:
   A = { a_0, a_1, ..., a_{n-1} }
   where a_0 is the script name.

2. The mapping of raw tokens to processed parameters:
   phi : S -> P
```

3. *The dynamic execution mapping:*
   f : P -> E
   where P is the set of validated parameters and E is the execution
   ↪ *outcome.*

The script uses the argparse module to parse the command-line
↪ *arguments,*
supporting both positional and optional arguments.
"""

```python
import sys
import argparse

def process_arguments():
    """
    Process command-line arguments.

    Raw command-line inputs are provided as an ordered sequence:

        A = { a_0, a_1, ..., a_{n-1} }

    where a_0 is the script name and a_i (i >= 1) are the
    ↪ substantive parameters.
    We define a mapping:

        phi : S -> P

    that converts raw string tokens S into a set of processed
    ↪ parameters P.

    This function uses argparse to validate and transform inputs.
    """
    parser = argparse.ArgumentParser(
        description="Dynamic Python script to perform arithmetic
        ↪ operations (sum or prod)"
    )

    # Positional argument for operation: either 'sum' or 'prod'
    parser.add_argument(
        "operation",
        choices=["sum", "prod"],
        help="Specify the operation: 'sum' to add numbers or 'prod'
        ↪ to multiply them."
    )

    # Positional argument for a list of numbers (as floats)
    parser.add_argument(
        "numbers",
        metavar="N",
        type=float,
        nargs="+",
        help="One or more numbers to be processed."
    )
```

313

```python
    # Optional verbosity flag
    parser.add_argument(
        "--verbose",
        action="store_true",
        help="If set, output detailed internal processing
        ↪ information."
    )

    # Parse the arguments from the command-line and return the
    ↪ result as a Namespace.
    args = parser.parse_args()
    return args

def dynamic_execution(params):
    """
    Execute the operation based on validated parameters.

    This function characterizes the mapping:

        f : P -> E

    where P represents the processed parameters and E the execution
    ↪ outcome.

    Depending on the operation ('sum' or 'prod'), the function
    ↪ calculates either
    the sum or the product of the provided numbers.
    """
    operation = params.operation
    numbers = params.numbers

    if params.verbose:
        print("Verbose Mode: Enabled")
        print("Operation Selected:", operation)
        print("Input Numbers:", numbers)

    if operation == "sum":
        # Calculate the sum of the numbers.
        result = sum(numbers)
    elif operation == "prod":
        # Calculate the product of the numbers.
        result = 1.0
        for num in numbers:
            result *= num
    else:
        # This branch is not expected to be reached because argparse
        ↪ restricts 'operation'.
        raise ValueError("Unsupported operation provided!")

    return result

def main():
```

```
    """
    Main function that orchestrates the argument processing and
    ↪   dynamic execution.

    The workflow is as follows:
    1. Convert raw input A to processed parameters P using phi: S ->
    ↪   P.
    2. Map the parameters P to an execution outcome E using f: P ->
    ↪   E.
    3. Output the computed result.
    """
    # Process command-line arguments to obtain P.
    params = process_arguments()

    # Compute execution outcome E via f: P -> E.
    result = dynamic_execution(params)

    # Display the final result.
    print("Result:", result)

if __name__ == "__main__":
    main()
```

Chapter 58

The sys Module: System-specific Parameters

Architectural Overview of the sys Module

The sys module constitutes a core component within the Python runtime environment, providing a unified interface to a multitude of interpreter-specific parameters and functionalities. Its design encapsulates both the state of the interpreter and the mechanisms for interacting with system-level resources. This module emerges as an essential abstraction layer for accessing internal variables and functions that govern the behavior of the Python execution engine. The inherent organization of sys reflects a rigorous adherence to system-level conventions, thereby enabling precise control over input/output streams, interpreter configuration, and system exit protocols.

Command-line Arguments: Representation and Structural Formalism

A central feature provided by the sys module is the facility for processing command-line arguments. The argument vector is internally represented as an ordered sequence, denoted by

$$A = \{a_0, a_1, \ldots, a_{n-1}\},$$

where the element a_0 corresponds to the identifier of the executing script, and each subsequent element a_i (with $i \geq 1$) embodies a distinct parameter introduced at process invocation. This formal representation underpins the dynamic configuration capabilities of Python programs, furnishing a well-ordered framework for subsequent validation and transformation of raw input tokens into semantically enriched parameters. The deterministic ordering guaranteed by this structure facilitates systematic analysis and robust handling of input data in environments that necessitate precision and flexibility.

Interrogation of Interpreter-Specific Variables

Beyond command-line parameters, the sys module provides access to a broad spectrum of interpreter-specific variables that illuminate the internal state of the Python execution environment. Variables such as

```
sys.version
```

and

```
sys.platform
```

serve as critical indicators of the interpreter's versioning and its operational platform, respectively. These parameters allow for a detailed examination of the runtime context, enabling software to adapt its behavior in response to the nuances of the underlying hardware and operating system. The consolidation of such metadata within the sys module exemplifies a systematic approach to environmental introspection, ensuring that the interpreter's characteristics are readily available for inspection and integration into high-level application logic.

Interfacing with System-level I/O and Execution Controls

The sys module also encompasses functionalities that extend to the management of standard input, output, and error streams. Variables such as

$$\texttt{sys.stdin, \ sys.stdout, \ sys.stderr}$$

form the cornerstones of interaction between the Python interpreter and its external execution context. These interfaces permit the redirection and calibration of data flow, thereby facilitating advanced techniques in logging, diagnostics, and inter-process communication. Furthermore, the module integrates a controlled mechanism for terminating program execution through a standardized exit protocol. This precise handling of exit conditions underscores the module's role in orchestrating the termination behavior of the interpreter in accordance with prevailing system-level conventions.

Python Code Snippet

```python
import sys

def display_interpreter_info():
    """
    Display interpreter-specific information such as Python version
    ↪   and platform.
    """
    print("Interpreter Information:")
    print("------------------------")
    print("Python Version:", sys.version)
    print("Platform:", sys.platform)
    print()

def display_command_line_arguments():
    """
    Display the command-line arguments in a structured formalism.
    The arguments are represented as an ordered sequence:
        A = { a_0, a_1, ..., a_{n-1} }
    where a_0 is the script identifier and subsequent a_i are
    ↪   additional parameters.
    """
    args = sys.argv
    print("Command-line Arguments (A = {a_0, a_1, ..., a_{n-1}}):")
    for i, arg in enumerate(args):
        print(f"  a_{i}: {arg}")
    print()

def process_standard_input():
    """
    Interact with standard input, output, and error streams.
    The user can type input which will be echoed.
    Typing 'error' will trigger a sample error message to standard
    ↪   error.
```

```python
    Typing 'exit' or reaching EOF will exit the input loop.
    """
    print("Enter input (type 'exit' to quit):")
    while True:
        # Read a line from the standard input (sys.stdin)
        user_input = sys.stdin.readline().strip()

        # Check if the command to exit is given
        if user_input.lower() == 'exit' or user_input == '':
            print("Exiting input loop.")
            break

        # Echo the input using standard output (sys.stdout)
        sys.stdout.write("Echo: " + user_input + "\n")
        sys.stdout.flush()

        # If the user enters 'error', demonstrate writing to
        ↪   standard error (sys.stderr)
        if user_input.lower() == 'error':
            sys.stderr.write("Error: The input 'error' is not
            ↪   permitted as valid data.\n")
            sys.stderr.flush()
    print()


def main():
    """
    Main function to demonstrate the usage of the sys module
    ↪   functionalities.
    This includes:
        - Displaying interpreter-specific variables.
        - Representing and processing command-line arguments.
        - Interacting with system-level I/O streams.
        - Terminating program execution in a controlled manner.
    """

    display_interpreter_info()
    display_command_line_arguments()
    process_standard_input()

    # Demonstrate controlled program termination using sys.exit
    print("Terminating the program using sys.exit(0).")
    sys.exit(0)


if __name__ == "__main__":
    main()
```

Chapter 59

The os Module: Interaction with the Operating System

Architectural Underpinnings and Functional Paradigms

The os module represents a rigorously engineered interface that abstracts the heterogeneity of underlying operating system services into a cohesive and consistent programming model. Its architectural design is founded upon the principle of encapsulating low-level system calls within a high-level semantic framework, thereby permitting applications to interact with operating system internals in a platform-agnostic manner. Underlying this framework is the systematic mapping of diverse operating system functionalities—ranging from file system interactions to environmental parameter retrieval—into a unified set of function calls and variables. In this context, the module functions as an intermediary that translates invocations into corresponding native system operations while preserving invariants such as error propagation and resource management. The inherent design adheres to established operating system standards, including the *POSIX* specifications where applicable, ensuring that the abstraction maintains fidelity to the original system-level semantics and guarantees consistent behavior across varying execution contexts.

File and Directory Manipulation

The management of files and directories is a core competency offered by the os module, providing a comprehensive suite of operations for navigating and manipulating the file system. The module exposes functions that facilitate the creation, deletion, and renaming of directory structures, as well as the traversal of intricate directory trees through both absolute and relative path specifications. The representation of paths is managed with careful consideration of the distinct separator conventions and case sensitivity characteristics inherent to different file systems. Moreover, the interface systematically encapsulates operations for querying file metadata, such as access permissions, modification timestamps, and other attributes, thereby allowing for a nuanced control over file system entities. The module's design accounts for the variability and complexity of underlying storage architectures by providing an abstraction layer that transparently manages the conversion between high-level path representations and the native, system-specific constructs.

Execution of System-Level Commands and Process Interactions

Beyond file system management, the os module extends its interface to the execution of system-level commands and the management of process-related activities. The functionality provided herein includes the capability to translate textual representations of commands into discrete system calls that initiate separate processes or subprocesses. This translation is executed in strict accordance with the scheduling and process control paradigms imposed by the operating system kernel, thereby ensuring that the instantiation and termination of processes adhere to standardized protocols. The module mediates this interaction through a well-defined set of functions that abstract the nuances of command interpretation and process synchronization. In this regard, high-level invocations are systematically decomposed into their constituent system calls, with stringent error handling mechanisms employed to manage potential anomalies in process execution. The interface is meticulously designed to safeguard system integrity and to enforce a controlled interaction with the operating system's native environment, thereby enabling seamless integration of system-level operations into broader application workflows.

Python Code Snippet

```python
import os
import sys
import subprocess
import datetime

def create_directory(path):
    """
    Create a directory if it does not already exist.
    """
    try:
        if not os.path.exists(path):
            os.makedirs(path)
            print(f"Created directory: {path}")
        else:
            print(f"Directory already exists: {path}")
    except Exception as e:
        print(f"Error creating directory {path}: {e}")

def list_files_and_directories(path):
    """
    List all files and directories in the given path along with
    ↪  their metadata.
    """
    try:
        print(f"\nListing contents of directory: {path}")
        with os.scandir(path) as entries:
            for entry in entries:
                if entry.is_file():
                    info = entry.stat()
                    mod_time =
                    ↪  datetime.datetime.fromtimestamp(info.st_mtime)
                    print(f"File: {entry.name} | Size:
                    ↪  {info.st_size} bytes | Last Modified:
                    ↪  {mod_time}")
                elif entry.is_dir():
                    print(f"Directory: {entry.name}")
    except Exception as e:
        print(f"Error listing contents of {path}: {e}")

def get_directory_size(directory):
    """
    Recursively calculate the total size of all files within a
    ↪  directory.
    This algorithm walks through each subdirectory and sums up file
    ↪  sizes.
    """
```

```python
    total_size = 0
    for dirpath, dirnames, filenames in os.walk(directory):
        for file in filenames:
            file_path = os.path.join(dirpath, file)
            if os.path.exists(file_path):
                total_size += os.path.getsize(file_path)
    return total_size

def execute_system_command(command):
    """
    Execute a system-level command and capture its output.
    Uses subprocess for reliable command execution.
    """
    try:
        print(f"\nExecuting command: {command}")
        result = subprocess.run(command, shell=True, check=True,
                                stdout=subprocess.PIPE,
                           ↪    stderr=subprocess.PIPE,
                           ↪    text=True)
        print("Command Output:")
        print(result.stdout)
        if result.stderr:
            print("Command Error Output:")
            print(result.stderr)
    except subprocess.CalledProcessError as e:
        print(f"Command '{command}' failed with return code
        ↪   {e.returncode}")
        print(e.stderr)

def rename_file(old_path, new_path):
    """
    Rename a file from old_path to new_path.
    """
    try:
        if os.path.exists(old_path):
            os.rename(old_path, new_path)
            print(f"Renamed file from {old_path} to {new_path}")
        else:
            print(f"File {old_path} does not exist")
    except Exception as e:
        print(f"Error renaming file: {e}")

def delete_file(file_path):
    """
    Delete the file at file_path.
    """
    try:
        if os.path.exists(file_path):
            os.remove(file_path)
            print(f"Deleted file: {file_path}")
        else:
            print(f"File {file_path} does not exist")
    except Exception as e:
```

```python
        print(f"Error deleting file: {e}")

def main():
    # Define a base directory for demonstration purposes
    base_dir = os.path.join(os.getcwd(), "demo_os_module")
    create_directory(base_dir)

    # Create a sample text file in the base directory
    sample_file = os.path.join(base_dir, "sample.txt")
    try:
        with open(sample_file, "w") as f:
            f.write("This is a sample text file for demonstrating os
            ↪ module operations.\n")
        print(f"\nCreated sample file: {sample_file}")
    except Exception as e:
        print(f"Error creating sample file: {e}")

    # List contents in the base directory
    list_files_and_directories(base_dir)

    # Calculate and print the total size of the base directory
    dir_size = get_directory_size(base_dir)
    print(f"\nTotal size of directory '{base_dir}' is: {dir_size}
    ↪ bytes")

    # Rename the sample file to a new name
    renamed_file = os.path.join(base_dir, "renamed_sample.txt")
    rename_file(sample_file, renamed_file)

    # Execute a system command to list directory contents
    # Use a cross-platform command: 'dir' for Windows, 'ls -l' for
    ↪ Unix-like systems.
    command = f"dir {base_dir}" if os.name == "nt" else f"ls -l
    ↪ {base_dir}"
    execute_system_command(command)

    # Delete the renamed file
    delete_file(renamed_file)

    # Clean up by removing the directory (will only succeed if
    ↪ directory is empty)
    try:
        os.rmdir(base_dir)
        print(f"\nRemoved directory: {base_dir}")
    except Exception as e:
        print(f"Error removing directory {base_dir}: {e}")

if __name__ == "__main__":
    main()
```

Chapter 60

File Paths and Directory Management with os and pathlib

Foundations of File Path Abstraction and Cross-Platform Uniformity

File paths represent more than mere string sequences; they constitute an intricate abstraction layer that bridges the complexities of varied file system architectures. The heterogeneity inherent in operating system conventions—such as the distinction between case sensitivity in *UNIX* and *Windows* environments—necessitates a mechanism that normalizes these differences. This abstraction is achieved by encapsulating hierarchically structured directory identifiers and file names into a coherent model that is both semantically rigorous and operationally robust. The design underpinning file path management integrates considerations of symbolic links, relative and absolute path distinctions, and the maintenance of metadata consistency, thereby ensuring that operations across disparate systems yield reliable and predictable outcomes.

Systematic File and Directory Operations via the os Module

The os module furnishes a procedural interface that maps high-level file system operations directly onto underlying system calls. This interface implements a set of deterministic routines that cover activities such as directory traversal, file metadata extraction, and the manipulation of path elements. Each routine adheres to a strict error propagation model, reflecting the native semantics of the operating system. Underlying functions perform explicit actions—such as concatenation of path segments, normalization of separator characters, and environment variable resolution—that are critical for maintaining the integrity of file system interactions. The procedural design ensures that every operation conforms to the established protocols of the host system, accommodating variations in file system encodings and directory structure paradigms. As a result, the os module serves as a dependable intermediary, reconciling low-level system intricacies with high-level operational requirements while preserving cross-platform consistency.

The Object-Oriented Paradigm of Path Management via pathlib

In contrast to the procedural paradigm, the pathlib module introduces an object-oriented framework that encapsulates file path manipulation within an immutable, context-aware structure. Here, paths are treated as first-class objects, endowed with methods that facilitate both the inspection and the transformation of file system entities. This paradigm supports method chaining and operator overloading, which streamline complex operations such as file resolution, property querying, and hierarchical traversal. The integrated design abstracts the underlying system details—such as divergent separator conventions and platform-specific path resolution rules—thereby enabling a more expressive formulation of file system logic. In this framework, the object representation of paths is intrinsically aligned with the operational semantics of both local and remote environments, ensuring that manipulations remain robust even under dynamic runtime conditions. The pathlib approach advances the state of file path handling by embedding cross-platform intelligence into the core of its object model, thereby providing a versatile and scalable solution for modern file system management.

Python Code Snippet

```python
import os
from pathlib import Path

def demo_os_operations():
    """
    Demonstrates file path and directory operations using the os
    ↪   module.

    Key operations:
        - Joining path segments to build a file path.
        - Normalizing the file path to conform with the host OS.
        - Checking for existence and creating directories/files as
        ↪   needed.
        - Listing directory contents with type checking (directory or
        ↪   file).
    """
    # Get the current working directory
    cwd = os.getcwd()
    print("Current Working Directory:", cwd)

    # Join path segments to create a new file path
    joined_path = os.path.join(cwd, "subdir", "file.txt")
    print("Joined Path:", joined_path)

    # Normalize the path (this resolves redundant separators and
    ↪   up-level references)
    normalized_path = os.path.normpath(joined_path)
    print("Normalized Path:", normalized_path)

    # Check if the file exists; if not, create the necessary
    ↪   directories and file.
    if os.path.exists(normalized_path):
        print("Path exists:", normalized_path)
    else:
        print("Path does not exist. Creating directories and file
        ↪   at:", normalized_path)
        try:
            # Create the directory path if it doesn't exist
            os.makedirs(os.path.dirname(normalized_path),
            ↪   exist_ok=True)
            # Create a new file and write a short demo text
            with open(normalized_path, "w") as file:
                file.write("Demo file created using os module.\n")
        except Exception as e:
            print("Error creating file or directory:", e)
```

```python
    # List the contents of the directory where the file was created
    directory = os.path.dirname(normalized_path)
    print("Listing directory contents for:", directory)
    try:
        for item in os.listdir(directory):
            item_path = os.path.join(directory, item)
            item_type = "Directory" if os.path.isdir(item_path) else
            ↪    "File"
            print(f"  - {item} ({item_type})")
    except Exception as e:
        print("Error listing directory contents:", e)


def demo_pathlib_operations():
    """
    Demonstrates file path operations using the pathlib module.

    Key operations:
      - Constructing paths using the '/' operator.
      - Resolving paths to absolute form.
      - Querying file attributes such as name, parent directory, and
      ↪   suffix.
      - Creating files using pathlib and recursively searching for
      ↪   files.
    """
    # Construct a Path object for the current working directory
    current_path = Path.cwd()
    print("Using pathlib, current directory is:", current_path)

    # Build a new path by chaining path segments using the '/'
    ↪    operator
    path_obj = current_path / "subdir" / "file.txt"
    print("Constructed Path using pathlib:", path_obj)

    # Resolve the path to get an absolute path
    try:
        absolute_path = path_obj.resolve(strict=False)
        print("Absolute Path:", absolute_path)
    except Exception as e:
        print("Error resolving path:", e)

    # If the file exists, display its attributes; otherwise, create
    ↪    it.
    if path_obj.exists():
        print("File Name:", path_obj.name)
        print("Parent Directory:", path_obj.parent)
        print("File Suffix:", path_obj.suffix)
        try:
            size = path_obj.stat().st_size
            print("File Size (bytes):", size)
        except Exception as e:
            print("Error accessing file stats:", e)
    else:
```

328

```
        print("Path does not exist. Creating file for
        ↪  demonstration.")
        try:
            # Ensure the parent directories exist, then write text
            ↪  to the file
            path_obj.parent.mkdir(parents=True, exist_ok=True)
            path_obj.write_text("Demo file created using pathlib
            ↪  module.\n")
        except Exception as e:
            print("Error creating file with pathlib:", e)

    # Recursively list all .txt files in 'subdir'
    print("Recursively searching for .txt files in:",
    ↪  path_obj.parent)
    for txt_file in path_obj.parent.rglob("*.txt"):
        print("Found text file:", txt_file)

def recursive_directory_traversal(path_obj):
    """
    Recursively traverses a directory structure using pathlib.

    This function represents an algorithm that explores directories
    ↪  and files.
    For every directory, it prints the directory name and iterates
    ↪  over its children.
    For files, it simply prints the file path.
    """
    if path_obj.is_dir():
        print("Directory:", path_obj)
        # Iterate over each item in the directory
        for child in path_obj.iterdir():
            recursive_directory_traversal(child)
    else:
        print("File:", path_obj)

if __name__ == "__main__":
    print("Demo: os module file path operations")
    demo_os_operations()

    print("\nDemo: pathlib module file path operations")
    demo_pathlib_operations()

    print("\nDemo: Recursive Directory Traversal using pathlib")
    # Start traversal from the 'subdir' directory created earlier
    start_path = Path.cwd() / "subdir"
    recursive_directory_traversal(start_path)
```

Chapter 61

Using the pickle Module for Object Serialization

Foundational Concepts of Object Serialization

Object serialization denotes the systematic conversion of in-memory data structures into a linear, byte-oriented representation that encapsulates both the intrinsic state and the interrelationships among constituent objects. This process entails the transformation of dynamic, hierarchical, and potentially cyclic object graphs into a streamed format amenable to storage, transmission, and later reconstitution. In this context, the term serialization is employed to describe the methodical reduction of complex software objects into a representation that preserves sufficient metadata—such as type information, attribute mappings, and reference identities—to enable complete state reconstruction. The procedure operates on the principle that every object, whether elementary or composite, may be decomposed into fundamental constituents whose serial form reflects the original structure, thus ensuring consistency upon deserialization.

The pickle Module: Design, Protocols, and Mechanisms

The pickle module is a core component within the Python standard library that facilitates the serialization and deserialization of Python objects. Its implementation is grounded on a series of protocols, each corresponding to distinct trade-offs between human-readability, efficiency, and backward compatibility. Early protocols were designed for simplicity and portability, while subsequent iterations have introduced optimizations that better accommodate large and complex object graphs. The module employs a deterministic traversal of an object's namespace, assigning unique identifiers to repeated references and resolving cyclic dependencies. This methodical approach ensures that multiple references to the same object within the original data structure are faithfully preserved in the sequential representation, thus maintaining object identity and reducing redundancy. Such design choices reflect a deep understanding of the dynamic and often unpredictable nature of Python's object model.

Preservation of Object State and Its Complexities

The preservation of object state via the pickle module necessitates a comprehensive capture of both explicit attributes and the implicit properties that define an object's behavior. The serialization process scrutinizes the internal state—typically represented by an object's attribute dictionary—and aggregates additional metadata that describes the object's class, inheritance hierarchy, and dynamic properties. During serialization, every attribute and reference is encoded in a manner that supports later reconstruction, thereby ensuring that the deserialized object mirrors the original in both structure and semantics. The conversion process copes effectively with nested objects, recursive data structures, and interdependent references by embedding markers and type descriptors within the byte stream. Such meticulous preservation extends not only to static user-defined objects but also to built-in types whose state may be derived from complex internal invariants. The fidelity of object state retention, therefore, is contingent upon the pickle module's capacity to introspect and serialize diverse attributes with precision.

Security Considerations and Limitations of Pickle Mechanisms

The flexibility inherent in the pickle module's design introduces notable security implications, particularly with respect to the deserialization of untrusted data. Since the process of reconstructing objects from a byte stream involves the instantiation and execution of object initializers, it may inadvertently permit the activation of arbitrary constructors, thus engendering potential vulnerabilities. This capability, while central to the module's power, demands a cautious approach to handling serialized data from uncertain origins. Moreover, the evolution of pickle protocols has occasionally precipitated challenges in backward compatibility, as improvements in efficiency and format may alter the interpretation of serialized data across different versions of the Python interpreter. Such constraints necessitate a rigorous analysis of the operational context in which object serialization is applied, particularly in environments where data integrity and security are paramount. The balance achieved by the pickle module between expressive versatility and the attendant risks underscores the need for judicious application when managing serialized objects.

Python Code Snippet

```python
import pickle

# Custom class to demonstrate object serialization with cyclic
↪    references
class CustomObject:
    def __init__(self, name, value):
        self.name = name
        self.value = value
        self.reference = None   # Placeholder for creating a cyclic
        ↪    reference

    def __repr__(self):
        return f"CustomObject(name={self.name!r},
        ↪    value={self.value!r})"

    # Customizing pickling behavior with __getstate__ and
    ↪    __setstate__
```

```python
    def __getstate__(self):
        # Return state as a copy of the attribute dictionary
        state = self.__dict__.copy()
        # Debug: state before pickling can be logged or manipulated
        ↪   here
        return state

    def __setstate__(self, state):
        # Restore instance attributes
        self.__dict__.update(state)

# Function to demonstrate handling of cyclic references and multiple
↪   references
def cyclic_reference_demo():
    print("=== Cyclic Reference Demo ===")
    # Create two objects that reference each other
    obj1 = CustomObject("Object1", 100)
    obj2 = CustomObject("Object2", 200)
    obj1.reference = obj2
    obj2.reference = obj1

    # Place both objects in a list structure
    data = [obj1, obj2]

    # Serialize the data using the highest available protocol
    serialized_data = pickle.dumps(data,
    ↪   protocol=pickle.HIGHEST_PROTOCOL)
    print("Serialized Data (byte stream):", serialized_data)

    # Deserialize back into Python objects
    deserialized_data = pickle.loads(serialized_data)
    obj1_loaded, obj2_loaded = deserialized_data

    print("Deserialized obj1:", obj1_loaded)
    print("Deserialized obj2:", obj2_loaded)
    # Verify cyclicity: check if the references are correctly
    ↪   re-established
    print("Cyclic check:",
          obj1_loaded.reference is obj2_loaded,
          obj2_loaded.reference is obj1_loaded)

# Function to demonstrate pickling of various built-in data types
def builtin_types_demo():
    print("\n=== Built-in Types Demo ===")
    sample_dict = {
        'integer': 42,
        'float': 3.1415,
        'string': 'pickle serialization',
        'list': [1, 2, 3, 4],
        'tuple': (5, 6, 7),
        'set': {8, 9, 10}
    }
    # Serialize the dictionary
```

```python
    serialized_dict = pickle.dumps(sample_dict,
    ↪   protocol=pickle.HIGHEST_PROTOCOL)
    # Deserialize the dictionary
    loaded_dict = pickle.loads(serialized_dict)

    print("Original Dictionary:", sample_dict)
    print("Deserialized Dictionary:", loaded_dict)

# Function to showcase exception handling during deserialization of
↪   corrupted data
def exception_handling_demo():
    print("\n=== Exception Handling Demo ===")
    try:
        # Create simple serialized data and corrupt it by slicing
        ↪   off bytes
        valid_data = pickle.dumps({"key": "value"},
        ↪   protocol=pickle.HIGHEST_PROTOCOL)
        corrupted_data = valid_data[:-10]   # Intentionally corrupt
        ↪   data
        _ = pickle.loads(corrupted_data)
    except Exception as e:
        print("Exception caught during deserialization:", str(e))

def main():
    print("Pickle Module Demonstration\n")
    cyclic_reference_demo()
    builtin_types_demo()
    exception_handling_demo()
    print("\nDemonstration Complete.")

if __name__ == "__main__":
    main()
```

Chapter 62

Object-Oriented Programming: Classes and Objects

Conceptualization of Classes

In object-oriented programming, a class is defined as an abstract blueprint that encapsulates both data and behavior within a unified structure. A class specifies the attributes, which represent the state, and the methods, which embody the operations that act upon that state. This conceptualization enables the systematic modeling of domain entities by segregating the intrinsic properties of an entity from the operations that manipulate those properties. The deliberate structuring inherent to a class establishes a framework in which complex systems are decomposed into manageable, interrelated components.

Definition and Composition of Class Structures

A rigorous definition of a class involves an exhaustive delineation of its constituent elements. Attributes, conceived as variables, capture the internal state of an instance, whereas methods delineate the set of operations permissible on that state. The organization of these elements adheres to the principles of encapsulation, ensuring that the internal representation of an object is accessible only through well-defined interfaces. This approach not only reinforces data integrity but also facilitates a clear demarcation between the interface and the underlying implementation. The structured composition of a class typically includes constructors for initialization and may also incorporate mechanisms for controlled deallocation, all of which contribute to the disciplined management of resources.

Instantiation and Object Creation

The process of instantiation transforms a class from an abstract definition into a tangible object. During object creation, memory is allocated to house the instance's state, and initialization routines are invoked to assign initial values to its attributes. Each object instantiated from a class retains a unique identity, while simultaneously conforming to the structural and behavioral specifications prescribed by its class. The instantiation mechanism embodies the separation between the abstract blueprint and its concrete realization, permitting the coexistence of multiple objects derived from a single class definition. This paradigm ensures that while objects share a common design, their individual states remain distinct and subject to independent evolution over the course of execution.

Binding of State and Behavior

The core of the object-oriented paradigm is the intrinsic binding of state and behavior within an object. The state is encapsulated in a set of attributes that define the current configuration of the object, whereas behavior is articulated through methods that operate on this state. This coupling ensures that all interactions with an object are mediated through its defined interface, thereby enforcing encapsulation and maintaining internal consistency. The binding of state and behavior provides a coherent semantic structure that governs how an object responds to external messages and stimuli. As a consequence, the object-oriented framework facilitates a systematic approach to modeling dynamic systems, wherein the evolution of state is intricately linked to the operations that modify it.

Python Code Snippet

```python
import math

class EquationSolver:
    """
    A class to solve quadratic equations of the form: ax^2 + bx + c
    ↪   = 0
    """
    def __init__(self, a, b, c):
        # Initialize coefficients for the quadratic equation
        self.a = a
        self.b = b
        self.c = c

    def discriminant(self):
        # Calculate the discriminant: b^2 - 4ac
        return self.b**2 - 4 * self.a * self.c

    def solve(self):
        """
        Solve the quadratic equation using the quadratic formula.
        Returns:
            A list of real roots if they exist, or a message
            ↪   indicating no real roots.
        """
        disc = self.discriminant()
        if disc < 0:
            return "No real roots"
        elif disc == 0:
            return [-self.b / (2 * self.a)]
        else:
            root1 = (-self.b + math.sqrt(disc)) / (2 * self.a)
            root2 = (-self.b - math.sqrt(disc)) / (2 * self.a)
            return [root1, root2]

class Shape:
    """
    An abstract class representing a geometric shape.
    This class demonstrates the binding of state (attributes) and
    ↪   behavior (methods).
    """
    def __init__(self, name):
        self.name = name  # Name of the shape

    def area(self):
        # Abstract method for computing the area
        raise NotImplementedError("Subclasses must implement this
        ↪   method!")

    def perimeter(self):
        # Abstract method for computing the perimeter
```

```python
        raise NotImplementedError("Subclasses must implement this
        ↪    method!")

    def __str__(self):
        # Provides a string representation combining the shape's
        ↪    state and behavior
        return f"{self.name} with area: {self.area():.2f} and
        ↪    perimeter: {self.perimeter():.2f}"

class Rectangle(Shape):
    """
    A Rectangle is defined by its width and height.
    It demonstrates inheritance and encapsulation by extending the
    ↪    Shape class.
    """
    def __init__(self, width, height):
        super().__init__("Rectangle")
        self.width = width
        self.height = height

    def area(self):
        # Compute the area of the rectangle
        return self.width * self.height

    def perimeter(self):
        # Compute the perimeter of the rectangle
        return 2 * (self.width + self.height)

class Circle(Shape):
    """
    A Circle is defined by its radius.
    This subclass extends the Shape class and overrides the area and
    ↪    perimeter methods.
    """
    def __init__(self, radius):
        super().__init__("Circle")
        self.radius = radius

    def area(self):
        # Compute the area of the circle
        return math.pi * (self.radius ** 2)

    def perimeter(self):
        # Compute the circumference of the circle
        return 2 * math.pi * self.radius

def main():
    # Demonstrate the EquationSolver for the quadratic equation: x^2
    ↪    - 3x + 2 = 0
    print("Quadratic Equation Solver Example:")
    solver = EquationSolver(1, -3, 2)
    roots = solver.solve()
    print("The roots of the equation x^2 - 3x + 2 = 0 are:", roots)
```

338

```python
    # Demonstrate object instantiation and binding of state and
    ↪   behavior using Shape classes
    print("\nShape Calculations Example:")
    rectangle = Rectangle(3, 4)   # Instantiate a Rectangle with
    ↪   width=3 and height=4
    circle = Circle(5)            # Instantiate a Circle with
    ↪   radius=5

    shapes = [rectangle, circle]
    for shape in shapes:
        print(shape)

if __name__ == "__main__":
    main()
```

Chapter 63

Defining Methods, Attributes, and the ___init___ Method

Instance Attributes as Encapsulated State

A central aspect of class design in contemporary object-oriented paradigms is the systematic encapsulation of state via instance attributes. These attributes constitute the individual data elements or properties that characterize an object, thereby defining its unique configuration within the class framework. The careful declaration and management of these attributes facilitate the segregation of internal state from the external interface. In a rigorous implementation, attributes are not merely storage mechanisms but are integral components that participate in defining an object's invariant properties and permissible state transitions. The analytic formulation of such attributes often necessitates explicit adherence to naming conventions and data type specifications, ensuring consistency and predictability across diverse instance populations. The encapsulation provided by this design not only aids in preventing unintended interference with object state but also promotes clear semantic boundaries between the object's internal mechanics and its externally observable behavior.

Instance Methods and Their Semantic Role

Complementing the state encapsulated by instance attributes is the suite of instance methods, which articulate the functional behavior associated with a class's instances. These methods are defined as operations that can manipulate, transform, or expose the attributes of an object, thereby engendering a dynamic interplay between state and behavior. The design of instance methods requires a precise understanding of the underlying object model; each method implicitly receives a reference to the object itself, enabling coherent access to its attributes and a consistent modification of its state. Such methods are not isolated functions but are deeply intertwined with the object's identity, contributing to the coherent execution of algorithms that operate on state. The careful delineation of method responsibilities, their input parameters, and the expected output is paramount; this delineation ensures that the object's interface remains both robust and reflective of its intended operational semantics.

Initialization via the ___init___ Method

The ___init___ method occupies a distinguished role in the lifecycle of an object by providing the primary mechanism for state initialization during instantiation. Upon allocation of memory for a new object instance, the ___init___ method is invoked to assign initial values to the instance attributes, thereby establishing a well-defined starting state. This process of initialization is not merely a procedural formality; instead, it embodies critical design decisions that dictate the operational readiness and internal consistency of the object. The structure of the ___init___ method often reflects a systematic decomposition of the initialization process, wherein dependencies between attributes are resolved, and invariants critical to the class's integrity are enforced. In this context, the ___init___ method serves as an essential point of integration that binds the abstract class definition to its concrete representation. Through the establishment of initial conditions, it ensures that subsequent method invocations operate upon a rigorously defined and predictable state, thereby reinforcing the disciplined management of object resources within the overarching system architecture.

Python Code Snippet

```python
import math

class QuadraticEquation:
    """
    A class to represent a quadratic equation of the form:

        ax² + bx + c = 0

    This class encapsulates the coefficients as instance attributes
    ↪ and
    provides methods to compute the discriminant and solve the
    ↪ equation
    using the quadratic formula.
    """

    def __init__(self, a, b, c):
        """
        Initialize the QuadraticEquation instance with coefficients
        ↪ a, b, and c.

        Parameters:
            a (float): Coefficient of x².
            b (float): Coefficient of x.
            c (float): Constant term.
        """
        self.a = a
        self.b = b
        self.c = c

    def discriminant(self):
        """
        Compute the discriminant of the quadratic equation.

        Returns:
            float: The discriminant, calculated as b² - 4ac.
        """
        return self.b ** 2 - 4 * self.a * self.c

    def solve(self):
        """
        Solve the quadratic equation using the quadratic formula.

        Returns:
            list: A list of roots.
                - For a quadratic equation (a  0):
                    * Two distinct real roots if discriminant > 0.
                    * One real root (repeated) if discriminant ==
                    ↪ 0.
                    * Two complex roots if discriminant < 0.
```

```
            - For a linear equation (a == 0 and b   0), returns
          ↪   a single root.

    Raises:
        ValueError: If the equation is invalid (i.e., a == 0 and
          ↪   b == 0).
    """
    # Handle linear case: when a is zero, the equation reduces
      ↪   to bx + c = 0.
    if self.a == 0:
        if self.b != 0:
            return [-self.c / self.b]
        else:
            raise ValueError("Invalid equation: both a and b are
              ↪   zero. No solution exists.")

    D = self.discriminant()

    if D > 0:
        # Two distinct real roots.
        root1 = (-self.b + math.sqrt(D)) / (2 * self.a)
        root2 = (-self.b - math.sqrt(D)) / (2 * self.a)
        return [root1, root2]
    elif D == 0:
        # One repeated real root.
        root = -self.b / (2 * self.a)
        return [root]
    else:
        # Two complex roots.
        real_part = -self.b / (2 * self.a)
        imag_part = math.sqrt(-D) / (2 * self.a)
        return [complex(real_part, imag_part),
          ↪   complex(real_part, -imag_part)]

def __str__(self):
    """
    Return a string representation of the quadratic equation.
    """
    # Construct the equation string with proper handling of
      ↪   signs.
    equation = f"{self.a}x\u00B2 "
    equation += f"+ {self.b}x " if self.b >= 0 else f"-
      ↪   {abs(self.b)}x "
    equation += f"+ {self.c}" if self.c >= 0 else f"-
      ↪   {abs(self.c)}"
    equation += " = 0"
    return equation

# Example usage of the QuadraticEquation class
if __name__ == '__main__':
    # Create an instance for the equation: x² - 3x + 2 = 0
    equation = QuadraticEquation(1, -3, 2)
```

```python
print("Quadratic Equation:", equation)
print("Discriminant:", equation.discriminant())

try:
    roots = equation.solve()
    print("Roots of the equation:", roots)
except ValueError as e:
    print("Error:", e)
```

Chapter 64

Inheritance and Method Overriding

Foundations of Inheritance

Inheritance constitutes a core paradigm within object-oriented systems, wherein a new class is formulated by extending an existing class through the establishment of an inheritance relationship. Such a relationship engenders a hierarchical structure that delineates a *superclass*—which encapsulates generalized properties and behaviors—and one or more *subclasses* that inherit these qualities while possessing the ability to introduce specialized features. This mechanism facilitates the abstraction of shared functionality, thus reducing redundancy and promoting a modular architectural design. In the context of rigorous software engineering, the deliberate reuse of code via inheritance supports both conceptual clarity and effective maintenance, as alterations to the generalized behavior in the superclass can propagate in a controlled manner to the subclasses. The formalization of this relationship is often represented in diagrammatic models and is underpinned by theoretical constructs such as the *is-a* relation, which rigorously defines the semantic correctness of the inheritance hierarchy.

Mechanics of Method Overriding

Method overriding emerges as a key facet that enables subclasses to refine or replace the implementation of methods inherited from a superclass. This process involves declaring a method in the subclass that bears an identical signature to that of the method in the superclass, while providing an alternative definition tailored to the specific behaviors intended for instances of the subclass. Overriding is instrumental in facilitating runtime polymorphism, where the invocation of a method on a reference that denotes a superclass type dynamically dispatches the call to the subclass implementation during execution. The overriding mechanism demands a strict adherence to type compatibility, ensuring that the contract defined by the superclass is preserved despite the introduction of specialized behavior. This form of bespoke redefinition enhances the adaptability of the design and supports the principle that, while the overarching interface remains invariant, the underlying operational semantics can be modified to address new or refined requirements.

Integration of Inheritance and Overriding in Behavioral Customization

The synthesis of inheritance with method overriding engenders a design architecture in which extended classes not only assimilate existing functionalities but also possess the capacity to customize and enhance them. In this framework, the strategic redefinition of methods allows for the alteration of dynamic behavior in accordance with the specific needs of distinct application domains. Such customization enhances the expressiveness and utility of the object-oriented model by enabling subclasses to implement refined algorithms, adjust invariants, and enforce domain-specific constraints while maintaining a consistent interface defined by the superordinate abstraction. Moreover, the deliberate maintenance of method signatures across the hierarchy ensures that substituted implementations are congruent with the expectations of polymorphic operations. This interplay between inherited structure and overridden behavior exemplifies the paradigm of ad hoc polymorphism, where dynamic dispatch mechanisms yield objects that respond to method invocations in a manner coherent with their extended roles. The meticulous integration of these concepts lays the groundwork for robust, scalable, and semantically rich software systems.

Python Code Snippet

```python
# Import math for mathematical operations
import math

class EquationSolver:
    """
    Base class for solving equations.
    Defines the interface for equation solvers.
    """
    def solve(self):
        raise NotImplementedError("Subclasses must implement the
        ↪   solve method.")

class LinearEquationSolver(EquationSolver):
    """
    Solves linear equations of the form: a*x + b = 0
    """
    def __init__(self, a, b):
        self.a = a
        self.b = b

    def solve(self):
        # Check if the equation is degenerate
        if self.a == 0:
            if self.b == 0:
                return "Infinite solutions (all x satisfy the
                ↪   equation)"
            else:
                return "No solution (inconsistent equation)"
        # Compute the solution: x = -b / a
        return -self.b / self.a

class QuadraticEquationSolver(EquationSolver):
    """
    Solves quadratic equations of the form: a*x^2 + b*x + c = 0.
    Uses the quadratic formula: x = (-b ± sqrt(b^2 - 4*a*c)) / (2*a)
    """
    def __init__(self, a, b, c):
        self.a = a
        self.b = b
        self.c = c

    def solve(self):
        # Handle the degenerate case where a is 0 (linear equation)
        if self.a == 0:
            return LinearEquationSolver(self.b, self.c).solve()

        discriminant = self.b**2 - 4 * self.a * self.c

        if discriminant > 0:
            # Two distinct real roots
```

```python
            root1 = (-self.b + math.sqrt(discriminant)) / (2 *
            ↪  self.a)
            root2 = (-self.b - math.sqrt(discriminant)) / (2 *
            ↪  self.a)
            return (root1, root2)
        elif discriminant == 0:
            # One real repeated root
            return -self.b / (2 * self.a)
        else:
            # Complex roots
            real_part = -self.b / (2 * self.a)
            imaginary_part = math.sqrt(-discriminant) / (2 * self.a)
            return (complex(real_part, imaginary_part),
            ↪  complex(real_part, -imaginary_part))


def main():
    """
    Demonstrate the use of inheritance and method overriding with
    equation solving examples.
    """
    # Solve a linear equation: 2*x + 4 = 0 should yield x = -2.0
    linear_solver = LinearEquationSolver(2, 4)
    linear_result = linear_solver.solve()
    print("Linear Equation (2*x + 4 = 0) Solution:", linear_result)

    # Solve a quadratic equation with real roots:
    # x^2 - 5*x + 6 = 0 should yield x = 2 and x = 3
    quadratic_solver = QuadraticEquationSolver(1, -5, 6)
    quadratic_result = quadratic_solver.solve()
    print("Quadratic Equation (x^2 - 5*x + 6 = 0) Solutions:",
    ↪  quadratic_result)

    # Solve a quadratic equation with complex roots:
    # x^2 + 2*x + 5 = 0 should yield complex solutions.
    quadratic_complex_solver = QuadraticEquationSolver(1, 2, 5)
    quadratic_complex_result = quadratic_complex_solver.solve()
    print("Quadratic Equation (x^2 + 2*x + 5 = 0) Complex
    ↪  Solutions:", quadratic_complex_result)


if __name__ == "__main__":
    main()
```

Chapter 65

Encapsulation and Data Hiding

Conceptual Foundations of Encapsulation

Encapsulation represents an essential object-oriented paradigm that aggregates an object's state and the operations acting upon that state into a unified abstraction. This design principle enforces a clear separation between the external interface and the underlying implementation, thereby safeguarding the internal representation from arbitrary and uncontrolled manipulation. The formal notion of encapsulation can be expressed by considering an object with state S and associated functions f_i such that every operation satisfies the invariant condition $I(f_i(S)) = I(S)$; here, I denotes a predicate verifying the consistency and integrity of S. Such a formulation underscores the deliberate isolation of critical data, ensuring that any alteration is mediated solely through a controlled set of operations which maintain the object's intended behavior.

Mechanisms for Protecting Class Data

Data hiding is achieved through a series of disciplined techniques that restrict direct access to an object's internal data. This is accomplished through the use of access specifiers in languages that support them, where members declared as private or protected are inaccessible from external entities except through predefined access methods. In environments lacking explicit access control, naming

349

conventions and design patterns serve a similar purpose, establishing boundary contracts that demarcate the internal state from the public interface. These strategies include defensive data copying, controlled exposure via accessor and mutator methods, and the enforcement of invariants that act as guards in the implementation. The systematic deployment of these techniques ensures that class data remains consistent and insulated from inadvertent or unauthorized modifications, thereby reinforcing the structural integrity of the software system.

Architectural Implications in Object-Oriented Systems

The rigorous application of encapsulation and data hiding yields significant benefits at the architectural level of software design. By constraining how and where object state is accessed and modified, encapsulation inherently reduces inter-module coupling, which in turn enhances modularity and facilitates independent evolution of system components. This restricted interaction pattern promotes a disciplined structure in which components interact exclusively via well-defined interfaces, alleviating the risk of unintended side effects in a dynamic system environment. Moreover, the isolation of internal details simplifies both reasoning about and maintaining the system, as each component adheres to a minimal interface that guarantees predictable behavior. The resultant architecture not only exhibits improved reliability and maintainability but also aligns with fundamental principles of robust system design, such as separation of concerns and single responsibility.

Python Code Snippet

```
class BankAccount:
    def __init__(self, initial_balance: float):
        """
        Initialize the bank account with a non-negative initial
        ↪  balance.
        This represents the object state S. The invariant I(S) is
        ↪  that the balance must be non-negative.
        """
        if initial_balance < 0:
            raise ValueError("Initial balance cannot be negative")
```

```python
        self.__balance = initial_balance  # Encapsulated (private)
        ↪   attribute
        self.__check_invariant()

    def deposit(self, amount: float) -> float:
        """
        Deposit a positive amount into the account.
        This method serves as one of the operations f_i that
        ↪   transform the state S.
        The invariant I(f_i(S)) = I(S) is enforced after updating
        ↪   the state.
        """
        if amount <= 0:
            raise ValueError("Deposit amount must be positive")
        self.__balance += amount
        self.__check_invariant()
        return self.__balance

    def withdraw(self, amount: float) -> float:
        """
        Withdraw a positive amount from the account if sufficient
        ↪   funds exist.
        This method also represents an operation f_i, and
        ↪   post-operation it rechecks the invariant.
        """
        if amount <= 0:
            raise ValueError("Withdrawal amount must be positive")
        if amount > self.__balance:
            raise ValueError("Insufficient funds for withdrawal")
        self.__balance -= amount
        self.__check_invariant()
        return self.__balance

    def __check_invariant(self) -> bool:
        """
        Private method to ensure the invariant I(S) holds.
        In this case, I(S): balance is non-negative.
        This check simulates the formal expression: I(f_i(S)) = I(S)
        """
        if self.__balance < 0:
            raise Exception("Invariant violation: Negative balance
            ↪   detected")
        return True

    def get_balance(self) -> float:
        """
        Public accessor method for the current balance.
        Direct access to __balance is prevented to support data
        ↪   hiding.
        """
        return self.__balance
```

```python
# Demonstration of the encapsulation paradigm and invariant
↪    enforcement
if __name__ == "__main__":
    # Create a bank account with an initial balance of 100.0
    account = BankAccount(100.0)
    print("Initial Balance:", account.get_balance())

    # Deposit 50.0 and check the updated balance
    updated_balance = account.deposit(50.0)
    print("After deposit of 50.0, Balance:", updated_balance)

    # Withdraw 30.0 and check the updated balance
    updated_balance = account.withdraw(30.0)
    print("After withdrawal of 30.0, Balance:", updated_balance)

    # Uncomment the lines below to see the invariant enforcement in
    ↪    action:
    # Attempting an invalid withdrawal that would breach the
    ↪    invariant (negative balance)
    # updated_balance = account.withdraw(150.0)
    # print("After attempting an invalid withdrawal, Balance:",
    ↪    updated_balance)
```

Chapter 66

Polymorphism and Operator Overloading

Foundational Concepts of Polymorphism

1 Definition and Conceptual Framework

Polymorphism is a fundamental attribute of object-oriented design that permits elements of different classes to be treated as instances of a common superclass. Formally, if an object o is an instance of a subclass S and S is derived from a superclass T, then o may be used in any context that expects an element of type T. This substitution is governed by the Liskov Substitution Principle, which asserts that objects of a derived type must be substitutable for objects of the base type without altering the correctness of the program. Such a framework enables the definition of generic interfaces where the specific details of an object's implementation remain abstracted behind a common contract. In type-theoretic terms, this can be expressed as an inclusion relation $S \subseteq T$, where the operations defined on T are guaranteed to behave correctly when applied to instances of S.

2 Polymorphism in Hierarchical Type Systems

In hierarchical type systems, polymorphism emerges naturally through inheritance and interface implementation. The inherent structure allows classes to define specialized behaviors while still conforming to a general interface. Dynamic dispatch mechanisms ensure that the method corresponding to the actual type of the object is invoked, regardless of the type through which the object is accessed. Such mechanisms are formalized by binding operations at runtime, thereby enabling a single interface to accommodate a spectrum of different behaviors. This dynamic binding is often contrasted with compile-time (or static) polymorphism, wherein the method call is resolved at compile time based on the static type of the object. The interplay between these modalities provides a layered approach to abstraction and reuse, whereby both hierarchical relationships and compositional strategies facilitate a robust design paradigm.

Operator Overloading: Extending Built-in Semantics

1 Formal Characterization of Operator Overloading

Operator overloading represents a syntactic and semantic extension that allows built-in operators to be reinterpreted in the context of user-defined types. In a conventional setting, an operator symbol such as $+$ is associated with a specific function, for example $f : T \times T \to T$, where T denotes a designated type. Operator overloading permits the definition of alternative functions f_i, each tailored to distinct type domains such that $f_i : U_i \times V_i \to W_i$, thereby extending the original semantic domain of the operator. This mechanism employs compile-time resolution to select the appropriate operator function based on the static types of the operands, ensuring that expressions maintain coherent semantic interpretations across divergent contexts. The redefinition adheres to the syntactic and precedence rules innate to the language, thereby providing a seamless integration within the overall type system.

2 Interaction Between Polymorphism and Operator Overloading

The integration of operator overloading within a polymorphic framework offers a sophisticated means by which objects may exhibit uniform behavior under overloaded operators. The polymorphic nature of an object allows the overloaded operator to invoke methods that are specific to the actual type of the operands, even when these operands are accessed through a common interface. This dual mechanism effectively combines static overloading resolution with dynamic dispatch, ensuring that the semantics of the operator remain consistent with the underlying type-specific implementations. Consequently, operator overloading becomes not merely a syntactic convenience but also a mechanism that enhances expressive power while preserving semantic integrity. The careful design of such operators necessitates rigorous adherence to well-defined invariants and type constraints, thereby ensuring that the extended behaviors remain mathematically coherent and consistent within the established paradigm.

Python Code Snippet

```python
# This code demonstrates polymorphism and operator overloading in
↪    line with the theoretical
# framework presented in the chapter "Polymorphism and Operator
↪    Overloading".
#
# Key concepts illustrated:
# 1. Liskov Substitution Principle: Derived types (Scalar, Vector)
↪    can be used wherever the
#    base type (Expression) is expected.
# 2. Operator Overloading: Redefining operators such as '+' and '*'
↪    to work with user-defined
#    types. For example, the addition operator implements a function
↪    of the form:
#        f: T × T → T,
#    where T is the type (Scalar or Vector). Alternative
↪    implementations (f_i) are provided
#    depending on the operand types.
#
# The following classes define an abstract base class 'Expression'
↪    and its derived classes 'Scalar'
# and 'Vector'. Overloaded operators enable:
#    - Scalar + Scalar : Simple numeric addition.
#    - Vector + Vector : Element-wise addition.
#    - Vector + Scalar : Adding a scalar to each element of a vector.
#    - Scalar * Scalar : Simple numeric multiplication.
#    - Vector * Scalar : Scalar multiplication (each component
↪    multiplied by the scalar).
#    - Vector * Vector : Dot product resulting in a Scalar.
#
# This code snippet correlates the mathematical notation and
↪    abstract definitions with concrete
# Python implementations.

class Expression:
    """
```

355

```python
    Abstract base class representing an arithmetic expression.
    Subclasses must implement the arithmetic operations.
    """

    def __add__(self, other):
        raise NotImplementedError("Addition is not implemented for
        ↪   base Expression")

    def __mul__(self, other):
        raise NotImplementedError("Multiplication is not implemented
        ↪   for base Expression")


class Scalar(Expression):
    """
    Represents a scalar numeric value.

    Operator overloading:
      __add__: Implements f: Scalar × Scalar → Scalar
      __mul__: Implements multiplication for scalars, i.e., f:
      ↪   Scalar × Scalar → Scalar
    """

    def __init__(self, value):
        self.value = value

    def __add__(self, other):
        if isinstance(other, Scalar):
            # f: Scalar × Scalar → Scalar defined as addition of
            ↪   underlying values.
            return Scalar(self.value + other.value)
        elif isinstance(other, Vector):
            # Delegate to Vector's addition to handle Scalar +
            ↪   Vector.
            return other + self
        else:
            return NotImplemented

    def __radd__(self, other):
        # Ensures commutativity: other + self
        return self.__add__(other)

    def __mul__(self, other):
        if isinstance(other, Scalar):
            # f: Scalar × Scalar → Scalar defined as multiplication
            ↪   of underlying values.
            return Scalar(self.value * other.value)
        elif isinstance(other, Vector):
            # Delegate to Vector's multiplication for Scalar *
            ↪   Vector.
            return other * self
        else:
            return NotImplemented

    def __rmul__(self, other):
```

356

```python
        # Ensures commutativity: other * self
        return self.__mul__(other)

    def __str__(self):
        return str(self.value)


class Vector(Expression):
    """
    Represents a vector with numerical components.

    Operator overloading:
      __add__:
            - Vector + Vector: Element-wise addition (f: Vector ×
              ↳  Vector → Vector).
            - Vector + Scalar: Adds the scalar to each component.
      __mul__:
            - Vector * Scalar: Scalar multiplication.
            - Vector * Vector: Dot product (resulting in a Scalar).
    """
    def __init__(self, components):
        # Ensure components is a list of numbers.
        self.components = list(components)

    def __add__(self, other):
        if isinstance(other, Vector):
            if len(self.components) != len(other.components):
                raise ValueError("Vectors must be the same dimension
                    ↳  for addition")
            # Element-wise addition for vectors.
            result = [a + b for a, b in zip(self.components,
                ↳  other.components)]
            return Vector(result)
        elif isinstance(other, Scalar):
            # Add a scalar to each element of the vector.
            result = [a + other.value for a in self.components]
            return Vector(result)
        else:
            return NotImplemented

    def __radd__(self, other):
        # Supports Scalar + Vector.
        return self.__add__(other)

    def __mul__(self, other):
        if isinstance(other, Scalar):
            # Scalar multiplication: multiply each component by the
                ↳  scalar.
            result = [a * other.value for a in self.components]
            return Vector(result)
        elif isinstance(other, Vector):
            if len(self.components) != len(other.components):
```

```python
                raise ValueError("Vectors must be the same dimension
                ↪  for dot product")
            # Dot product: sum(a_i * b_i) yielding a Scalar.
            dot = sum(a * b for a, b in zip(self.components,
            ↪  other.components))
            return Scalar(dot)
        else:
            return NotImplemented

    def __rmul__(self, other):
        # Supports Scalar * Vector.
        return self.__mul__(other)

    def __str__(self):
        return "Vector(" + ", ".join(map(str, self.components)) +
        ↪  ")"


def main():
    # Demonstration of polymorphism with Scalar objects.
    a = Scalar(10)
    b = Scalar(20)
    sum_scalars = a + b    # Implements f: Scalar × Scalar → Scalar
    print("Sum of Scalars (10 + 20):", sum_scalars)

    # Demonstration of vector addition.
    v1 = Vector([1, 2, 3])
    v2 = Vector([4, 5, 6])
    sum_vectors = v1 + v2  # Element-wise addition of vectors.
    print("Sum of Vectors ([1,2,3] + [4,5,6]):", sum_vectors)

    # Mixed-type addition: adding a Scalar to a Vector.
    mixed_add = v1 + a     # Adds the scalar value 10 to each
    ↪  component of v1.
    print("Vector + Scalar ([1,2,3] + 10):", mixed_add)

    # Demonstration of multiplication:
    # Scalar multiplication: multiplying a Vector by a Scalar.
    scaled_vector = v1 * b # Each component of v1 is multiplied by
    ↪  20.
    print("Scalar Multiplication (Vector * 20):", scaled_vector)

    # Dot product of two vectors resulting in a Scalar.
    dot_product = v1 * v2
    print("Dot Product of Vectors ([1,2,3] • [4,5,6]):",
    ↪  dot_product)


if __name__ == "__main__":
    main()
```

www.ingramcontent.com/pod-product-compliance
Lightning Source LLC
Chambersburg PA
CBHW070932050326
40689CB00014B/3172